KITCHEN COLLECTIBLES

An Identification Guide

Kenneth L. Cope

ASTRAGAL PRESS
Mendham New Jersey

Library of Congress Card Number 00-104382
International Standard Book Number 1-879335-93-X

Cover design by Donald Kahn

Published by
THE ASTRAGAL PRESS
5 Cold Hill Road, Suite 12
P.O. Box 239
Mendham, New Jersey 07945-0239

Manufactured in the United States of America

DEDICATION

Dedicated to the memory of my mother, mother-in-law, and grandmothers. How I would love to see their reaction to the attention now paid to kitchen items they couldn t wait to get rid of.

INTRODUCTION

Collectors of all stripes spend a good deal of time and effort trying to determine the WHO, WHAT, WHEN, WHERE and sometimes WHY of items now in their collections or being considered for their collections. WHO made it? WHAT, exactly, is it? WHEN was it made? WHERE was it made? And, with some items, WHY would anyone make such a thing? This book is intended to help those interested in kitchen collectibles answer these very basic questions.

Hundreds of illustrations, found under the maker's name, place of business, and a short history, provide the answer to many of the questions. Cross reference lists of patent dates and tradenames allow the user to indentify the maker of a collectible marked only with a patent date or tradename. A list of foreign terms and abbreviations identifies the country of origin for non-U.S. items. A separate index helps to identify all makers who manufactured each type of collectible.

Taken together, this information will put a complete face on many items previously of uncertain origin, age, and use.

Kenneth L. Cope
Milwaukee, WI
July, 2000

A.B.C. CAN OPENER CO., San Francisco, CA

Maker of the *A.B.C.* can opener, introduced in 1895.

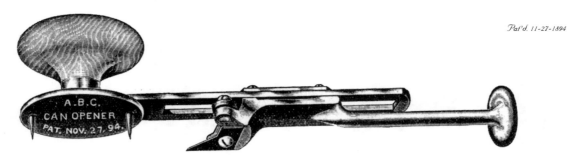

Pat'd. 11-27-1894

—The A. B. C. Can Opener.

A. & J. MFG. CO., Binghamton, NY

Formed 1908 by Benjamin T. Ash and Edward H. Johnson. Johnson became sole owner in 1919. The Edward Katzinger Co. bought the firm in 1929 and, in 1931 moved it to Chicago, IL.

Their first product was the *A & J* egg beater and cream whip (below). Later products included a line of eggbeaters patented October 9, 1923, can openers, and a great variety of small kitchen tools.

Pat'd. 10-15-1907

The A. & J. Egg Beater and Cream Whip.

ABBOTT & BOUTELL, Rochester, NY

Formed about 1890 as a successor to Kelsea & Boutell. W.H.Boutell, who had been associated with the Goodell Co., was a partner in both firms. Maker of the *REX* apple paring, coring and slicing machine. By 1908 the firm was doing business as the Boutell Mfg. Co.

Pat'd. 2-18-1902

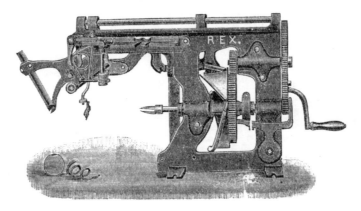

The Rex Apple Parer and Corer.

ACE HARDWARE MFG. CO., Philadelphia, PA

Maker, begining in 1924, of the *ACE* wall or shelf mounted knife sharpener (Fig. 1) and the *ACE* potato creamer "more than a masher" (Fig.2).

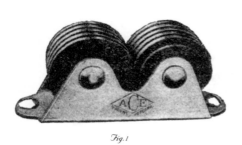

Fig.1

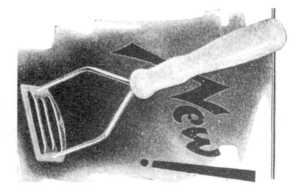

Fig.2

ACME FREEZER CO., Philadelphia, PA

Maker of *ACME* ice cream freezer, patented February 15, 1910, and July 23, 1912. The freezer was originally made by the Polar Star Co.

ACME METAL GOODS MFG. CO., Newark, NJ

Founded in 1900 by August C. Fischer. Maker of kitchen tools and gadgets such as potato peelers, food graters, egg slicers, tongs, ice picks, food choppers, etc.

ACME PEA SHELLER CO., New York, NY

Maker of the cast iron *ACME* pea sheller, introduced in 1897 *(Illustration at right)*.

Acme Pea Sheller.

ACME SHEAR CO., Bridgeport, CT

Primarily a maker of scissors and shears, the firm was also the maker of the *ACME* nut cracker introduced in 1892.

Pat'd. 9-27-1892

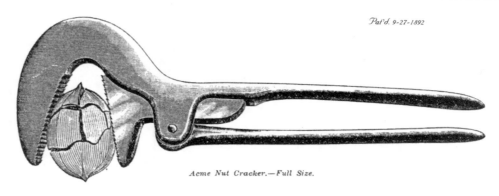

Acme Nut Cracker.—Full Size.

ADAMS CO., Dubuque, IA

Formed in 1892 by Eugene Adams (1860-1939) and his brother Herbert Adams (1863-1945). The company made a variety of cast iron goods including cook stove accessories such as stove pipe shelves (Fig.1), stove lifters (Fig.2), and stove covers (Fig.3). The firm remained active into the 1960's, but in later years concentrated on a line of machine tools.

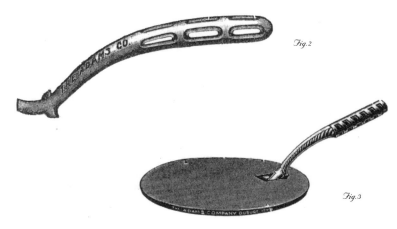

Fig.2

Fig.1

Fig.3

ADAMS CO., F.F., Erie, PA

Founded in 1874 by F.F. Adams; incorporated in January, 1883. Maker of the *KEYSTONE* washer machines and wringers, ladders and household articles. These included the ACME combination lemon squeezer and knife, introduced in 1888 (Fig.1); *HURLEY'S* cork puller, patented October 5, 1886; and the *KEYSTONE* can holder (Fig.2).

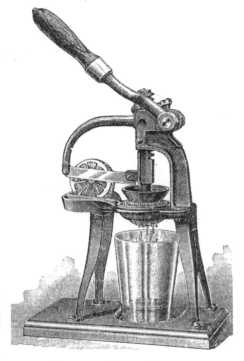

The Acme Lemon Squeezer.

Fig.1 - Pat'd. 12-20-1887

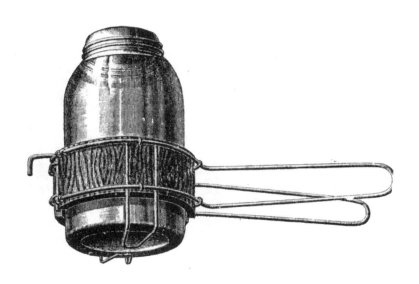

—Keystone Can Holder on Can.

Fig.2

ADAMS & WESTLAKE CO., Chicago, IL

Maker of a variety of kitchen metal ware including a vertical crank flour sifter, patented January 13, 1885; the *A & W* flour sifter introduced in 1888 (Fig.1); a milk-shake machine (Fig.2), an ice shaving machine (Fig.3) and a plane type ice shaver (Fig.4), introduced in 1889; and a flue broiler introduced in 1890 (Fig.5).

The A. & W. Flour Sifter.

Fig.1

— Ice-Shaver.

Fig.4

–The A. & W. Milk-Shake Machine.

Fig.2 - Pat'd. 11-28-1888

–Ice-Shaving Machine.

Fig.3

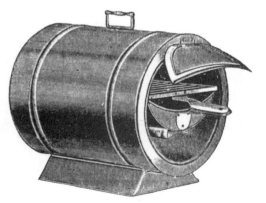

The Adams & Westlake Flue Broiler.

Fig.5

ALASKA FREEZER CO., Winchendon, MA

Maker, in 1913, of *ALASKA* and *NORTH POLE* metal ice cream freezers. *(Illustration at right)*

THE ALASKA FREEZER CO.
547 Lincoln Avenue,
Winchendon, Mass.

NORTH POLE ALL METAL FREEZER

ALBUM MFG. CO., Freeport, IL

No listing for this firm in the Freeport city directories was found, so it was apparently in business for a very short time. Maker, in 1898, of the *20TH CENTURY* juice extractor. The identical unit was offered by Beaumont & Callahan, earlier in 1898, as the *ALBUM* lemon squeezer. *(Illustration at right)*

ALFORD & BERKELE, New York, NY

Agent, in 1886, for Leavitt's *COMMON SENSE* can opener (Fig.1), made by the New England Specialty Co. Maker of the *ELECTRIC* rotary expansive can opener, introduced in 1891 (Fig.2); and the *PERFECT* cork extractor introduced in 1890 (Fig.3).

20th Century Power Juice Extractor
JUST OUT
Lemon, Beef, Onion and Fruit Squeezer

It produces more juice for less money. **No Seeds, No Pulp** Acid absolutely free from oil of rind. Actually pays for itself the first season. No soiled fingers, no stained clothes. It is neat, clean and simple. SOLID ALUMINUM HOLDER, PLUNGER AND CUP. Lemonade making made easy. Having it on hand will keep the men folks home many evenings. Child can operate it. Turn the wheel and the plunger will do the rest. USE LEMON JUICE IN YOUR TABLE WATER. ORANGE, ONION AND BEEF JUICE ALSO EXTRACTED. Write for Circular and Testimonials. Express charges prepaid to any part of U. S. on receipt of price, $2.00.

ALBUM MFG. CO., Freeport, Ill.

LEAVITT'S
"COMMON SENSE"
CAN OPENER.
Patented Dec. 19, 1882.

The Best, Simplest, Most Practical and the Easiest - Working Can Opener in the Market.

It cuts the end out the full size of Can. No parts to adjust, nothing to get out of order. A plain Knife, with a lip to rest on the edge of can, using the can for a fulcrum.

The Alford & Berkele Co.
AGENTS,
77 Chambers Street, New York,
P. O Box, 2002.

Fig. 1

Fig. 2

Electric Rotary Expansive Can Opener.

Fig. 3

—The Perfect Cork Extractor.

ALLIGER, HASBROUCK, New York, NY

Inventor and maker of the *BEST YET* can opener patented July 29, 1890. *(Illustration at right).*

—Best Yet Can Opener, Preparing to Cut.

ALUMINUM COOKING UTENSIL CO., Pittsburgh, PA

Formed in 1901 with capital of $50,000. Its first product was the *IDEAL* percolating coffee pot (Fig.1). In 1903, the firm began making a line of aluminum cookware under the *WEAR-EVER* trade name (Fig.2). The firm became a subsidiary of the Aluminum Company of America in 1931 and changed its name to Wear-Ever Aluminum, Inc. in 1954.

The Ideal Percolating Coffee Pot.

Fig.1

Fig.2

ALUMINUM GOODS MFG. CO., Two Rivers, WI

Founded 1898 by Henry Vits (1842-1921) as the Aluminum Novelty Co., maker of combs and other small items. Vits reorganized as the Aluminum Goods Mfg. Co. in 1909 and absorbed the New Jersey Aluminum Co. in 1911. Early products were small table ware such as the 1910 items shown below. In 1917 a line of aluminum kitchenware was introduced under the *MIRRO* tradename with a cheaper line offered under the *VIKO* name. The firm reorganized as the Mirro Aluminum Co. in 1957.

ALUMINUM NOVELTY CO., Canton, OH

Maker of *BALL'S* diagonal corrugated bread and cake knife, introduced in 1894.

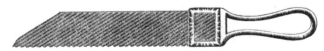

Ball's Diagonal Corrugated Bread and Cake Knife.

AMERICAN AUTOMATIC VENDING MACHINE MFG. CO, New York, NY

Maker, in 1891, of the *JACK FROST* ice cream freezer. By 1893, the freezer was a product of the Jack Frost Freezer Co.

ICE CREAM MADE IN THIRTY SECONDS.

Throw Away Your Old Freezer.

Will save its cost a dozen times a year in ice, salt, time and labor.

A child can operate it.

2 Qts., $3.75 ; 4 Qts., $4.50 ; 6 Qts., $5.50 ; 8 Qts., $6.50.

Send for Descriptive Pamphlet.

AMERICAN AUTOMATIC VENDING MACHINE MANUF'G CO.,
43 Park Street, New York.

AMERICAN AXE & TOOL CO., New York, NY

A very large conglomerate of axe makers formed in 1889. In 1895, it introduced Blood's *CHAMPION* ice pick and hammer. *(Illustration at right.)*

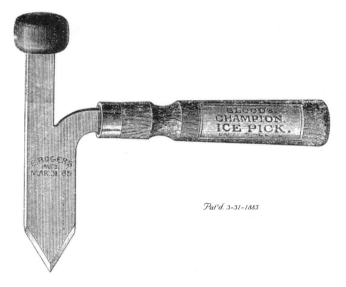

Pat'd. 3-31-1885

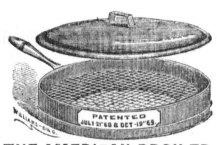

THE AMERICAN BROILER,

THE NE PLUS ULTRA OF BROILERS,

HAS NOW A NATIONAL REPUTATION, and is admitted by all who have used it, having any appreciation for a

Delicious, Healthy Broiled Steak,

as an indispensable article in all well-regulated families. Try one and be convinced. **Price, $2.00.** For sale by Stove, Tin, House-Furnishing, and Hardware Dealers everywhere.

American Broiler Mfg. Company,

Office, 28 Barclay Street, N. Y., and 158 West Fourth Street, Cincinnati, Ohio

AMERICAN BROILER MFG. CO., Cincinnati, OH

Maker, in 1871, of stove top broilers, patented July 21, 1868, and October 19, 1869. *(Illustration at left)*

AMERICAN CHEESE CUTTER CO., Anderson, IN

Maker of the *AMERICAN* combination cheese cutter introduced in 1906. The cutter was furnished with both hinged and hand knives. *(Illustration at right)*

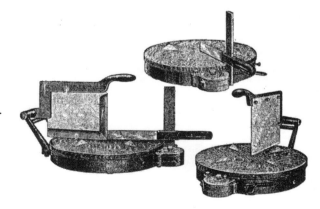

American Combination Cheese Cutter.

AMERICAN CUTLERY CO., Chicago, IL

Maker of the *AMERICAN* bread knife (Fig.1) introduced in 1894; carving sets introduced in 1895 (Fig.2); and the *KITCHEN FRIEND* utensil set (Fig.3) introduced in 1909.

Fig.1

The American Cutlery Company s Carvers.

Fig.2

American Bread Knife.

Kitchen Friend Set and Cover Rack.

Fig.3

AMERICAN ENAMEL CO., Providence, RI

Maker of the *ROYAL* (Fig.1) and *GEM* (Fig.2) ice picks, introduced in 1891.

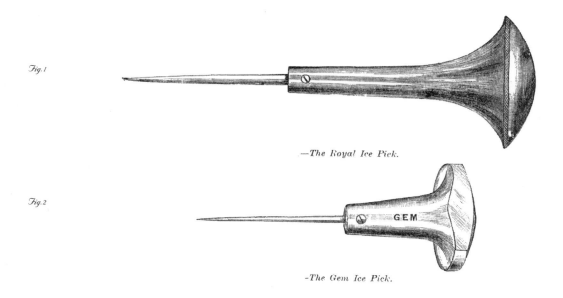

Fig.1

—The Royal Ice Pick.

Fig.2

-The Gem Ice Pick.

AMERICAN MACHINE CO., Philadelphia, PA

Maker, beginning about 1879, of the *AMERICAN* ice chisel (Fig.1); *CROWN* can opener (Fig.2); and *CROWN* lemon squeezer (Fig.3). Later products included the *CROWN* ice chipper (Fig.4); *GEM* ice shave, introduced in 1889 (Fig.5); *CROWN* meat cutter, introduced in 1888 (Fig.6); the improved *PERFECTION* meat cutter (Fig.7); and the *GEM, CROWN* (in two styles), *STAR,* and *AMERICAN* ice cream freezers offered in 1890 (Fig.8). Most of these products were continued by the North Bros. Mfg. Co., which bought the firm in 1892.

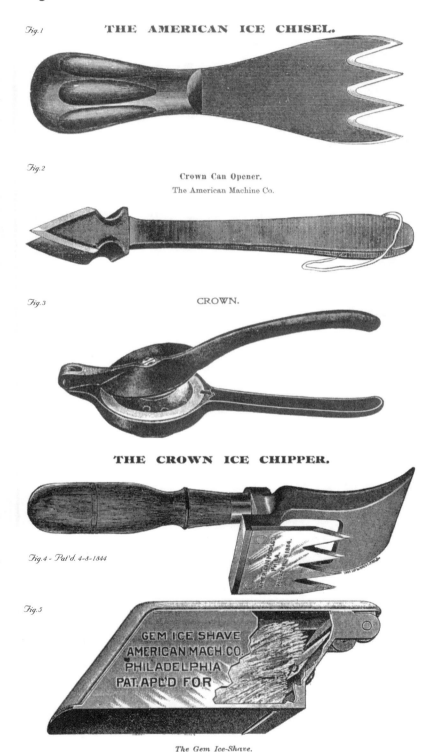

Fig.1
THE AMERICAN ICE CHISEL.

Fig.2
Crown Can Opener.
The American Machine Co.

Fig.3
CROWN.

THE CROWN ICE CHIPPER.

Fig.4 - Pat'd 4-8-1844

Fig.5

GEM ICE SHAVE
AMERICAN MACH. CO.
PHILADELPHIA
PAT. APL'D FOR

The Gem Ice-Shave.

—*The Crown Meat Cutter.*

Fig.6 - Pat'd 8-9-1887 & 12-6-1887

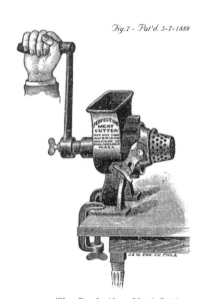

Fig.7 - Pat'd 5-7-1889

—*The Perfection Meat-Cutter.*

Illustrations continued on next page.

American Machine Company's Ice Cream Freezers.

American.

Star.

Crown, Single Action.

Crown, Double Action.

Gem.

Fig. 8

Best Quality Cedar Tubs, Galvanized Iron Hoops.

AMERICAN MFG. CO., Philadelphia, PA

Maker, in 1878, of a combination glass cutter, knife sharpener, cork screw and can opener.

AMERICAN MFG. CO.

120 Exchange Place, Phila., Pa.,

MANUFACTURERS OF

Hardware Novelties, &c.

COMBINATION NOVELTY TOOLS

Pat'd. 8-17-1875

GLASS CUTTER AND PUTTY KNIFE.

Glass Cutter, Knife Sharpener, Cork Screw,
Can Opener, &c.

AMERICAN MFG. CO., Waterbury, CT

Maker, in 1905, of tea and coffee strainers for attachment to tea and coffee pot spouts.

—Attached to Coffee Spout.

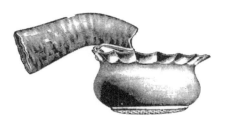

—Attached to Tea Spout.

AMERICAN SPECIALTY CO., Hartford, CT

Maker of the *EZY* raisin seeder (Fig.1) and the *PERFECTION* hot vegetable peeler (Fig.2), both introduced in 1895.

Fig.2

Perfection Hot Vegetable Peeler.

Fig.1- Pat'd. 5-21-1895

The Ezy Raisin Seeder.

Fig.3

--Vegetable Peeler in Use

AMERICAN VAPOR STOVE CO., Cleveland, OH

Maker of *NORTH'S* ventilated broiler, introduced in 1888.
(Illustration at right)

North's Ventilated Broiler.

AMERICAN WOODENWARE CO., Toledo, OH

Maker, in 1907, of the *MAGIC* churn (Fig.1). A wooden churn with a steel cover, it was made in 6, 10, and 15 gallon sizes. In 1908, the firm introduced their fireless *MAGIC* cooker (Fig.2) which consisted of an outer barrel (similar to the churn) with a steel inner can and utentsils (Fig.3) that fit inside the inner can. In use, the food was boiled for a time and, still in the utentsil, placed in the cooker can with / to 1 gallon of boiling water. The cooker was then sealed and the food left to finish cooking.

Fig.1 — The Magic Churn.
—The Magic Cooker. *Fig.2*
—Inner Can to Cooker.
—Cooking Utensils that Fit Inside of Cooker Can. *Fig.3*

ANDERSON & SONS, W.H., Detroit, MI

Maker of a cabbage corer introduced in 1903. *(Illustration at right)*

The Anderson Cabbage Corer.

ANDERSON, ELWIN S., Gloversville, NY

Maker, in 1893, of a ring-shaped chopping knife (Fig.1). He later offered a grater (Fig.2).

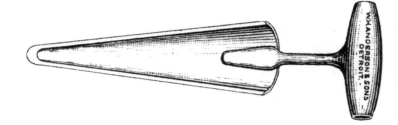

Fig.1 Chopping Knife.
Fig.2 - Pat'd 6-11-1901

ANDERSON, JOHN A.E., Indianapolis, IN

Inventor and maker of the *IDEAL* ice cream freezer, patented December 12, 1899. Made in a one gallon size only, the freezer was designed with a rotating shell, containing the ice, and a stationary cream can and dasher. Anderson claimed that it would "freeze three quarts in five minutes".

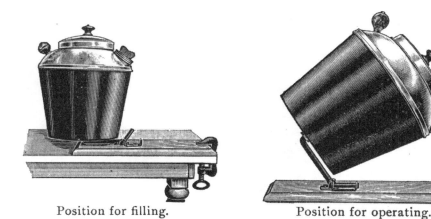

Position for filling.   Position for operating.

ANDREWS WIRE AND IRON WORKS, Rockford, IL

Founded by Charles Andrews in 1885 and incorporated March 6, 1893. There were 125 employees in 1916, with annual sales at $250,000. Maker of formed wire household goods under the *ANDROCK* tradename. The firm was bought by the Wire Goods Co. in 1917 and merged into the Washburn Co. when the latter was formed in 1922.

Products included plate scrapers, patented June 26, 1906, (Fig.1); *ANDROCK* toy kitchen tools (Fig.2); soap savers (Fig.3); several styles of potato mashers (Figs.4-6), offered in 1910; the *TELLER* knife (Fig.7); a "saucepan" style flour sifter operated with a squeeze handle, patented October 4, 1910; dish drainers, patented June 18, 1912; and the *ANDROCK* can opener (Fig.8) introduced in 1924. *(continued next page)*

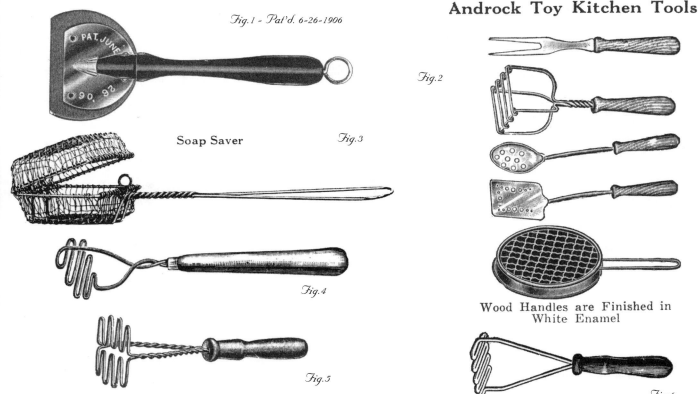

Fig.1 - Pat'd. 6-26-1906

Androck Toy Kitchen Tools

Fig.2

Soap Saver   Fig.3

Fig.4

Fig.5

Fig.6

Wood Handles are Finished in White Enamel

The *VROOMAN* sink strainer, previously made by F.E.& E.B. VROOMAN (Fig.9) was introduced in 1907 and later offered in an improved model, patented July 20, 1909 (Fig.10). By 1911, the strainer was offered in a 9 1/2" x 10 1/2" size as *MRS. VROOMAN'S* (Fig.11) and a 8" x 9" size as *AUNT DINAH'S* (Fig.12). Toaster offerings included *KRISPY* (Fig.13) and *ANDROCK* (Fig.14) stove top models; *KITCHEN KUMFORT* (Fig.15) and *RADIANT* (Fig.16) stove top models; and *CROSS* (Fig.17) and *REVERSIBLE* (Fig.18) hand held toasters offered in 1910.

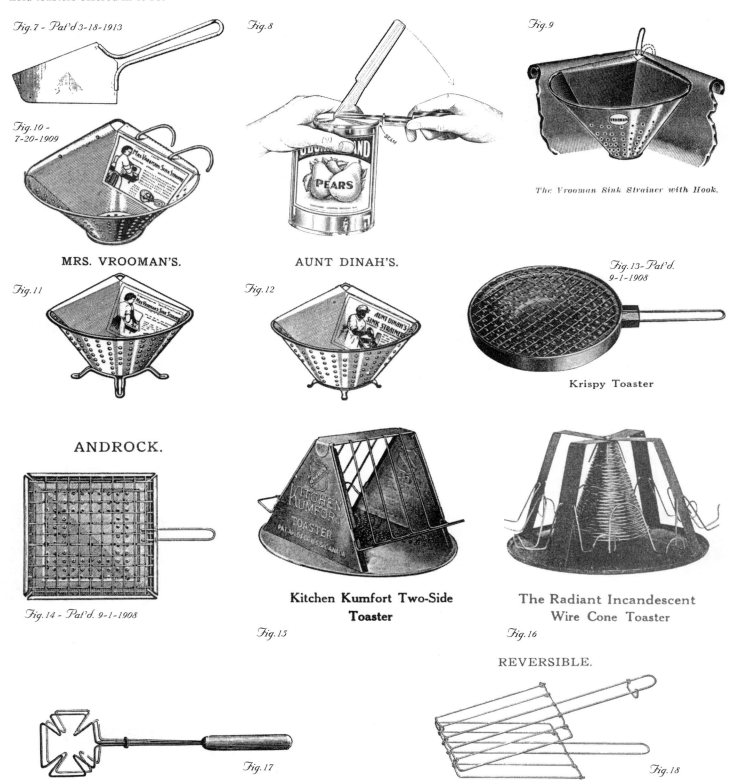

Fig.7 - Pat'd 3-18-1913

Fig.8

Fig.9

The Vrooman Sink Strainer with Hook.

Fig.10 - 7-20-1909

MRS. VROOMAN'S.

Fig.11

AUNT DINAH'S.

Fig.12

Fig.13- Pat'd. 9-1-1908

Krispy Toaster

ANDROCK.

Fig.14 - Pat'd. 9-1-1908

Kitchen Kumfort Two-Side Toaster

Fig.15

The Radiant Incandescent Wire Cone Toaster

Fig.16

REVERSIBLE.

Fig.17

Fig.18

ANNETA MFG. CO., Pittsburgh, PA

Maker of an ice cream disher introduced in 1903. *(Illustration at right)*

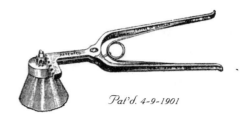

Pat'd. 4-9-1901

—*The Sanitary Ice Cream Disher.*

ANTHONY WAYNE MFG. CO., Fort Wayne, IN

Primarily a maker of washing machines, the firm also made, in 1897, the *CYCLONE* churn in 4, 6 and 8 gallon sizes. The churn used a screw propeller rather than traditional paddles and therefore "could be worked by a child of ten without exertion".

Fig. 1.—The Cyclone Churn.

Fig. 2.— Cyclone Churn in Detail.

ARCADE MFG. CO., Freeport, IL

Formed in 1885 by Albert Baumgarten, Cyrus Tobias and Edward H. Morgan as a reorganization of the Novelty Iron Works, previously operated by Morgan. Early products were hinges and cork extractors, but a line of coffee mills was added in 1887. Loyal L.

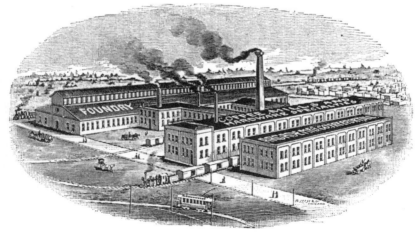

THE ARCADE PLANT.

Munn became a partner in 1893 and was later elected president. L.M. Devore & Co. was bought in 1899 and those products continued under the Arcade name.

In 1901, the firm employed 150 hands, making 600 dozen coffee mills and 1500 hinges daily. The coffee mills were offered in 50 different styles and sizes. Cast iron toys were also offered and became an important part of their business through the 1930's. In 1910 the firm began production of a miniature, toy coffee mill and soon claimed to be shipping a million of them each year to France alone. All the early products were discontinued during World War II, the company was sold to the Rockwell Mfg. Co. in 1945 and was closed in 1953.

Coffee mills included the *IMPERIAL* series (Figs.1-3), introduced in 1888 and made well into the 1920's; the *FAVORITE* series (Figs.4-5), also made into the 1920's; the *TELEPHONE* mill "ring up for coffee" (Fig.6), introduced in 1892; the *ROYAL* mill, introduced in 1894 (Fig.7); the *CRYSTAL* mill, introduced in 1899 (Fig.8), with an improved version available by 1910 (Fig.9); the *X-RAY* mill, introduced in 1900 (Fig.10); the *JEWEL* mill, introduced in 1901 (Fig.11); and the *BELL* mill, introduced in 1904 (Fig.12). An improved wall mill was patented July 16, 1912.

Fig.1 - Pat'd 9-25-1888 & 3-19-1889

The Imperial Coffee Mill, No. 177.

Fig.2 - Pat'd 9-25-1888 & 3-19-1889

Fig.3 - Pat'd 9-25-1888 & 3-19-1889

Fig.4 - Pat'd. 9-25-1888, 3-19-1889, 1-13-1891, & 10-20-1891

Fig.5 - Pat'd. 9-25-1888, 3-19-1889, 1-13-1891, & 10-20-1891

The Telephone Mill.

Fig.6 - Pat'd. 4-15-1890, 6-7-1892 &
4-11-1893

New Royal Pound Mill.

Fig.7

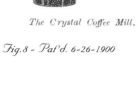

The Crystal Coffee Mill.

Fig.8 - Pat'd. 6-26-1900

Fig.9

The X Ray Coffee Mill.

Fig. 10

The Jewel Coffee Mill.

Fig. 11

Cork pullers included: the *ARCADE (Fig.13); PHOENIX* in two styles (Figs.14-15) and *DAISY* (Fig.16); and the *CLIPPER* in two styles (Figs.17-18), introduced in 1903. Its last model, the *PIX*, patented August 24, 1915, was made for the Albert Pick Co.

Fig.14 -
Pat'd 5-19-1903

—*Phœnix Cork Puller No. 30.*

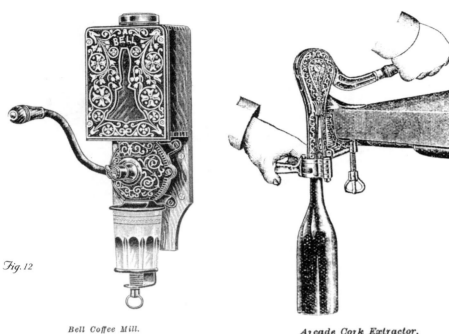

Fig.12

Bell Coffee Mill.

Arcade Cork Extractor.

Fig.13 - Pat'd. 6-9-1896, 9-7-1897, and 3-14-1899

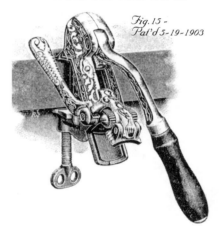

Fig.15 -
Pat'd 5-19-1903

—*Phœnix Cork Puller No. 60.*

Fig.16 - Pat'd. 1-15-1895
11-12-1895 & 9-17-1901

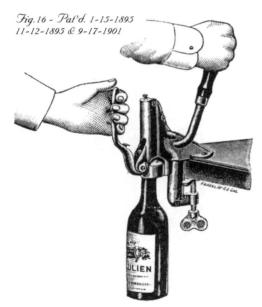

THE "DAISY" CORK EXTRACTOR.

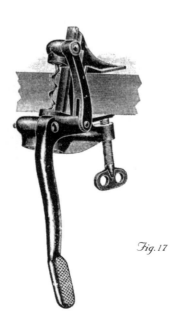

Fig.17

Fig.18

Lemon squeezers included the *CHAMPION* (Fig.19), introduced in 1900; *PERFECT* (Fig.20), introduced in 1903; the *X-RAY* (Fig.21), introduced in 1904; and a rack and pinion type, patented October 5, 1915.

Other products included the *ARCADE* nut cracker (Fig.22), introduced in 1900; *JEWEL* cake turner (Fig.23), introduced in 1905; *ARCADE* ice scraper (Fig.24) introduced in 1909; a *"Dragon"* bottle opener (Fig.25) and the *ARCADE* flour mill (Fig.26) introduced in 1917.

Fig. 19 - Pat'd. 8-8-1899

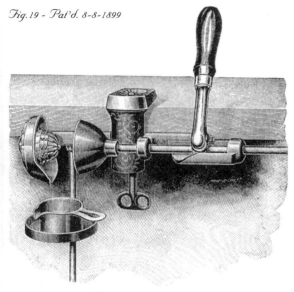

Champion Lemon Squeezer.

Fig.20

—The Perfect Squeezer No. 10, Fastened to Wall.

The Arcade Adjustable Nut Cracker.   *Fig.22*

X-Ray Lemon Squeezer.   *Fig.21*

The Jewel Cake Turner.   *Fig.23*

Arcade Ice Scraper with Points Sharply Ground.

ARCADE

Designed to produce perfect flour from any small grain such as wheat, corn, barley, rye and rice.

Requires but little effort and works rapidly.

Can be adjusted to grind the finest flour or coarse poultry feed.

Fig.26

Fig.25 - Pat'd. 1-24-1911

ARCADE MFG. CO., Newark, NJ

Maker, in 1891, of a combination slicing machine for bread, meat, cabbage, fruit, etc. They claimed the machine would cut slices "from the thickness of a sheet of paper" to one inch. *(Illustration at right)*

—*Combination Slicing Machine.*

ASBURY-PAINE MFG. CO., Philadelphia, PA

Maker of self-pouring tea pots introduced in 1895. The lid acted as a pump, forcing the water through the tea leaves and out the spout.

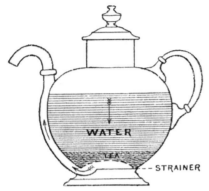

Fig. 1.—*Sectional View of Self Pouring Tea Pot.*

Fig. 2.—*Self Pouring Tea Pot.*

Pat'd. 5-1-1860

Greatest Convenience of the Age.

ASHLEY'S PATENT SCREW EGG-BEATER,

The only one that can be used in a small vessel, or that will beat from one egg to any required number. All other beaters must be attached to some place to be used; this needs only to be held in the hand. Will do the work thoroughly *in less than a minute!* Durable, simple, and cheap. Warranted to give satisfaction. For sale by all house-furnishing and hardware stores. Sample postpaid for 50 cts. Circulars free. K. E. ASHLEY, Sole Manufr., Office 95 Maiden Lane, New York. Box 5646 Post-Office.

ASHLEY, K.E., New York, NY

Maker, in 1865, of Ashley's patent screw egg-beater. Ashley was granted a second eggbeater patent, June 26, 1866. *(Illustration at right)*

ATHOL MACHINE CO., Athol, MA

Formed in 1868 for "the special purpose of making Starrett's food chopper and other articles of Mr. Starrett's invention." George T. Johnson was president and capitalization was $25,000. The first product was a food chopper that was made in family sizes (Fig.1) with 8" or 10" cylinders; hotel size (Fig.2) with 12" cylinder; and butchers' sizes (Figs.3-4) with 15", 18" or 20" cylinders. Other products included a food press (Fig.5) offered in three sizes; 6x9x4 , 8x12x5 , and 10x14x6 .

Hotel Sizes.

(continued on next page)

Family Sizes.

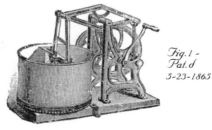

Fig.1 -
Pat.d
5-23-1865

Fig.2

The firm was taken over in 1905. The new owners announced that food chopper production would continue, but it ceased sometime prior to the 1925 reorganization as the Athol Machine & Foundry Co.

Butchers' Sizes.

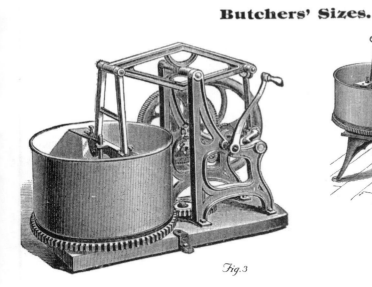

Fig.3

Fig.4

DOMESTIC MEAT PRESS.

Fig.5 - Pat'd. 4-15-1873

ATKINS & CO., E.C., Indianapolis, IN

A very large maker of saws and edge tools, the firm also made cutting blades for other firms such as the Tucker & Dorsey Mfg. Co. In 1900, Atkins introduced the *QUEEN* vegetable slicer, but in 1904 turned it over to Tucker & Dorsey Mfg. Co. and ceased competing with a large customer.

The Queen Vegetable Slicer.

AUGUSTA MACHINE WORKS, Augusta, ME

Maker, in 1893, of the *ELECTRIC* vegetable parer and slicer. *(Illustration at right)*

The Electric Parer and Slicer.

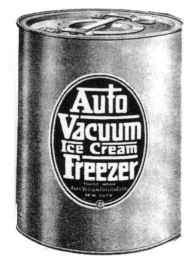

AUTO VACUUM FREEZER CO., New York, NY

Makers of a double walled, metal ice cream freezer offered in one to three quart sizes, patented January 2, 1912, and offered as late as 1924. In use, the cream mixture was poured in the inner can, ice and salt placed between the inner and outer cans, the freezer sealed and then left to stand. *(Illustration at left)*

AUTOSPIN CO., Middletown, CT

Formed about 1908 as a reorganization of FRED J. BURR, maker of the *AUTOSPIN* ice cream freezer. The firm also made a tandem version of the freezer, patented June 29, 1909. By 1910, both freezers were products of the New England Enameling Co.

BADGER IRON & WIRE WORKS, Milwaukee, WI

Maker, in 1911, of *BADGER* fruit jar wrenches (Fig.1) and fruit jar holders (Fig.2). The jar holder was adjustable to any size between 2 1/4" and 4 1/2".

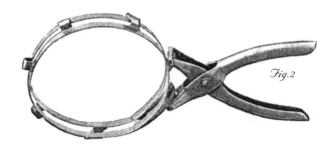

Fig. 1   *Fig. 2*

BADGER, L.V., Chicago, IL

Inventor and maker of a wood and tin nutmeg grater, patented January 8, 1867. The nutmeg was held in a tin tube which was rotated against a perforated metal segment. *(Illustration at right)*

BALL, R.M., Muncie, IN

Maker, in 1891, of the *LIGHTNING* can opener (Fig.1). The opener was made of heavy cast iron designed to be heated in the stove fire, then lifted out and placed on the can top to melt the solder, "thus preserving the can for future use." The double tank *THERMOMETER* churn (Fig.2) was introduced in 1894.

Lightning Can Opener.

Fig.1

—Double Tank Thermometer Churn.

—Parts of Double Tank Churn.

Fig.2 - Pat'd. 6-21-1881

BARNES, JOSHUA, New York, NY

Inventor and probably maker of a double helix corkscrew. *(Illustration at right)*

Pat'd. 6-27-1876

BEATTY & SON, WM., Chester, PA

Maker, in 1908 and well into the 1920's, of *DIAMOND* 6" kitchen size meat cleavers (Fig.1) and larger butchers' cleavers (Fig.2) offered in seven sizes from 7" to 13".

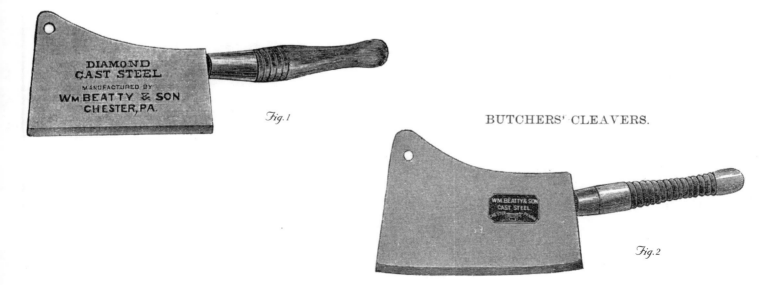

DIAMOND CAST STEEL MANUFACTURED BY WM. BEATTY & SON CHESTER, PA.

Fig.1

BUTCHERS' CLEAVERS.

Fig.2

BEAUMONT & CALLAHAN, Milwaukee, WI

A partnership of H.H. Beaumont and John Callahan, listed in the city directory as makers of patent specialties. Maker, in 1898, of the *CRACKER-JACK* nut cracker (Fig.1); *ALBUM* lemon squeezer (Fig.2), patented by Albert Baumgarten; and the *CHAMPION* cork puller (Fig.3), patented by Charles Morgan. Both Baumgarten and Morgan were associated with the Arcade Mfg. Co., Freeport, IL, which may have been the actual maker. Later in 1898, the *ALBUM* lemon squeezer was advertised by the Album Mfg. Co., Freeport, IL.

Fig.1

Cracker-Jack, Sr., Nut Crack.

Album Lemon or Fruit Squeezer.

Fig.2 - Pat'd. 11-9-1897

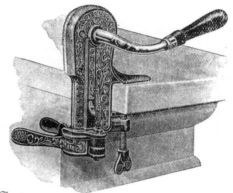

Fig.3 - Pat'd. 3-14-1899

Champion Cork Puller.

BEAUMONT & GUERNSEY, New Britain, CT

Maker, in 1866, of a "condensing" coffee pot, patented November 6, 1860. The grounds were held in the lower chamber; the upper chamber, filled with cold water, acted as a condenser for the steam rising in the pot, with the resulting hot water dripping into the lower chamber.
(Illustration at right)

BEAVER MFG. CO., Beaver, PA

Maker of stamped ware with universal covers and anti-scorcher insert, introduced in 1908.

Fig. 1.—Pot Cover.　　Fig. 2.—Anti-Scorcher.

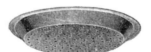

Fig. 3.—Pot Fitted with Cover and Anti-Scorcher.

BEESE, A.F., Davenport, IA

Maker of *CLEAN CUT* cake tins in 1896. The sliding knife design is still popular.
(Illustration at right)

BELLAIRE STAMPING CO., Harvey, IL

Maker of *COLUMBIAN* enameled cookware c1892-1900 (Fig.1). Products included drip pans (Fig.2) and the *QUEEN* percolator (Fig.3).

Columbian **Triple Coated** Enameled Ware

Is absolutely non-poisonous and so highly finished that hot water is all that is needed to make it clean and sweet even after years of constant use.
We know that **50,000** readers of The Ladies' Home Journal use this ware and will readily recognize the value of the following combination.

KITCHEN OUTFIT—18 pcs., Standard Sizes

1 only, 3-qt. Coffee Pot	$0.95	1 only, 3-qt. Milk Pan	$0.35
1 " 7-qt. Tea Kettle	1.45	1 " 4-qt. Pudding Pan	.45
1 " 2-qt. Rice Cooker	1.35	1 " ¾-qt. Dipper	.35
1 " 3-qt. Sauce Pan	.50	1 " 3½ x 1¾-in. Ladle	.20
1 " 6-qt. Preserving Kettle	.65	1 " 14-in. Spoon	.20
1 " 11¾ x 3¾-in. Basin	.35	1 " 4 x 2¾-in. Cup	.17
1 " 17-qt. Dish Pan	1.30	3 " 9-in. Pie Plates	.60
1 " 2-qt. Milk Pan	.30	1 " 9¾ x 1¾-in. Fry Pan	.50
			$9.67

This set complete will be sent, **freight charges prepaid** by us, for **$8.75**

Fig.1

Seamless Flanged Drip Pan.

Fig.2

Fig.3

The Queen Percolator.

BERTELS, SONS & CO., W.B., Wilkes-Barre, PA

Maker, in 1894, of a screw cup dinner pail (Fig.1). Its improved *SUN* dinner pail was introduced in 1902 (Fig.2).

Fig.1- Pat'd. 3-8-1892

Fig.2

Screw Cup Dinner Pail.

—Sun Dinner Pail.

BERTHOUD, R.J., Swanton, OH

Maker of a fruit jar wrench, introduced in 1904. By 1920 the wrench was a product of Cassady-Fairbank Co. *(Illustration at right)*

Pat'd. 6-28-1904

—The Berthoud Fruit Jar Wrench.

BEST-S CO., Lancaster, PA

Maker of a fruit jar wrench, patented by Emanuel L. Fenstermaker. *(Illustration at right)*

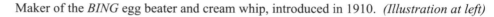

Pat'd. 5-8-1917

BING MFG. CO., Minneapolis, MN

Maker of the *BING* egg beater and cream whip, introduced in 1910. *(Illustration at left)*

The Bing Beater, Showing Up Stroke.

BISHOP & CO., GEO. H., Cincinnati, OH

A large saw maker, the firm also made, about 1910, some kitchen tools including the mincing knives shown below.

BLANCHARD, PARKER & CO., Boston, MA

Maker, in 1888, of the *BUFFER* ice pick designed to prevent flying pieces of ice.

The Buffer Ice Pick.

26

BLANCHARD'S SONS, PORTER, Nashua, NH

Maker, in 1900, of *LIGHTNING* churns (Fig.1) in four sizes, from two to five gallons; and *BLANCHARD* churns (Fig.2) in five sizes, from two to 16 gallons.

THE LIGHTNING CHURN.

Fig.1

BLANCHARD CHURN.

Fig.2

Made in 3 Sizes

BLANTON & McKAY CO., Cincinnati, OH

Maker, in 1914, of the *FAYWAY* butter separator. The firm claimed it revolutionized buttermaking because, rather than paddles or blades, the separator used a stream of air to "blow millions of butter globules to the top." The butter "tastes better, keeps longer, than ordinary churned butter." *(Illustration at left)*

BLEAKLEY, W.M., Verplank, NY

Inventor and maker of a can opener. A two-handed device, the left hand piece held the can stationary while the right hand piece was rotated to cut out the top.

Pat'd. 10-19-1869

BLUFFTON SLAW CUTTER CO., Bluffton, OH

Maker, in 1923, of *RAPID* slaw and vegetable cutters. Selling for 40 cents, it was 4¼" by 13". *(Illustration at right)*

Pat'd.
11-3-1868

THE "MONITOR" COFFEE-POT.

BLUNT, E., New York, NY

Maker of the *MONITOR* coffee pot. The design included a cold water reservoir in the lid assembly and a steam whistle. When the whistle indicated the water was boiling, a rod in the center of the reservoir was lifted, dumping the cold water into the pot and thus settling the grounds. *(Illustration at left)*

Pat'd. 6-12-1900

The Bolton Bread Crumb Crusher.

BOLTON, OGDEN, Canton, OH

Maker of a bread crumb crusher, introduced in 1900. *(Illustration at right)*

Pat'd.
1-29-1895

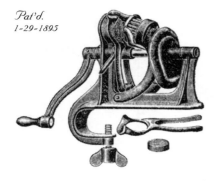

American Wonder Raisin Seeder.

BORGFELDT & CO., GEORGE, New York, NY

Maker of the *AMERICAN WONDER* raisin seeder introduced in 1902. Turning the crank forced a series of small pins through the fruit. *(Illustration at left)*

BOSTON MFG. ASSOC., Boston, MA

One of several makers of "Neverslip" pattern can openers, the firm offered the *BAY STATE* can opener in 1911.

BAY STATE.

BOUTELL MFG. CO., Rochester, NY

Formed about 1908 as the successor to Abbott & Boutell. The firm continued the apple parer line, adding new models patented July 7, 1908, and November 1, 1910, by William H. Boutell.

BOYE NEEDLE CO., Chicago, IL

Founded 1905 by John L. Flannery (1847-1920) and J.H. Boye. Maker of knitting needles, hair pins, and a variety of kitchen tools and novelties. Kitchen tools included a combination can opener and knife sharpener, patented September 10, 1912; a nutmeg grater, patented September 29, 1914, by J.H. Boye; a jar wrench (Fig.1); and a can-opener (Fig.2).

Fig.1 - Pat'd. 11-28-1916 & 5-22-1917

Fig.2 - Pat'd. 6-15-1920

BRADLEY, BLINN & LYON, New Haven, CT

Maker, in 1891, of the *CONE CUP* potato masher and fruit press, patented by Joseph S. Blinn.

Pat'd. 8-4-1891

Blinn "Cone Cup" Potato Masher and Fruit Press.

BRADLEY MFG. CO., New Haven, CT

Maker, in 1896, of the iron handled *DIAMOND* ice pick with triangular head for cracking ice (Fig.1) and the *WEBB* ice shaver and crusher (Fig.2).

Fig.2 - Pat'd. 3-18-1884

Diamond Ice Pick.

Fig.1 - Pat'd. 3-20-1894

CHAPMAN'S PATENT CHURN.

BRADLEY, WILLIAM L., Boston, MA

Maker of the *EUREKA* churn, patented by Nathan Chapman. The patented features were the hollow shaft and hollow arms used on the dasher "to introduce air into the churn." *(Illustration at left)*

Pat'd. 1-30-1866

BRECHT, GUSTAVUS A., St. Louis, MO

Maker, in 1886, of rack and gear drive sausage stuffers offered in 20 pound (Fig.1) and 35 pound (Fig.2) sizes.

Fig.1

Fig.2

BREWINGTON, BAINBRIDGE & CO., Baltimore, MD

Maker of flour sifters (Fig.1); a larger style sifter patented May 14, 1889; and skillets with a vent to allow odors and smoke to vent through the fire and out the chimney (Fig.2). All patents were issued to Henry S. Brewington. *(Illustrations on next page)*

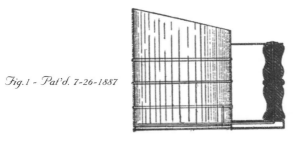

Fig.1 - Pat'd. 7-26-1887

Improved Frying Skillet.

Fig.2 - Pat'd. 3-11-1890

BRIDGEPORT BRASS CO., Bridgeport, CT

Maker of the *NATIONAL* fly fan, introduced in 1892. These wind-up fans were designed to set in the middle of the dining table and shoo flys during meal time.

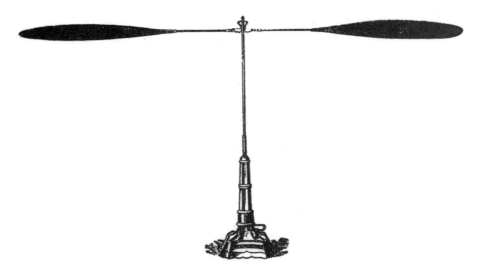

National Fly Fan.

BRIDGEPORT MFG. CO., Bridgeport, CT

Maker of a variety of hand tools, the firm also made the *CYCLONE* can opener, introduced in 1898.

Cyclone Can Cutter.

BRIDGEPORT WIRE GOODS CO., Bridgeport, CT

Maker of a smokeless and odorless broiler (Fig.1) and griddle (Fig.2).

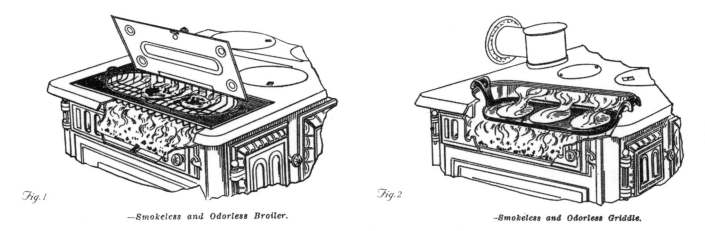

Fig.1

—*Smokeless and Odorless Broiler.*

Fig.2

—*Smokeless and Odorless Griddle.*

BRITTAN, GRAHAM & MATHES CO., Pittsburgh, PA

Maker of the *ACME* cold handle, introduced in 1896.

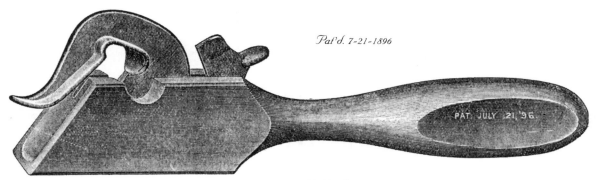

Pat'd. 7-21-1896

PAT. JULY 21, '96

The Acme Cold Handle.

BRONSON SUPPLY CO., Cleveland, OH,   <u>later</u>
BRONSON-WALTON CO., Cleveland, OH

Formed about 1888 by Adelbert E. Bronson to make the *NEVER BREAK* line of stamped steel cooking utensils (Fig.1-5). The *PURITAN* coffe pot (Fig.6), which used a cloth filter was introduced in 1893. Coffee mill production began in 1899 with introduction of the *NONE-SUCH* (Fig.7). *(continued on following two pages)*

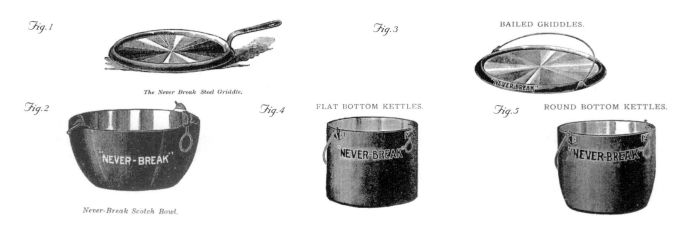

Fig.1

The Never Break Steel Griddle.

Fig.2

Never-Break Scotch Bowl.

Fig.3

BAILED GRIDDLES.

"NEVER-BREAK"

Fig.4

FLAT BOTTOM KETTLES.

NEVER-BREAK

Fig.5

ROUND BOTTOM KETTLES.

"NEVER-BREAK"

Fig.6

Puritan Coffee Pot, with Section Cut
Away, Showing Filter.

Fig.7

–None-Such Canister Coffee Mill.

Fig.8

—B-W Prospect All Steel Coffee Mill No. 103.

In April, 1900, the firm reorganized as the Bronson-Walton Co. Coffee mill production continued with the *PROSPECT* (Fig.8) and *TIGER* (Fig.9) introduced in 1901. The *OPLEX* double grinder (Fig.10) was introduced in 1902 and was also made under *AROMA* and *SILVER LAKE* trade names. *EVER READY* (Fig.11) and *MAHOGANY* (Fig.12) wall mount mills were introduced in 1906 and the *MONITOR* table top mill (Fig.13) was available by 1910.

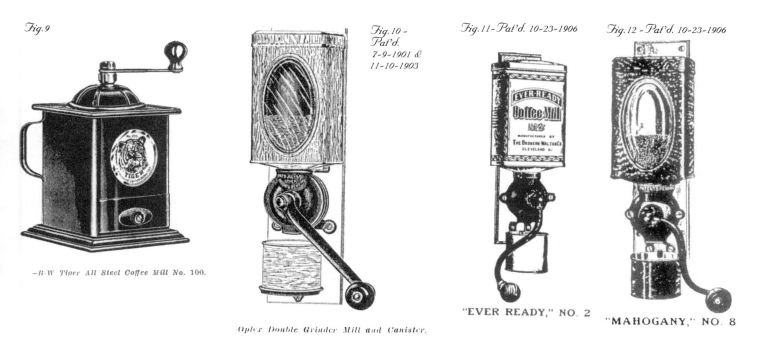

Fig.9

—B-W Tiger All Steel Coffee Mill No. 100.

*Fig.10 -
Pat'd.
7-9-1901 &
11-10-1903*

Oplex Double Grinder Mill and Canister.

Fig.11 - Pat'd. 10-23-1906

"EVER READY," NO. 2

Fig.12 - Pat'd. 10-23-1906

"MAHOGANY," NO. 8

Steel pans included the *NEVER-BURN* drip pan (Fig.14); the *BROWN BEAUTY* roaster (Fig.15), introduced in 1902; and a multiple baking pan, patented January 26, 1904. *(Illustrations continued on next page)*

Fig.13 - Pat'd. 4-24-1906
& 5-11-1909

"MONITOR"

Fig.14 - Pat'd. 10-21-1902

Never-Burn Drip Pan.

Fig.15

Roaster Closed, Showing Self Basting Device.

Eclipse Can Opener and Cover.

BROOKLYN NOVELTY CO., Brooklyn, NY

Maker, in 1895, of the *ECLIPSE* can opener made especially for opening condensed milk cans and then left in place as a cover. *(Illustration at left)*

BROWN, CHARLES D., New York, NY

Maker, in 1900, of the *STAR* food cutter, patented August 28, 1900, by Hurbert K. Wood. *(Illustration at right)*

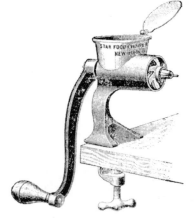

Star Food Cutter.

BROWN, EDMUND, Lynn, MA

Maker, in 1857, of nutmeg graters, patented October 13, 1857, by Nathan Ames. He may have also been the maker of coffee and tea pot strainers, patented September 17, 1861, by Ames. *(Illustration at left)*

BROWNE & DOWD MFG. CO., Meriden, CT

Makers, in 1898, of potato mashers and beaters, mincing knives, meat tenderers, egg beaters and cream whips, kettle scrapers, fish and griddle cake turners, ice picks, nut crackers and picks.

Can opener offerings in 1895 included *NEVER SLIP* (Fig.1); *KING* (Fig.2) and *QUEEN* (Fig.3). By 1910 its can opener line included the improved *KING* (Fig.4), now equipped with a bottle opener; a cheaper version of the *KING,* patented November 3, 1908; and improved *NEVER SLIP* (Fig.5) with a wooden handle. *(Illustrations on next page)*

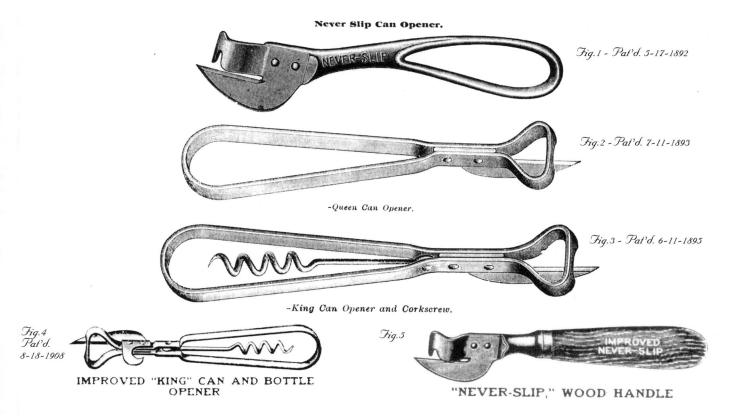

Never Slip Can Opener.

Fig.1 - Pat'd. 5-17-1892

-Queen Can Opener.

Fig.2 - Pat'd. 7-11-1893

Fig.3 - Pat'd. 6-11-1895

-King Can Opener and Corkscrew.

Fig.4 Pat'd. 8-18-1908

IMPROVED "KING" CAN AND BOTTLE OPENER

Fig.5

"NEVER-SLIP," WOOD HANDLE

BROWNE MFG. CO., WILLIAM G., Kingston, NY

Maker, in 1902, of the *CYCLONE* egg beater (Fig.1) and the *ROYAL* vegetable masher (Fig.2). 1902 can opener offerings included the model in (Fig.3) and the *SHEAR CUT CLIPPER (Fig.4)*. Additions to the line by 1910 included the *BEST* can opener (Fig.5), complete with corkscrew, milk bottle cap remover and bottle opener; *NONE SUCH* can opener and corkscrew (Fig.6); and the *I.X.L.* iron handle (Fig.7).

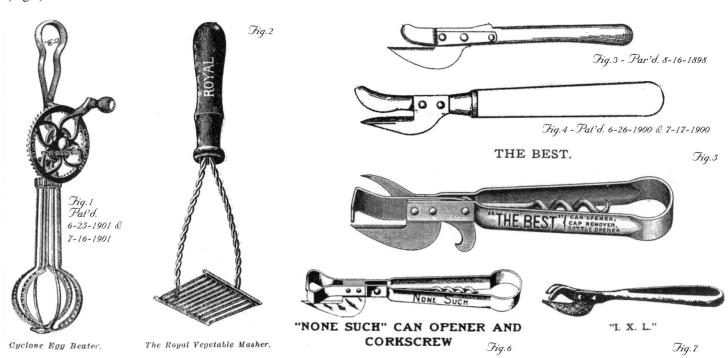

Fig.2

Fig.3 - Pat'd. 8-16-1898

Fig.4 - Pat'd. 6-26-1900 & 7-17-1900

THE BEST.

Fig.5

Fig.1 Pat'd. 6-25-1901 & 7-16-1901

Cyclone Egg Beater.

The Royal Vegetable Masher.

"NONE SUCH" CAN OPENER AND CORKSCREW *Fig.6*

"I. X. L." *Fig.7*

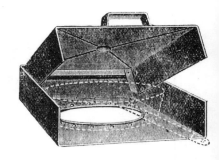

The Odorless Frying Oven.

BROWNLOW, D.R., Middletown, CT

Maker of an odorless frying oven, introduced in 1897. *(Illustration at right)*

BUCKEYE CHURN CO., Sidney, OH

Maker, in 1893, of the *BUCKEYE* churn. The churn operated by rocking the barrel and had no dasher or paddles. *(Illustration at left)*

—*The Buckeye Churn.*

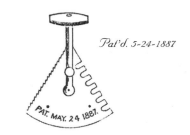

Pat'd. 5-24-1887

Combined Meat Chopper, Mincing Knife, &c.

BULLOCK, O.W., Springfield, MA

A maker of hand tools, especially jeweler's tools, in 1888 the firm introduced a combination meat chopper, bone saw, mincing knife and steak tenderer. *(Illustration at right)*

BURPEE CAN SEALER CO., Chicago, IL

Maker, in 1924, of a home can sealer which allowed housewives to use tin cans for home canning. Their ad claimed "big profits selling to city familes, restaurants, hotels." *(Illustration at left)*

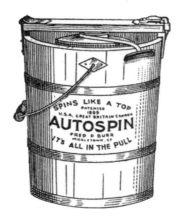

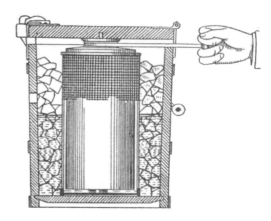

BURR, FRED J., Middletown, CT

Maker, in 1901, of the *AUTOSPIN* ice cream freezer patented November 14, 1899, and made in 2, 3 and 4 quart sizes. The unique action was much like starting today's lawn mowers. By 1908, the firm had reorganized as the Autospin Co.

—*The Autospin Ice Cream Freezer.*

Sectional View of the Autospin.

BUTLER, KATTENHORN & ELLSWORTH, New York, NY

Maker, in 1894, of *BUTLER'S* ice cream freezer. It was a unique type with 22 small cups in which the ice cream was frozen, rather than a single container.

Pat'd. 6-5-1894

Family Ice Cream Freezer.

CADMUS PRODUCTS CO., Bayonne, NJ

Maker, in 1922, of the *MASTER BAKE POT* stove top oven. *(Illustration at right)*

CALDWELL MFG. CO., Rochester, NY

Maker of the *GEM* nutmeg grater, introduced in 1900 (Fig.1) and the *JUMBO* nut cracker (Fig.2), introduced in 1905.

Jumbo Nut Cracker.

Fig.2

The Gem Nutmeg Grater.   *Fig.1*

CARPENTER ELECTRIC HEATING MFG. CO., St. Paul, MN

Maker of a nickel-plated, electrically heated, chafing dish. Made with a cast iron bottom plate and copper body, it had a capacity of only one quart. Introduced in 1893, it was one of the first electric kitchen appliances.

General View of Chafing Dish Heated by Electricity.

CARTER, JOHN S., Syracuse, NY

Maker, in 1888, of the *O.K.* churn and *O.K.* butter worker. *(Illustration at right)*

CASSADY-FAIRBANK MFG. CO., Chicago, IL

A major maker of small kitchen tools beginning about 1905, the firm was bought by the Wire Goods Co. in 1914 and merged into the Washburn Co. when formed in 1922.

Products included the *FOUR POUR* ladle (Fig.1) and a salad chop (Fig.2), introduced in 1907; *REYNOLDS'* ball joint pudding stirrer (Fig.3), introduced in 1909; a combination knife for paring, slicing, eyeing and coring vegetables, offered in 1910 (Fig.4); kitchen sets offered in 1911 (Fig.5); *DUPLEX* serving forks previously made by the Duplex Serving Fork Co. (Fig.6); *TURBINE* egg beaters (Fig.7); *PRIDE* (Fig.8) and *BULLDOG* (Fig.9) nutcrackers; an improved nutcracker (Fig.10); and a combination doughnut and biscuit cutter with a removeable center (Fig.11).

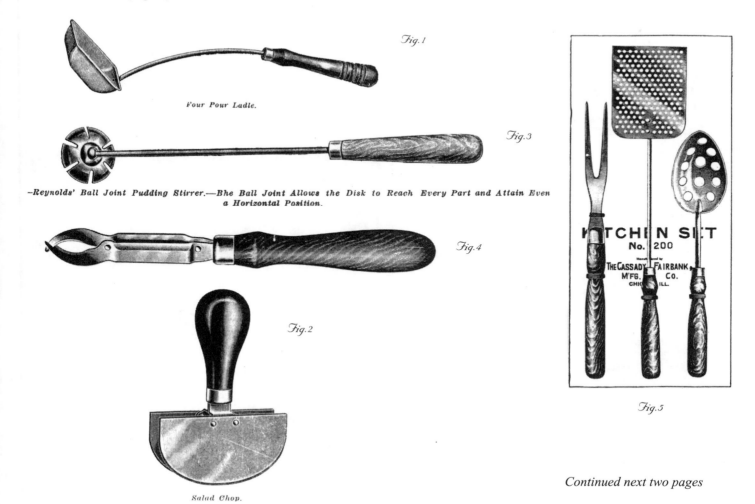

Fig.1

Four Pour Ladle.

Fig.3

—Reynolds' Ball Joint Pudding Stirrer.—Bhe Ball Joint Allows the Disk to Reach Every Part and Attain Even a Horizontal Position.

Fig.4

Fig.2

Salad Chop.

Fig.5

Continued next two pages

By 1925, additions included aluminum omelet pans (Fig.12); spring operated ice picks (Fig.13); *SHOOT-A-LITE* gas lighters (Fig.14); *SAFETY* crank operated can openers (Fig.15); and a variety of can openers (Figs.16-17); chopping and mincing knives (Figs.18-19); and fruit jar wrenches (Figs.20-21).

Duplex Serving Fork *Fig.6*

TURBINE *Fig.7 - Pat'd. 8-20-1912*

Fig.8 - Pat'd. 10-30-1900

Fig.9 - Pat'd. 10-30-1900

Fig.10 - Pat'd. 10-22-1918

Fig.11

Pure Aluminum Diameter 2¾ in.

Aluminum Omelet Pan *Fig.12*

Folding

Ice Picks *Fig.13*

With spring in handle

LARSEN'S "SHOOT-A-LITE" SAFETY GAS "LITER"

Fig.14 - Pat'd. 8-30-1917

MONTCLAIR BRAND LOBSTER

Fig.15

Fig. 16

Cast Iron Handle
Bright Steel Blade 2¾x5⅞"
Ground Edge   Fig. 18

Rubberoid Handle
Bright Steel Blades 6¼x2 in.
Ground Edges
Fig. 19

Fig. 17

Fig. 20

Fig. 21

CENTAUR MFG. CO., Chicago, IL

Maker of *SMITH'S PAT*. egg separators (Fig.1) in 1898 and the *CENTAUR* can and bottle opener (Fig.2) by 1911.

CENTAUR.

Fig. 2

Centaur Egg Separator.

CENTRAL STAMPING CO., New York, NY

Organized January 1, 1885, by David H. James (1835-1905). Products included a drop spout copper tea kettle (Fig.1), introduced in 1900; the *CENTRAL* seamless bread and cake mixer (Fig.2) and the *CENTRAL* bread mixer (Fig.3), both introduced in 1909. *(Illustrations on next page)*

Fig.1

—*Drop Spout Nickeled Copper Tea Kettle.*

Fig.2

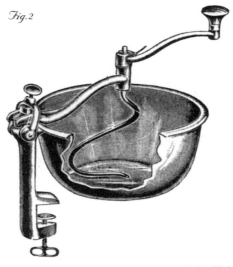

—*Central Seamless Bread and Cake Make*

Fig.3

—*Central Seamless Bread Mixer.*

—*Champion Egg Opener.*

CHAMPION EGG OPENER CO., Hartford, CT

 Maker, beginning in 1890, of *CHAMPION* egg openers. By 1905, the openers were a product of the Taplin Mfg. Co. *(Illustration at left)*

Pat'd. 1-4-1887 & 12-22-1903

CHAMPION GRATER CO., Boston, MA

 Maker of a nutmeg grater, patented October 9, 1866, and April 2, 1867.

CHAMPLIN & CO., J.R., Laconia, NH

 Maker of ice cream freezers that came in several sizes from six quarts to 15 gallons. They featured a design where the can and dasher were rotated in opposite directions.
(Illustration at right)

Pat'd. 11-1-1864 & 3-16-1869

CHANDLER, N.S., Springfield, MA

Maker, beginning in 1882, of *CHANDLER'S* ice cutting machine, patented by Edwin S. Field. Made in three sizes, the device was offered as late as 1900. *(Illustration at right)*

Pat'd. 11-16-1880

CHAPMAN, C.A., Geneva, NY

Maker of the *VAN DEUSEN* line of stamped tinware; including an egg whip (Fig.1); measuring cups (Fig.2); and several types of cake pans (Figs.3-6). The cake pans featured metal tabs which acted as handles and, when pulled up, exposed slots which admitted a knife blade for loosening the cake from the pan bottom.

Fig.1 - Pat'd. 3-13-1894

Fig.2

Fig.3

SQUARE, FOR LAYER CAKES, SHEET
CAKES, ETC.

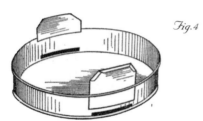

Fig.4

ROUND, FOR LAYER CAKES, SHEET
CAKES, ETC.

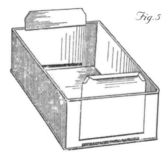

Fig.5

OBLONG, FOR LOAF CAKES.

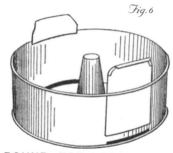

Fig.6

ROUND, FOR LOAF CAKE.
WITH TUBE.

Pat'd. 4-2-1895

Star Raisin Seeding Machine.

CHASE & CO., F.H., Chicago, IL

Maker of the *STAR* raisin seeding machine introduced in 1894. *(Illustration at left)*

CHATILLON & SONS, JOHN, New York, NY

Primarily a maker of scales patented December 10, 1867, and January 4, 1876, the firm made other items such as the *DUPLEX* knife sharpener (Fig.1), and the *LOWNDES* combination cleaver, twine cutter and skewer puller (Fig.2). The cleaver was offered with 8" or 10" blade.

Fig. 1 - Pat'd. 10-27-1891

Duplex Steel for Sharpening Knives.

Fig.2 - Pat'd. 3-19-1895

Lowndes Butchers' Cleaver.

CHICAGO COFFEE MILL CO., Chicago, IL

Maker, in 1890, of the *CHICAGO* double-grinder coffee mill. The mill was made in five sizes, with either sunken or exposed hoppers and in bronze, copper, or japan finish. *(Illustration at right)*

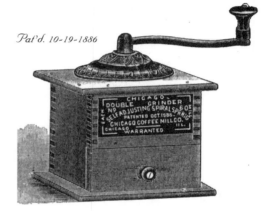

Pat'd. 10-19-1886

—Chicago Double-Grinder Coffee-Mill, Sunken Hopper.

CHICAGO NICKEL WORKS, Chicago, IL

Maker, in 1877, of *BALDWIN'S* pyrometer oven door knob (Fig.1), one of the earliest externally mounted oven thermometers. In 1890, Smith's patent *PALACE* cork extractor (Fig.2) and *DISTELHORST'S* grating machine (Fig.3) were introduced.

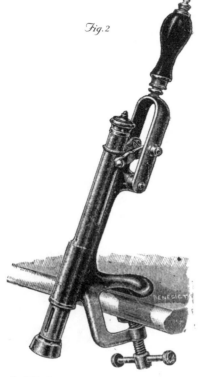

Fig.2

Smith's Patent Palace Cork Extractor.

Baldwin's Pyrometer Oven Door Knob.
Useful as well as Ornamental. The great Fuel Saver –a Stove Thermometer.
Pointer hand on nickel dial knob indicates *exact heat of oven.* It takes place of usual *oven door knob;* can be applied in a moment by any person to any *stove* or *range* now in use. It will not burn the hands. It *insures economy in fuel.* It tells exactly how to regulate your fire for baking bread, pastry, or meats.
Agents wanted. Samples, post paid, $1.50; Agts., $9.00 per doz. Send for circular. CHICAGO NICKEL WORKS, 150 Lake St., Chicago.

Fig.1

Distelhorst's Patent Grating Machine.

Fig.3 - Pat'd. 12-18-1888

CHIEFTAIN CO., Canton, OH

Maker of *CYCLONE* (Fig.1) and *LIGHTNING* (Fig.2) can openers and *GEM* vegetable mashers (Fig.3), all introduced in 1891.

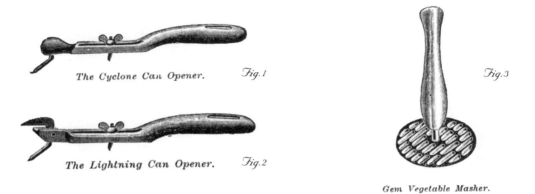

The Cyclone Can Opener. *Fig.1*

The Lightning Can Opener. *Fig.2*

Fig.3

Gem Vegetable Masher.

CHRISTY KNIFE CO., Fremont, OH

Founded about 1890 by Russ J. Christy. Maker of a variety of special wavy edge bread and carving knives, including the *CHRISTY* bread knife introduced in 1892 (Fig.1). The *CHRISTY* razor ground paring knife (Fig.2) was also introduced in 1892 and a 12" meat and household saw (Fig.3) in 1893. 1894 offerings included bread, ham, and carving knives (Fig.4). A wooden handle version of their bread knife (Fig.5) was introduced in 1895.

A special mayonnaise mixer was introduced in 1900 (Fig.6). A small funnel, attached to the beater, allowed the oil to be fed in away from the side of the bowl and at a controlled rate.

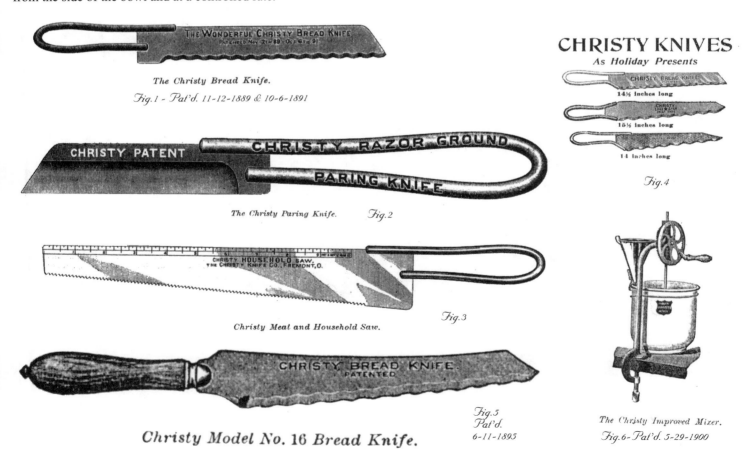

The Christy Bread Knife.
Fig.1 - Pat'd. 11-12-1889 & 10-6-1891

The Christy Paring Knife. *Fig.2*

Christy Meat and Household Saw. *Fig.3*

Christy Model No. 16 Bread Knife.

Fig.5 Pat'd. 6-11-1895

CHRISTY KNIVES
As Holiday Presents

14½ inches long

15½ inches long

14 inches long

Fig.4

The Christy Improved Mixer.
Fig.6- Pat'd. 5-29-1900

CINCINNATI STAMPING CO., Cincinnati, OH

Maker of coffee pots (Fig.1) and coffee boilers (Fig.2), introduced in 1890.

Fig.1

Improved Coffee Pots.—Fig. 1.—Side View
of Coffee Pot.

Fig.2

Fig. 2.—General View of Coffee Boiler.

CINCINNATI TOOL CO., Cincinnati, OH

Formed in 1879 to make a variety of woodworking tools. The firm was taken over by E.H. Hargrave in 1899 and reorganized as the Hargrave Tool Co. in 1925. The only kitchen tool thus far encountered is the *PERFECTION* coal tongs designed for use with kitchen stoves and introduced in 1895. *(Illustration at right)*

Perfection Coal Tongs.

Fig.1-
Pat'd.
1-8-1884

Clad's Patent Ice-Cream Machine.

CLAD, VALENTINE, Philadelphia, PA

Maker, in 1888, of Clad's ice cream machine (Fig.1); the *CLEWELL* ice cream disher, in five sizes (Fig.2); and the *CLEWELL* ice cream measure (Fig.3). *(Illustrations at left and below)*

—The Clewell Ice-Cream Disher.

Fig.2 - Pat'd. 11-12-1878

—The Clewell Ice-Cream Measure.

Fig.3 - Pat'd. 11-12-1878

Lifter for Hot Dishes.

CLARK & CO., W.J., Canton, OH

Maker of a hot dish lifter, introduced in 1890.
(Illustration at right)

CLARK HARDWARE CO., Rockford, IL

Founded in 1874 by J.L. Clark as a retail hardware store. In 1904 it announced that it would withdraw from the retail trade and devote all its attention to the manufacture of *CRISPY* toasters and *GEM* sifters.

The Gem Sifter.

The Clark Crispy Toaster.

CLARK MFG. CO., Fond du Lac, WI

Maker of the *BOSS* fire kindler introduced in 1897. The kindler was filled with asbestos which was soaked in kerosene when ready for use.

Boss Fire Kindler, One-Half Size.

CLARK & PARSONS, East Wilton, ME

Makers, in 1910, of the *LIGHTNING* 9 inch bread knife.

CLARK NOVELTY CO., Rochester, NY

Maker of a pear and apple corer introduced in 1890 (Fig.1) and *SMITH'S* peach cutter and stoner, introduced in 1892 (Fig.2). The peach stoner was equipped with two spring loaded, revolving knives which followed the contour of the stone as they sliced the peach in half.
(Illustrations at right and below)

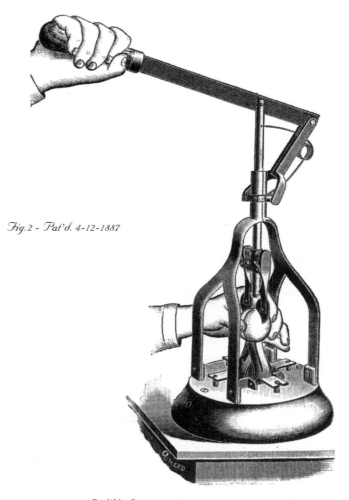

Fig.2 - Pat'd. 4-12-1887

Fig.1

New Pear and Apple Corer.

Smith's Improved Peach Cutter and Stoner.

CLAUSS SHEAR CO., Fremont, OH

Founded in 1878 by John H. Clauss (1855-1919). Primary products were scissors and shears but some other household goods were also made. Clauss scalloped edge knives (Fig.1) were introduced in 1892; a flexible pot and kettle cleaner in 1893 (Fig.2), and the *VICTOR* chopping and mincing knife (Fig.3), previously made by Corbin & Kenyon, was offered in 1894. *(Illustrations continued on next page)*

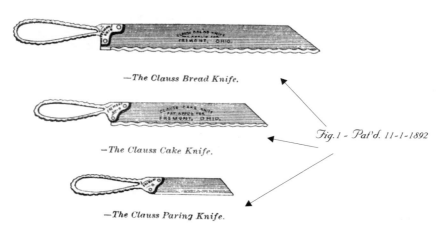

—*The Clauss Bread Knife.*

—*The Clauss Cake Knife.*

Fig.1 - Pat'd. 11-1-1892

—*The Clauss Paring Knife.*

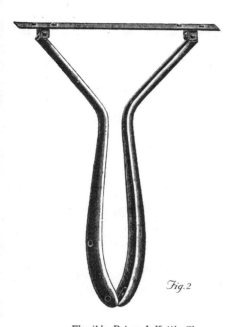

Fig.2

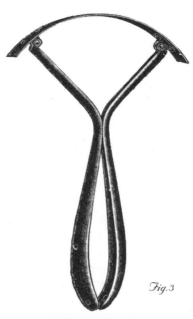

Fig.3

Fig.4

Victor Chopping and Mincing Knife.

—Flexible Pot and Kettle Cleaner.

—As Used for Round Surfaces.

CLEANLY EGG SHELLER CO., Pittsburgh, PA

Maker of egg shellers introduced in 1909. The device was a spring loaded striker which would "crack and prepare hot soft boiled eggs in a cleanly manner." *(Illustration at right)*

Fig. 1.—The Cleanly Egg Sheller.

CLEMENT & DUNBAR, Philadelphia, PA

Maker, in 1894, of the *HERO* ice cream freezer. *(Illustration at left)*

Hero Double Action Ice Cream Freezer.

CLEVELAND METAL PRODUCTS CO., Cleveland, OH

Maker, during the 1920's, of aluminum ware and a line of *ALADDIN* enamel cookware.

CLIMAX MFG. CO., Cleveland, OH

Maker of the one hand *CLIMAX* flour sifter, introduced in 1894. *(Illustration at right)*

The Climax Sifter.

CLIPPER MFG. CO., Cincinnati, OH

Maker of *CENTENNIAL* cake pans in 1890. The side, bottom and tube were all detachable. *(Illustration at right)*

CLOUGH & WILLIAMSON, Newark, NJ, later
CLOUGH CO., ROCKWELL, Alton, NH

A partnership of William Rockwell Clough (1844-1920) and Cornelius T. Williamson formed in 1875 to make wire corkscrews (Fig.1). A pocket corkscrew (Fig.2) was introduced in 1880; as well as folding corkscrews (Figs.3-4).

In 1885, the partnership was dissolved and Clough moved to Alton, NH, where he operated as the Rockwell Clough Co. Williamson remained in Newark, NJ, where he operated as the Williamson Co.

The Rockwell Clough Co. became a very large maker of wire corkscrews, claiming an output of 30,000,000 corkscrews in 1904 alone. Offerings included a small pocket corkscrew (Fig.5); the 99 solid handle steel cork screw (Fig.6), and the *NEWIRE* corkscrew (Fig.7) introduced in 1902.

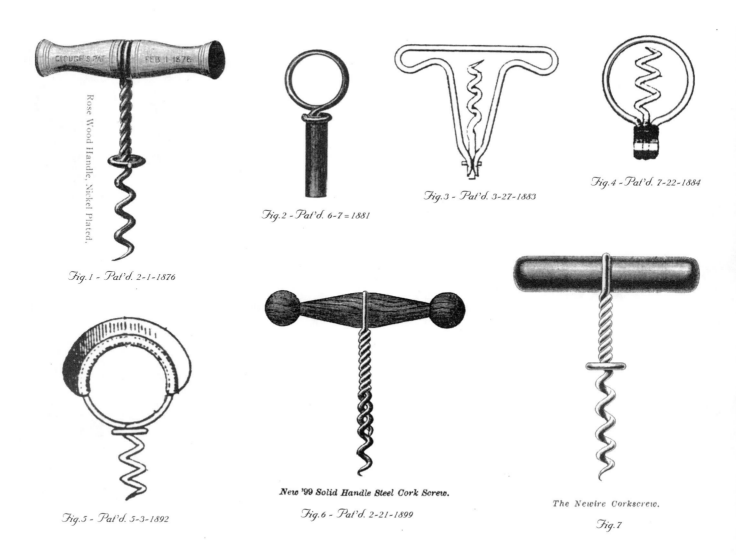

Fig.1 - Pat'd. 2-1-1876

Rose Wood Handle, Nickel Plated.

Fig.2 - Pat'd. 6-7 = 1881

Fig.3 - Pat'd. 3-27-1883

Fig.4 - Pat'd. 7-22-1884

Fig.5 - Pat'd. 5-3-1892

New '99 Solid Handle Steel Cork Screw.
Fig.6 - Pat'd. 2-21-1899

The Newire Corkscrew.
Fig.7

COBIN MFG. CO., New York, NY

Maker of a crank operated wine or beverage cooler, introduced in 1893.

Wine or Beverage Cooler.

COLBROOKDALE IRON CO., Pottstown, PA

Maker of the *CONNECTICUT* meat chopper, introduced in 1895 (Figs.1-3) and the *KEYSTONE* food chopper, introduced in 1906 (Fig.4). By 1906, the *CONNECTICUT* meat chopper was a product of O.D. Woodruff.

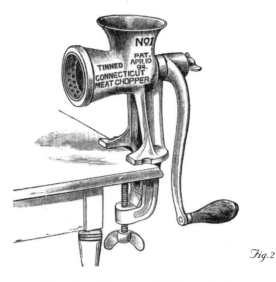

Fig.2

—*Connecticut Chopper with Clamp No. 1.*

Connecticut Chopper No. 2.
Fig.1 - Pat'd. 4-10-1894

Fig.3

—*Connecticut Sausage Stuffing Attachment.*

Fig.4

Keystone Food Chopper.

COLE, DAVID H., Brooklyn, NY

Inventor, and probably maker, of the *SAFETY* can opener. The name refered to the spur which protected the fingers during use.

Pat'd. 5-12-1914

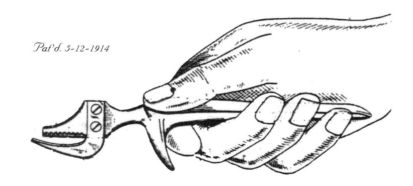

COLUMBIAN ENAMELING & STAMPING CO., Terre Haute, IN

Founded about 1900 to make a line of *ONYX,* mottled white on brown, enameled ware. Two hundred different items were offered, included a self-basting turkey roaster introduced in 1908. About 1920, the firm added a more expensive line, *SANITROX* ware, made with white porcelain enamel. *(Illustration at right)*

Enameled Self-Basting Roaster.

COMSTOCK-BOLTON CO., Kansas City, MO

Maker, in 1924, of the *MAGUIRE* aluminum egg poacher, "no more soggy toast." The firm also made the *C-B-CO* bottle capper. *(Illustration at left)*

CONSOLIDATED MFG. CO., Hartford, CT

Maker, in 1909, of a glass ice cream freezer priced at $1.25. *(Illustration at right)*

CONSTANCE CO., Mansfield, OH

Maker of the *BLUST* self-recommending churn introduced in 1908. *(Illustrations below)*

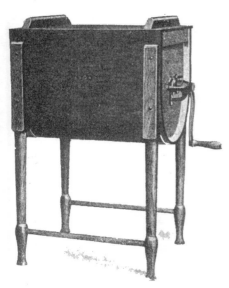

The Blust Self-Recommending Churn.

The Blust Dasher.

CONVERSE, E.M., Southington, CT

Maker of hollow ware formed from sheet metal, patented July 20, 1831, and tinware patented November 19, 1833.

CONVERSE, M.D., New York, NY

Maker, as late as 1910, of the QUICK AS A WINK cork puller.
(Illustration at right)

QUICK AS A WINK.

Pat'd. 5-9-1899

COOK, BURTON H., Brooklyn, NY

Maker of *COOK'S* grater and slicer (Fig.1); and lemon juice extractors (Figs.2-3), introduced in 1907.

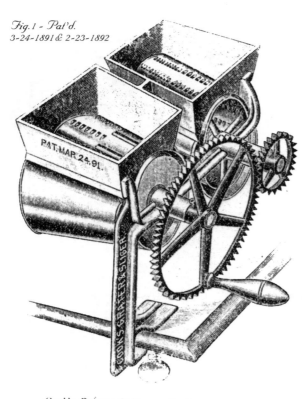

Fig.1 - Pat'd.
3-24-1891 & 2-23-1892

Cook's Rotary Culinary Grater and Slicer.

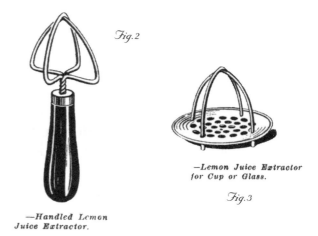

Fig.2

—Handled Lemon
Juice Extractor.

—Lemon Juice Extractor
for Cup or Glass.

Fig.3

COOK CO., FRANK B., Chicago, IL, <u>later</u> COOK ELECTRIC CO., Chicago, IL

Maker of the *IDEAL* nut cracker, patented by Cook. The first type (Fig.1), introduced in 1919, was furnished with knobs on the T handle. The second type (Fig.2), offered in 1920 when the company name was changed to Cook Electric Co., was made without knobs. Both types were offered in plain nickel at 75 cents and highly polished nickel at $1.

Fig.1
Pat'd.
8-6-1918

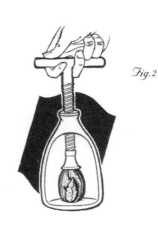

Fig.2

COOK FLOUR BIN CO., Homer, MI

Maker, in 1893, of *COOK'S* flour bin and sieve. The bin was made primarily of wood except for the sieve. *(Illustration at right)*

CORBIN & KENYON, Owego, NY

Maker of the *VICTOR* mincing or chopping knife, introduced in 1892. The Clauss Shear Co. took over production in 1894. *(Illustration at left)*

Victor Mincing or Chopping Knife.

Cook Flour Bin and Sieve.

CORDLEY & HAYES, New York, NY

Maker of fiber ware items, including a surprisingly old-fashioned churn, introduced in 1890 (Fig.1) and the *EASY* ice cream freezer (Fig.2).

INDURATED
FIBRE
WARE

ALWAYS
SWEET

ALWAYS
TIGHT

Churn of Indurated Fiber Ware.

Fig.1

—Easy Freezer Complete.

Fig.2

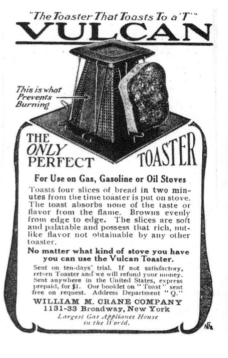

"The Toaster That Toasts To a 'T'"

VULCAN

This is what Prevents Burning

THE ONLY PERFECT TOASTER

For Use on Gas, Gasoline or Oil Stoves

Toasts four slices of bread in two minutes from the time toaster is put on stove. The toast absorbs none of the taste or flavor from the flame. Browns evenly from edge to edge. The slices are soft and palatable and possess that rich, nut-like flavor not obtainable by any other toaster.

No matter what kind of stove you have you can use the Vulcan Toaster.

Sent on ten-days' trial. If not satisfactory, return Toaster and we will refund your money. Sent anywhere in the United States, express prepaid, for $1. Our booklet on "Toast" sent free on request. Address Department "Q."

WILLIAM M. CRANE COMPANY
1131-33 Broadway, New York
Largest Gas Appliance House in the World.

CRANE CO., WILLIAM M., New York, NY

Maker of VULCAN toasters in 1905. *(Illustration at right)*

Crane's "76" Potato Masher.

PATENT. 1875.

Efficient, durable, and easily cleaned. Supplied to the trade only. Samples sent free to responsible houses. Agents wanted in every State. Send for illustrated circulars and price list to

ROBERT CRANE, Jr., Columbia, Lancaster Co., Pa.

CRANE, ROBERT,
Columbia, PA

Maker, beginning in 1876, of Crane's "76" potato masher, patented December 28, 1875. *(Illustration at left)*

CROWN THROAT & OPENER CO., Chicago, IL

Maker, beginning in 1911, of a series of bottle openers, some of them risque by the standards of the time. All were made under design patents issued to Harry L. Vaughan.

Patent 12/26/11   *Patent 4/30/12*   *Patent 6/17/13*   *Patent 11/25/13*   *Patent 12/8/14*

CRYSTAL PERCOLATOR CO., New York, NY

Maker of a glass percolator, patented July 6, 1915, by Fiore Ricciardelli. Note the close likeness to the Silex Co. coffee maker introduced a year earlier. *(Illustration at right)*

CURLEY, THOMAS, Troy, NY

Inventor and maker of a self-extracting corkscrew (Fig.1); and moulded lemon squeezers (Figs.2-3).

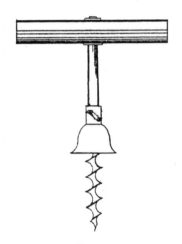

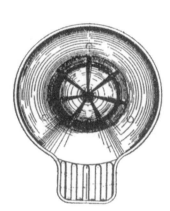

Fig.1 - Pat'd. 4-22-1884   *Fig. 2 - Pat'd. 12-15-1891*   *Fig.3 - Pat'd. 10-20-1896*

DAIRY QUEEN CHURN CO., Monmouth, IL

Maker of the *DAIRY QUEEN* churn in 1908. Made in two quart capacity, it was claimed to make butter in two minutes. *(Illustration at right)*

The Dairy Queen Churn.

DAME, STODDARD & KENDALL, Boston, MA

Introduced, in 1888, Curley's patent corkscrew. They were probably agents rather than makers. *(Illustration at right)*

Pat'd. 3-22-1884

DANA & CO., Cincinnati, OH

Operated by George F. Dana. Maker, beginning in 1895 when it took over the line from the Peerless Freezer Co., of the *PEERLESS ICELAND* line of ice cream freezers (Fig.1), including a toy, one pint, model (Fig.2). The *FREZO* model (Fig.3) was added in 1900. In 1906, the firm introduced the *DANA* food chopper (Fig.4). *(Illustrations continued on next page)*

DANA & CO.
Ninth and Sycamore Streets.
Manufacturers of Peerless Iceland Ice Cream Freezers.

The *only* way to be sure that ice-cream is fit for the home table is to *make* it at home. This is a simple matter with a Peerless Iceland Freezer. It *never* turns hard; freezes cream smooth, fine and firm in *three minutes*; is easily cleaned—has the fewest parts.

If not on sale in your town order direct from us. We pay the express. You may try it several times. If it doesn't make *good cream easily* we will pay for its return and refund your money at once. Dealers sell Peerless Iceland the same way.

The new cook book— "Ice Creams and Ices by Well-Known Cooks"— is splendid. We send it with name of a Peerless Iceland dealer if you write us. Address THE DANA MFG. CO., Dept. H, CINCINNATI.

Fig. 1

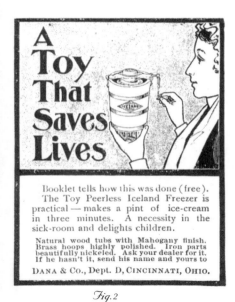

Fig. 2

Frezo Ice Cream Freezer.

Fig. 3

The Dana Food Chopper.

Fig. 4

DARLING FILTER CO., Cleveland, OH

Operated by Cornelius Darling and R.R. Darling. Maker, in 1894, of an ice pick. The pick was made with a sliding head and a cast bell to guide the pick and prevent flying chips. *(Illustration at right)*

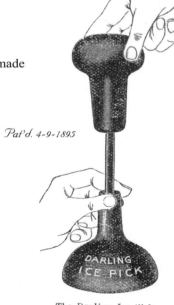

Pat'd. 4-9-1895

The Darling Ice Pick.

Pat'd. 8-28-1894

DAVIDSON & CO. O.E., Nashville, TN

Maker of the *ELECTRIC* cider press, introduced in 1894. *(Illustration at left)*

Davidson's Electric Cider Press

DAVIS CAN-SERVER CORP., New York, NY

Maker, in 1919, of a special pitcher made to punch, and hold, a can of evaporated milk "the Cleanly Way".

DAY & CO., J.H., Cincinnati, OH

Maker of the *CYCLONE* kraut and vegetable cutter, introduced in 1892. It claimed that "two large boys can cut 300 heads of cabbage in one hour." *(Illustration at right)*

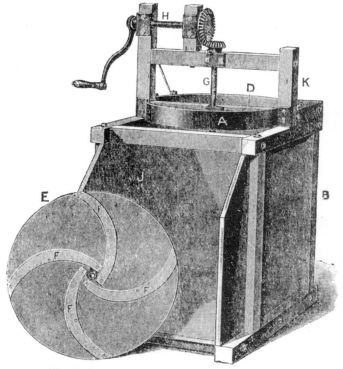

The Cyclone Revolving Kraut and Vegetable Cutter.

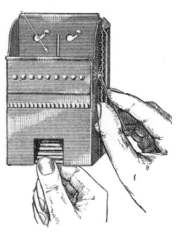

The Lusk Match Safe.

DAYTON CO., Buffalo, NY

Maker of the *LUSK* match safe, introduced in 1908. *(Illustration at left)*

DAZEY CHURN & MFG. CO., St. Louis, MO

Incorporated in 1906 by Nathan P. Dazey (1856-1945) to make the *DAZEY* home butter churn. Dazey served as president and later chairman until his death in 1945. *DAZEY* family churns were first offered in a glass version (Fig.1) made in four sizes from 3 to 9 pints. Later offerings included an all metal version (Fig.2), made in one-half and one gallon sizes; and an improved glass model (Fig.3) made in 4, 6, and 8 pint sizes. The *SHARPIT* knife sharpener (Fig.4), 5" high with 1/" wheels, was introduced in 1925. Other products included straw dispensers, patented November 28, 1911, wall mount can openers, fruit juicers and ice crushers.

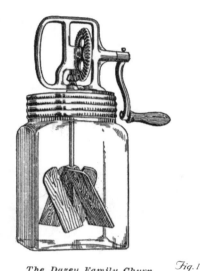   

Fig.2 - Pat'd. 12-18-1917 & 12-20-1921

Fig.3 - Pat'd. 2-14-1922

Fig.4

The Dazey Family Churn. *Fig.1*

DE STEIGER, J.L., La Salle, IL

Inventor, and probably maker, of a fruit jar wrench. The wrench was equipped with a small wheel that rode on the jar as the wrench was turned. *(Illustration at right)*

Pat'd. 3-5-1907

DEAN'S.

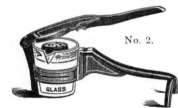

No. 2.

DEAN, WILLIAM B., New York, NY

Inventor and maker of a lemon squeezer fitted with a removeable glass cup. *(Illustration at left)*

Pat'd. 2-8-1882

DELPHOS MFG. CO., Delphos, OH

Maker of a sheet iron corn popper, introduced in 1908. These poppers were popular for years. *(Illustration at right)*

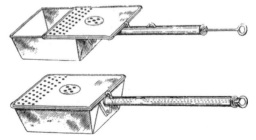

The Delphos Improved Sheet Iron Corn Popper.

DETROIT CORKSCREW CO., Detroit, MI

Maker, in 1893, of the *DAVIS* combination corkscrew, knife and wire cutter (Fig.1); and the *PUDDLEFOOT* corkscrew (Fig.2).

Fig. 1.—The Davis Corkscrew.

Fig.1 - Pat'd. 7-7-1891 & 7-14-1891

—The Puddefoot Corkscrew.

Fig.2 - Pat'd. 7-11-1893

JEWEL.

DETROIT STOVE WORKS, Detroit, MI

A large maker of kitchen stoves and ranges, the firm also offered, in 1911, the *JEWEL* stove top toaster. The toaster would handle four slices which were reversed with the action of a "patent swinging bracket." *(Illustration at right)*

THE DE VORE PLANT.

DEVORE & CO., L.M., Freeport, IL

Founded in 1892 to make cast iron hardware specialties, including hinges, stove lid lifters patented March 17, 1891; cork extractors (Fig.1); nut crackers (Fig.2); and a variety of bicycle items. The firm was absorbed by the Arcade Mfg. Co. in 1899. *(Illustrations at left and below)*

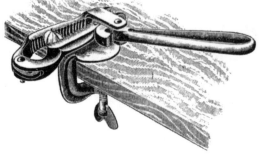

De Vore's Universal Nut Crack.

Fig.2

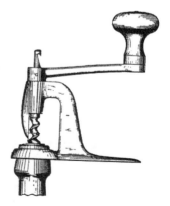

Fig.1 - Pat'd. 9-4-1888 & 9-25-1888

DIAMOND CUTLERY CO., New York, NY

Maker of the *DIAMOND* scissors sharpener (Fig.1), introduced in 1894 and the *DIAMOND* knife sharpener (Fig.2), introduced in 1895.

The Diamond Knife Sharpener.

Fig.2

Diamond Sharpener.

Fig.1

DILVER MFG. CO., Pittsburgh, PA

Maker, beginning in 1921, of the *DILVER* combination colander and strainer claimed to "remove seed and skins from a bushel of tomatoes, grapes or pitted fruit in ten minutes." *(Illustration at right)*

DISSTON & SONS, HENRY, Philadelphia, PA

The largest saw maker in the U.S., the firm also made a variety of edge tools and kitchen tools which contained cutting edges. Products offered in 1899 included slaw cutters in one and two knife versions (Fig.1); "crout" cutters in adjustable knife and fixed knife versions (Fig.2); potato or turnip shredders (Fig.3); and fresh corn graters (Fig.4). By 1915, the firm included mincing knives (Fig.5) in its catalogs. *(Illustrations continued on next page)*

ONE KNIFE.

Fig.1

TWO-KNIFE SLAW CUTTER.

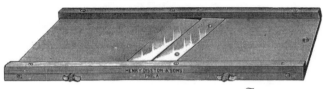

Fig.2

ADJUSTABLE CROUT CUTTERS.

Fig.3

CROUT CUTTERS.

Fig.4

CORN GRATER.

Fig.6

POTATO OR TURNIP SHREDDER.

Fig.5

No. 8

Fig.7

DOVER STAMPING CO., Boston, MA, <u>later</u>
DOVER STAMPING & MFG. CO., Boston, MA

Founded by Horace Whitney in 1833 to make tin ware in Dover, NH. In 1857, a branch was opened in Boston and the firm was reorganized as the Dover Stamping Co. The entire operation was moved to Boston in 1866. By 1869 the firm, in addition to tin ware, also offered hollow ware, Britannia ware, and a variety of other household goods such as the *HERSEY* double action apple parer (Fig.1); the *ICE KING* ice cream freezer (Fig.2) in 2 to 23 quart sizes; coffee roasters (Fig.3); *BLOOD'S* flour and cornmeal sifter (Fig.4); *EARLES'S* patent egg beater (Fig.5); and *MONROE'S* patent egg beater (Fig.6). Dover was likely the agent, rather than the maker, of some of these goods.

The firm reorganized as the Dover Stamping & Mfg. Co. when Horace Whitney's son, Edward Whitney took control in 1883. Horace F. Whitney, Edward's son, took over when his father died in 1906. *(continued on next page)*

Fig.1 - Pat'd 6-18-1861 & 8-30-1864

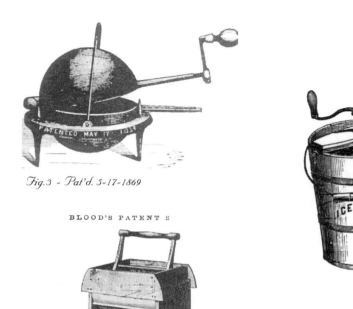

Fig.3 - Pat'd. 5-17-1869

BLOOD'S PATENT S

Fig.4 - Pat'd. 9-17-1861 & 1-9-1866

Fig.2

Beginning about 1870, the firm made a wide variety of *DOVER* egg beaters under one or more patents (Figs.7-11). A tumbler model (Fig.12) was introduced in 1895 for beating one or two eggs in a glass and the improved *DOVER*, with an idler gear (Fig.13), was introduced in 1897. By the turn of the century, the name *DOVER* appears to have become a generic term for this type of egg beater and was used as a trade name by several other makers.

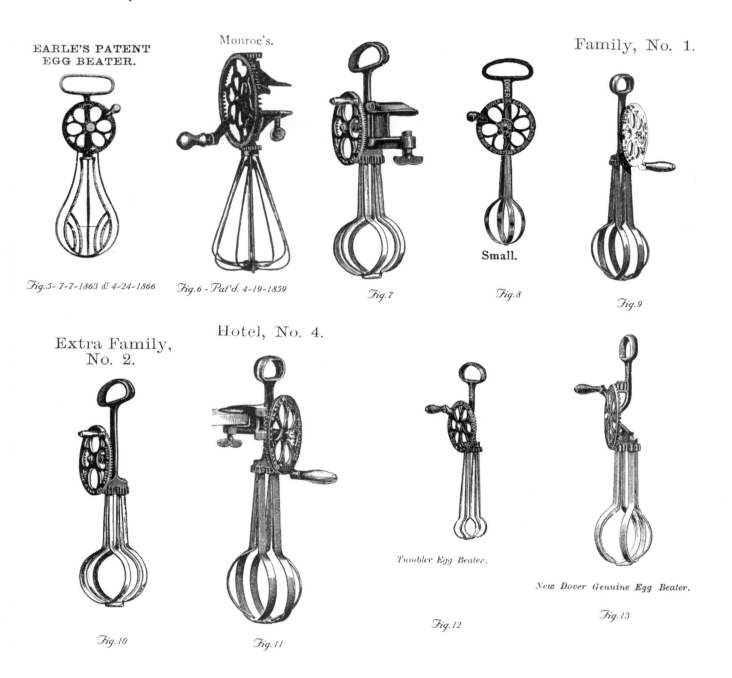

EARLE'S PATENT
EGG BEATER.

Monroe's.

Family, No. 1.

Small.

Fig.5- 7-7-1863 & 4-24-1866

Fig.6 - Pat'd. 4-19-1859

Fig.7

Fig.8

Fig.9

Extra Family,
No. 2.

Hotel, No. 4.

Tumbler Egg Beater.

New Dover Genuine Egg Beater.

Fig.13

Fig.10

Fig.11

Fig.12

Figs.7-11 - Pat'd 5-31-1870, 5-6-1873, 7-14-1885, 4-3-1888, & 11-24-1891

DOYLE, J.J., Sharon, CT

Inventor and maker of a "beefsteak crusher", patented November 14, 1865. The top roller was held by rubber bushings which allowed the unit to self-adjust for thickness of the meat or to "allow bones to pass through." *(Illustration at right)*

DRAKE & MILLS, Cleveland, OH

Maker of the PERFECTION fruit jaw wrench and PERFECTION jar holder, introduced in 1902. *(Illustration at left)*

The Perfection Fruit Jar Wrench and Jar Holder.

DUNDEE MFG. CO., Boston, MA

Maker, in 1922, of the DUPLEX cast aluminum, dripless, smokeless broiler. *(Illustration at right)*

DUNLAP, C.W., New York, NY

Maker, in 1890, of kitchen tools including mincing knives, paring knives and cake turners.

DUNLAP, J.S., Chicago, IL

Maker of *DUNLAP'S* nutmeg razor (Fig.1) and DUNLAP'S silver blade cream and egg whip (Fig.2), both introduced in 1906; and *DUNLAP'S* coffee extractor (Fig.3), which operated on the drip principle. *(continued next page)*

The cream and egg whip came with a special stoneware bowl, made with a dimple in the bottom to support and center the rotating blade. It was offered, through distributer Casey- Hudson Co., well into the 1920's. Dunlap also had a version, patented February 26, 1907, equipped with a dasher adjustable for curvature.

4/7 SIZE

Dunlap's Nutmeg Razor.

Fig.1 - Pat'd. 7-301907

Dunlap's Silver Blade Cream and Egg Whip.

Fig.2 - Pat'd. 5-15-1906

—Dunlap's Coffee Extractor.

Fig.3 - Pat'd. 11-19-1907

DUPLEX FORK CO., Fremont, OH

Maker of the *MARVELOUS DUPLEX* serving fork, introduced in 1893. The same fork was later made by Cassady-Fairbank Co.

DUPLEX MFG. CO., Cincinnati, OH

Maker, in 1898, of the combination *DUPLEX* butter churn and *KLONDIKE* ice cream freezer shown below

Fig 1.—The Duplex Churn.   *Fig. 2.—The Klondike Freezer.*

EAGLE MFG. CO., Lancaster, PA

Maker, in 1925 and before, of a line of wine and cider presses and crushers. Offerings included the *EAGLE* fruit press in three sizes (Fig.1); *EAGLE* combination apple grinder and press (Fig.2); and the *EAGLE* grape crusher (Fig.3).

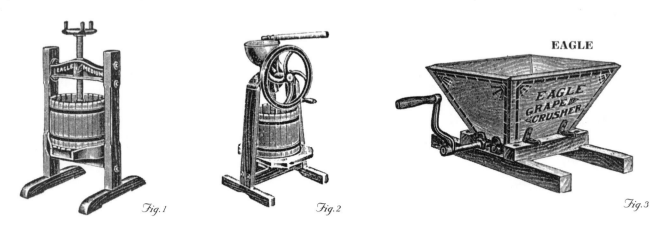

Fig.1   *Fig.2*   *Fig.3*

EASLEY MFG. CO., WILLIAM F., New York, NY

Maker, as late as 1910, of Easley's *DIAMOND POINT* lemon squeezers. Made of moulded glass, they were offered in a tumbler model (Fig.1), for squeezing directly into a glass, and solid dish model (Fig.2). Other styles of glass lemon squeezers were patented February 5, 1895, November 15, 1898, and March 6, 1900. *(Illustrations at right)*

Fig.1   *Pat'd. 9-10-1888*   *Fig.2*

EAST MFG. CO., Black Rock, NY

Maker of the X-RAY raisin seeder, introduced in 1896. *(Illustration at right)*

Pat'd. 12-24-1895

The X Ray Raisin Seeder.

EDGAR MFG. CO., Reading, MA

Maker of *EDGAR* nutmeg graters (Fig.1). An improved model (Fig.2) was introduced in 1897.

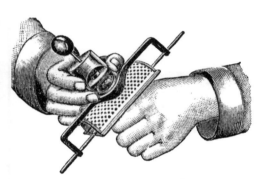

The Edgar Nutmeg Grater.

Fig.1 - Pat'd. 8-18-1891

The Edgar Nutmeg Grater.

Fig.2 - Pat'd. 11-10-1896

EDLUND CO., Burlington, VT

Founded by Henry J. Edlund about 1925 to make *EDLUND, JR.* (Fig.1) and institutional (Fig.2) can openers. Edlund also made the *TOP- OFF* jar lid remover and the *SURE-SHARP* knife sharpener. *(Illustrations at right)*

Fig.1 - Pat'd. 4-21-1925

Fig.2 - Pat'd. 5-12-1925

EDMONDS-METZEL MFG. CO., Chicago, IL

Maker of a combination egg cup and cutter, introduced in 1901. Rotating the top neatly cuts the end off the egg. *(Illustration at right)*

Combination Egg Cup and Cutter.

EDWARDS, M.L., Salem, OH

Operated by Martin L. Edwards. Maker of meat and vegetable choppers, patented August 15, 1871, June 3, 1873, and November24, 1874. In 1892, *EDWARDS'* improved lard and tallow press was introduced. *(Illustration at left)*

Edwards' Improved Lard and Tallow Press.

OPENRIGHT

EHRLICH, M. & L., Brooklyn, NY

Operated by Morris and Louis Ehrlich, inventors and makers of the *OPENRIGHT* can opener. "Cuts smoothly and leaves a rolled edge; no ragged edges to cut your hands." *(Illustration at right)*

Pat'd. 2-21-1922

Monarch Can Opener.

ELECTRIC LETTER BOX CO., Meriden, CT

Maker of the *MONARCH* can opener, introduced in 1894. The opener was aluminum plated. *(Illustration at left)*

ELIZABETH MFG. CO., Elizabeth, NJ

Maker of *ALPHA* dish tongs, introduced in 1895. "Designed for use when washing dishes in scalding water." *(Illustration at right)*

Alpha Dish Tongs.

ELLRICH HARDWARE MFG. CO., Plantsville, CT

Operated by Robert C. Ellrich from about 1883 until joining Peck, Stow & Wilcox about 1898. Maker of the *ELLRICH* meat cutter. *(Illustration at right)*

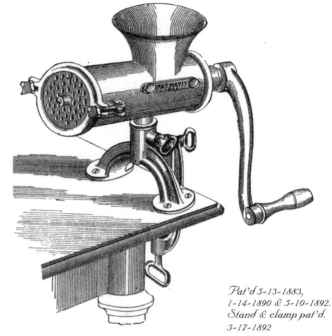

Pat'd 5-13-1883, 1-14-1890 & 5-10-1892. Stand & clamp pat'd. 5-17-1892

—*The Ellrich Meat Cutter.*

West's Percolator.

ELLSWORTH, T.G., New York, NY

Maker of WEST'S coffee percolator, introduced in 1893. Although called a percolator, the device was actually a perforated basket with enough sealed air space to float. It was placed in a pot of boiling water "where the agitation is the greatest and the action of the water forces the strength out of the coffee." *(Illustration at left)*

EMPIRE KNIFE CO., West Winsted, CT

Maker of the *EMPIRE* automatic cork extractor (Fig.1). An improved version was introduced in 1893 (Fig.2). *(Illustrations at right)*

Empire Automatic Cork Extractor.

Fig.1 - Pat'd. 4-16-1889

The Empire Automatic Cork Puller, No. 3.

Fig.2

71

EMPIRE STATE MFG. CO., Buffalo, NY

Maker, in 1877, of spun copper and half copper tea kettles (Fig.1). In 1886, the firm introduced copper tea kettles with a patented handle (Fig.2).

EMPIRE STATE MFG. CO., 37 Washington St., BUFFALO, N. Y.
BIXBY & DRULLARD, Proprietors,
MANUFACTURERS OF
HARDWARE SPECIALTIES,
SPUN COPPER and HALF COPPER TEA KETTLES,
MOULDERS' TOOLS, AWLS, COUNTER PEG FLOATS, CRIMP MACHINES,
METAL SPINNING AND NICKEL PLATING.
SEND FOR CATALOGUE.

Fig.1

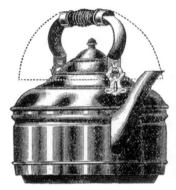

Fig.2

–Handle in Vertical Position.

ENTERPRISE ENAMEL CO., Bellaire, OH

Maker of the *CROWN* roaster (Fig.1), introduced in 1907; enameled churns (Fig.2) in 1908; *PEERLESS* enameled ware (Fig.3) in 1909 and *CORONA* enamel ware (Fig.4) in 1910. The line of *CORONA* enamel ware was also available "with highly decorative designs by a celebrated American artist and is the only decorative enamel ware of its kind made."

—Crown Roaster.

Fig.1

Enameled Churn.

Fig.2

The Peerless Seamless One-Piece Enameled Tea Kettle.

Fig.3

Crown Your
Kitchen With
CORONA
Enamel Ware

When you *invest* in CORONA Enamel Ware you get the very best — the kind *made* better than any other — that *looks* better — that gives longest service — and that will be an ornament to the kitchen.

CORONA Enamel Ware will not easily chip, and with ordinary use will not burn or rust. Colors are varied, and unusually beautiful and durable. Inside white linings are easily freed from strong fruit stains that permanently mar other ware. Steel shapes are *very* strong and do not easily dent.

Also made with highly decorative designs by a celebrated American artist. This is the only Decorative Enamel Ware of its kind made.

CORONA Ware crowns the kitchen and saves its own cost many times over because of its great durability. Awarded several gold medals, the last at the Alaska Yukon Pacific Exposition.

The Corona Roaster will delight any housewife's heart. *Cannot dry or burn the roast.* Made in one piece — not a single seam to retain grease or cooking odors. Easily cleaned. Also a full line of other enamel ware, from churns to toilet sets. Sold by dealers everywhere. Write us for interesting literature and name of Corona dealer nearest you.

The Enterprise Enamel Co.,
110 18th St., Bellaire, Ohio

Fig.4

ENTERPRISE MFG. CO., Everett, MA

Maker, in 1901, of *ORIGINAL* measuring spoons. The three spoons, 15, 30, and 45 drops (¼, ½, and ¾ teaspoons), were held together with an eyelet. *(Illustration at right)*

—*Original Measuring Spoon.*

ENTERPRISE MFG. CO., Philadelphia, PA

Formed May 8, 1866, by T. Henry Asbury (1838-1907) to make a self-measuring faucet for dispensing molasses. The firm soon branched out into a wide variety of cast iron kitchen and household goods, and by 1907, employed 900 workmen. Business continued well past 1925.

Products included fruit, wine and jelly presses, introduced about 1880 (Figs.1-2) and an improved version (Fig.3); fruit, lard and jelly presses, offered by 1885 (Fig.4); and a combination fruit and meat juice extractor (Fig.5).

Coffee and spice mills were important products, beginning with the *CHAMPION* model (Fig..6). A wall mounted coffee, drug and spice mill (Fig.7) was introduced in 1894; clamp-on (Fig.8) and free standing (Fig.9) home models were available by 1906. An improved wall mount model, adjustable for fineness of grind (Fig.10) was brought out in 1915. *(continued on next five pages)*

No. 46, $20.00

Capacity of Hopper, 3 quarts.   Height, 19 inches.
Length, 18 inches.   Weight, 36 lbs.

Fig.1 - Pat'd. 9-30-1879

No. 48, $30.00.

Capacity of Hopper, 8 qts.   Length, 25 in.   Height, 26
Weight, 90 lbs.

Fig.2 - Pat'd. 9-30-1879

Fig.3 - Pat'd. 6-5-1888

Fig.4

Enterprise Juice Extractor No. 21.

Fig.5 - Pat'd. 8-20-1895

Coffee, Corn, Spice & Drug Mill.
Three Sizes.

Fig. 6 - Pat'd. 6-21-1870

Fig. 7

Enterprise Coffee, Spice and Drug Mill

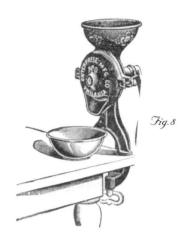

Fig. 8

Fig. 9

Fig. 10

Enterprise Coffee Mill
Number 100.

A wide variety of larger mills, primarily for stores, was offered in 1906. These included cast iron hopper models in 4, 8, and 12 ounce capacity (Fig.11), 1¾, 3 & 5 pound capacity with a drawer receiver (Fig.12), and 3½, 5 & 6½ pound capacity with a scoop receiver (Fig.13). Nickel hopper models were offered in ¾ & 2¼ pound capacity (Fig.14), and 4½ pound capacity (Fig.15). Free standing models were offered in iron hopper style with 6½ pound capacity with drawer receiver (Fig.16) or scoop receiver (Fig.17), and nickel hopper style with 7½ pound capacity (Fig.18). Most models were made well into the 1920's.

Fig. 11

Fig. 12

Fig. 13

Fig. 14

Fig. 15

Capacity of Iron Hopper—6½ lbs. of Coffee

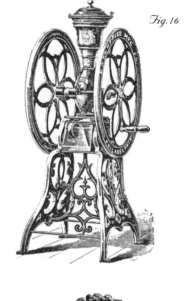

Fig. 16

Capacity of Iron Hopper—6½ lbs. of Coffee

Fig. 17

Capacity of Nickel-Plated Hopper—7½ lbs. of Coffee

Fig. 18

No. 5 Chopper.

Fig. 19 - 1-30-1883, 8-30-1892, 11-8-1892

No. 22 Chopper.

Fig. 20 - Pat'd. 1-30-1883, 8-30-1892, 11-8-1892

*Fig. 21 - Pat'd.
1-30-1883,
8-30-1892,
11-8-1892*

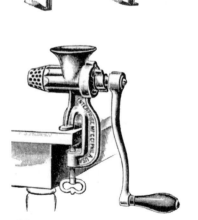

New No. 2 Chopper.

Fig. 22 - Pat'd. 9-17-1895

Fig. 3.— No. 44 Meat Chopper.

Meat choppers were made in a variety of sizes from #1 to #44 (Figs.19-21). There was a new #2 model (Fig.22); an improved #3 model was introduced in 1893 (Fig.23); and the new design #100 with three changeable cutters (Fig.24) was introduced in 1899. By 1906, a food masticator (Fig.25), designed for mounting on the dining table, was offered for use by those with poor teeth.

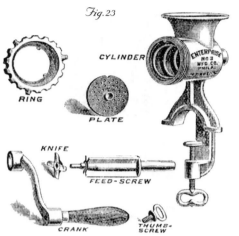

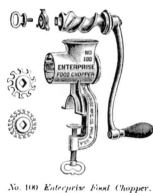

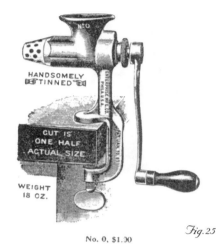

Fig.23

CYLINDER

RING

PLATE

KNIFE

FEED-SCREW

CRANK

THUMB-SCREW

Fig. 1.—No. 3 Enterprise Meat Chopper.

No. 100 Enterprise Food Chopper.
Fig.24

HANDSOMELY TINNED

CUT IS ONE-HALF ACTUAL SIZE

WEIGHT 18 OZ.

No. 0, $1.30

Fig.25

Cherry stoners included the #1 (Fig.26); #12 (Fig.27); a new model (Fig.28) introduced in 1901; and an improved model (Fig.29). Raisin seeders (Fig.30) were also offered.

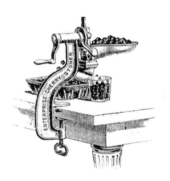

Fig.26 - Pat'd. 4-24-1883

Enterprise Cherry Stoner No. 12.
Fig.27 - Pat'd. 6-5-1894

Fig.28

Fig.29 - Pat'd. 3-31-1903

Sausage stuffers and lard presses were available in screw drive (Fig.31) or rack movement (Fig.32) in 1899. A double cylinder model was patented June 27, 1905, and an improved nozzle for the stuffers was patented July 17, 1906.

Also available in 1906 were self-gauging cheese cutters (Fig.33); tincture presses (Fig.34); cork pressers (Fig.35); ice shredders in two styles (Figs.36-37); tobacco shavers (Fig.38); and three styles of tobacco cutters (Fig.39).

Other products included the *ENTERPRISE* cork puller (Fig.40) introduced in 1889; *ENTERPRISE* ice shredder (Fig.41); new slaw cutter (Fig.42); a vegetable slicer by 1899 (Fig.43); the *CHAMPION* smoked beef shaver (Fig.44); an improved #23 smoked beef shaver (Fig.45) equipped with a sharpening attachment; a bottle capper in 1915 (Fig.46); and the *ENTERPRISE* home grain mill (Fig.47) introduced in 1917 "to supply a war-time need." *(Illustrations continued on next two pages)*

Fig. 30 - Pat'd. 4-2-1895 & 8-30-1895

Screw movement.

Fig. 31 - Pat'd. 4-10-1883

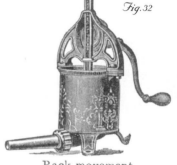

Rack movement.

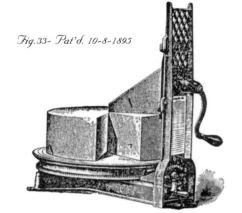

Fig. 33- Pat'd. 10-8-1895

Lift of Knife, 10 inches   Diameter of Table, 19 inches

Fig. 34

Fig. 36

Fig. 37

Fig. 35

Fig. 40

OUR Tobacco Cutters are undoubtedly the best in the world. The blades are of tempered steel, and in cutting have a draw cut movement which is very effective. Other Cutters have been put on the market, imitating ours in shape and finish, but inferior in mechanical principle and construction.

PRICES

No. 1—Cuts Plug 4⅜ inches wide - - - - $1.75

No. 1—Cuts Plug 4⅜ inches wide - - - -

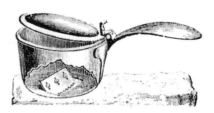

Fig. 38

No. 0,   - $1.00

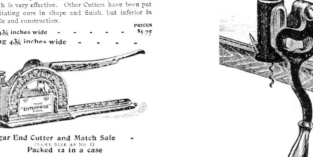

No. 3—With Cigar End Cutter and Match Safe -
(SAME SIZE AS No. 1)
Packed 12 in a case

Enterprise Cork Puller.

The Enterprise Ice Shredder.

Fig. 41 - Pat'd. 7-4-1893

"GOOD CHEER" is the most handsome Tobacco Cutter made. It is elegantly finished with rich nickel-plated mountings, and is of the same size as our No. 1.

No. 4—"Good Cheer" - - - - - $3.00

Fig. 39 - Pat'd. 4-13-1875 & 1-20-1885

Enterprise New Slaw Cutter No. 94.

Fig. 42 - Pat'd. 11-28-1893

Fig. 43

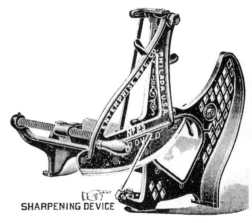

SHARPENING DEVICE

Fig. 45-Sharpening device pat'd. 8-6-1901

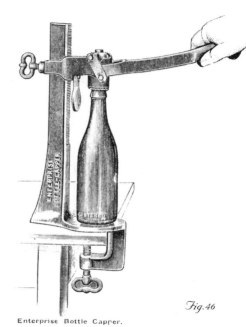

Champion Smoked Beef Shaver.

Fig. 44 - Pat'd. 10-5-1875, 11-19-1878 &
7-12-1881

Fig. 47

Durable and heavily tinned
—inside and out; can't rust;
easily operated and cleaned;
extra long handle.

Small Family Size
No. 54 . . $2.50

Large Family Size
No. 64 . . $5.00

Extension Hoppers
50c and 75c.

LARGER SIZED MILLS
FOR COMMUNITY USES

Fig. 46

Enterprise Bottle Capper.

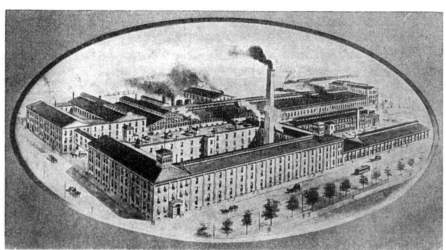

Factory in 1916

The Present Enterprise Plant, Covering Two City Blocks In Philadelphia.

ERIE SPECIALTY MFG. CO., Erie, PA, <u>later</u>
ERIE SPECIALTY CO., Erie, PA

Formed in 1888 as a partnership of Edwin Walker (1847-1917), Thomas A. Thomas and Benjamin D. Brown. Starting with 20 employees, the firm made a variety of household items patented by Walker. In 1892, Walker bought out his partners and reorganized as the Erie Specialty Co. which incorporated in 1902 with a capital of $100,000 and 67 employees. Walker's son, Clarence L. Walker, joined the new corporation and reorganized it as the C.L. WALKER CO. soon after his father's death in 1917.

Many products were made for the iced beverage market. *WALKER'S* ice plane (Fig.1), *WALKER'S* ice shave and adjustable ice grip (Fig.2), and *WALKER'S* beverage mixer (Fig.3) were all introduced in 1889.

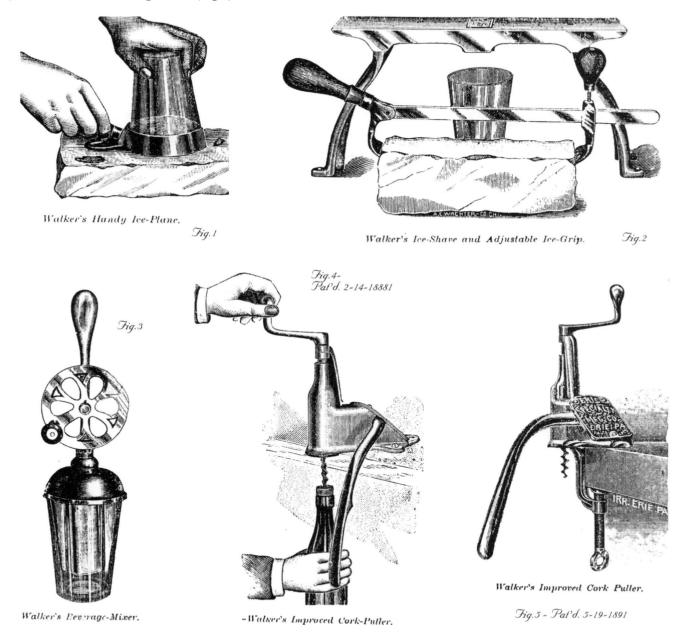

Walker's Handy Ice-Plane.

Fig.1

Walker's Ice-Shave and Adjustable Ice-Grip.

Fig.2

Fig.3

*Fig.4 -
Pat'd. 2-14-18881*

Walker's Beverage-Mixer.

-Walker's Improved Cork-Puller.

Walker's Improved Cork Puller.

Fig.5 - Pat'd. 5-19-1891

Cork screws and pullers were important items and included *WALKER'S* improved cork puller introduced in 1889 (Fig.4); another improved model introduced in 1890 (Fig.5); *WALKER'S* hand corkscrews, made in three styles (Figs.6-8), introduced in 1892; *WALKER'S SELF-PULLING* cork screw (Fig.9); *WALKER'S CROWN LIFTER* and *SELF PULLER* (Fig.10); *WALKER'S QUICK &*

EASY cork puller introduced in 1894 (Fig.11), with an improved form introduced in 1895 (Fig.12- shown on next page); and a pocket cork screw introduced in 1898 (Fig.13). Related products included a champagne tap (Fig.14) and an improved model (Fig.15).

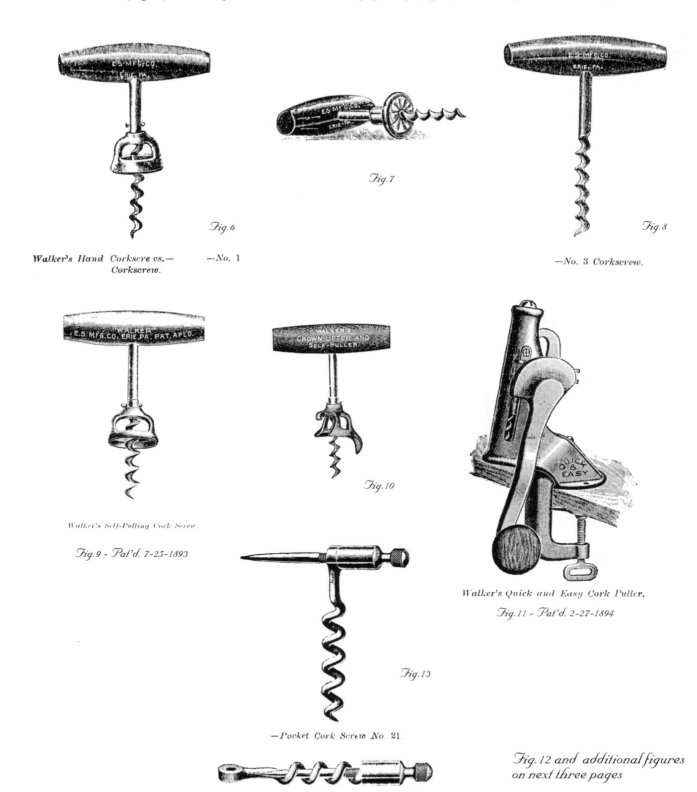

Fig.6

Fig.7

Fig.8

Walker's Hand Corkscrews.—   **—No. 1**   **—No. 3 Corkscrew.**
Corkscrew.

Fig.10

Walker's Self-Pulling Cork Screw.

Fig.9 - Pat'd. 7-25-1893

Walker's Quick and Easy Cork Puller.

Fig.11 - Pat'd. 2-27-1894

Fig.13

—*Pocket Cork Screw No. 21.*

Fig.12 and additional figures
on next three pages

—*Cork Screw in Shape for Pocket.*

The firm introduced *WALKER'S* improved lemon squeezer in 1888 (Fig.16); its *TABLE* model (Fig.17) and another improved style (Fig.18) in 1890. Still another improved model, the *QUICK & EASY*, patented February 9, 1897, (Fig.19) was introduced in 1897 along with an iron stand (Fig.20). The *QUICK & EASY* meat and fruit press (Fig.21) was introduced in 1905, but not patented until June 28, 1910.

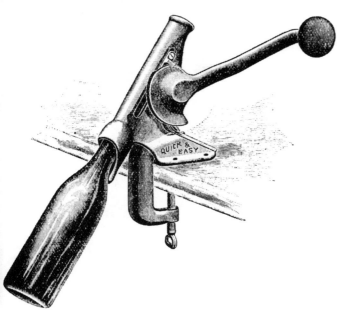

—*Walker's Quick and Easy Cork Puller.*

Fig. 12 - Pat'd. 7-23-1895 & 4-7-1896

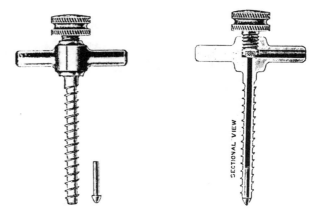

Walker's Champagne Tap.

Fig. 14 - Pat'd. 2-11-1902

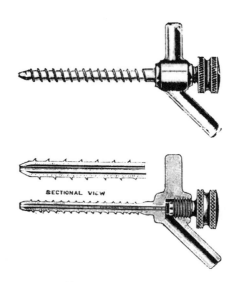

-*Walker's Champagne Tap No. 210.*

Fig. 15 - Pat'd. 4-19-1904

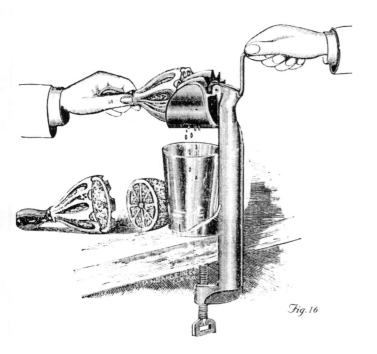

Fig. 16

Walker's Improved Lemon Squeezer.

Walker's Table Lemon Squeezer. — Fig. 17

Walker's Improved Lemon Squeezer. — Fig. 18

ALUMINUM CUP

GLASS RECEIVER

Fig. 19 - Pat'd. 2-9-1897

Improved Lemon Squeezer.

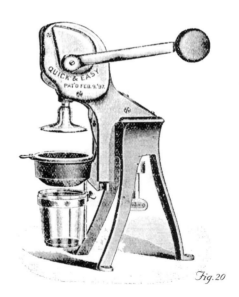

Fig. 20

Iron Stand for Lemon Squeezer.

Other products included *WALKER'S* improved cigar cutter, introduced in 1889 (Fig.22); a later model (Fig.23) introduced in 1890 along with an improved tobacco cutter (Fig.24); the *QUICK & EASY* shaker, introduced in 1898 (Fig.25); and the *QUICK & EASY* orange knife and peeler (Fig.26) introduced in 1906.

The last new products introduced were bottle openers, patented July 21, 1914, (Fig.27); lime squeezers (Fig.28); a variety of *QUICK & EASY* ice cream dippers patented July 7, 1908, December 26, 1911, May 11, 1915, and November 30, 1915, and *QUICK & EASY* ice picks (Fig.29). Production of the ice picks and ice cream dippers was continued by the C.L. WALKER CO., formed in 1918.

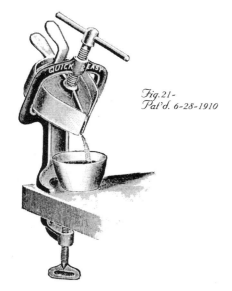

Fig.21-
Pat'd. 6-28-1910

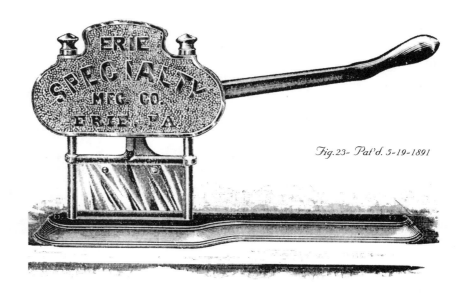

Fig.23- Pat'd. 5-19-1891

Walker's Quick and Easy Meat and Fruit Juice Press.

Walker's Improved Tobacco Cutter.

Fig.22

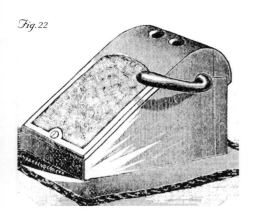

Fig.24

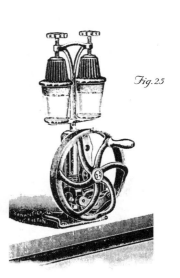

Fig.25

Walker's Improved Tobacco Cutter.

Quick and Easy Shaker No. 48½.

Fig.27- Pat'd. 7-21-1914

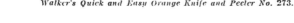

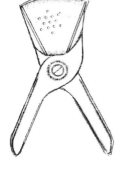

Fig.26

Walker's Quick and Easy Orange Knife and Peeler No. 273.

Fig.28- Pat'd. 12-7-1915

Fig.29

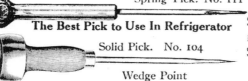

ESTATE STOVE CO., Hamilton, OH

Maker, beginning about 1923, of the *ESTATE* electric toaster, claimed to be the first four slice toaster. All four slices were reversed with a single lever.

ESTATE

Pat'd. 6-27-1911 & 4-14-1925

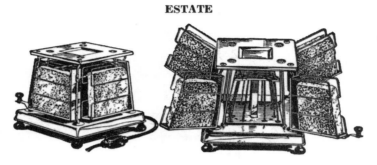

ESTES & CO., Nashua, NH

Maker of the *POLAR* ice pick, introduced in 1895.
(Illustration at right)

EUSTIS MFG. CO., Boston, MA, and New York, NY

Maker of the *PURITAN* cooker (Fig.1) with metal outer pot and ceramic inner pot; and the *PURITAN* egg poacher (Fig.2), both introduced in 1891. A tea strainer (Fig.3) was introduced in 1898 and a dish drainer (Fig.4) was introduced in 1902.

Fig.1

—*Puritan Cooker.*

Three-Ring Puritan Egg Poacher.

Fig.2 - Pat'd. 4-14-1891

Fig.3 - Pat'd. 7-19-1898

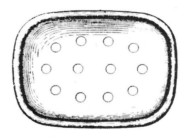

Fig.4 - Pat'd. 2-4-1902

EVEREDY CO., Frederick, MD

Maker, in 1924, of the *EVEREDY* jelly bag and stand (Fig.1) and the *EVEREDY* bottle capper (Fig.2). *(Illustrations at right)*

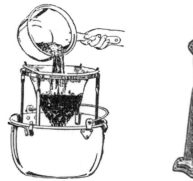

Fig.1

Fig.2

Pat'd. 10-10-1893 & 1-2-1894

EVERETT SPECIALTY CO., Boston, MA

Maker, in 1895, of a 15 cent raisin seeder. It was claimed to seed a pound in 10 minutes. *(Illustration at left)*

FABER, A.E., Plainfield, NJ

Maker of the *HANDY* household ice scraper introduced in 1904. *(Illustration at right)*

The Handy Household Ice Scraper.

FAHNESTOCK & CO., GEORGE E., Lancaster, PA

Maker, in 1892, of rather ornate egg holders and egg tongs which "obviate burnt fingers."

Pat'd. 7-27-1897

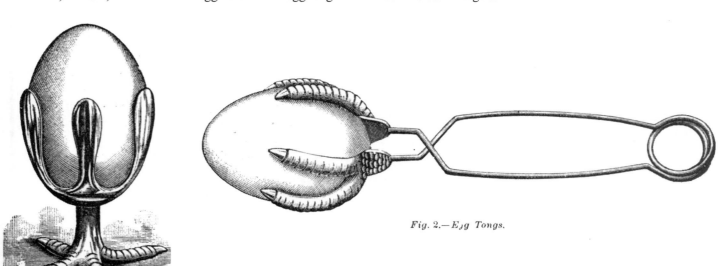

Fig. 2.—Egg Tongs.

Fig. 1.—Egg Holder.

FANNER MFG. CO., Cleveland, OH

Maker of a combination ice pick and ice chopper (Fig.1), patented by George J. Fanner and a fruit press, also patented by Fanner (Fig.2). The *ARCTIC* fruit jar wrench (Fig.3) was introduced in 1903. The fruit press was later made by the Silver Co.

Fig.2 - Pat'd. 6-23-1903

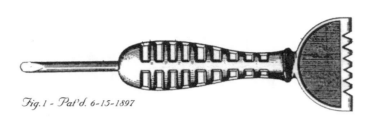

Fig.1 - Pat'd. 6-15-1897

Fig.3   —The Arctic Fruit Jar Wrench.

FARNSWORTH & CO., San Francisco, CA

Maker, in 1889, of the *EUREKA* fruit pitter for peaches, plums, apricots, nectarines, etc. *(Illustration at right)*

FARWELL, OZMUN, KIRK & CO., Minneapolis, MN

Maker, in 1895, of the *MACKLETT STAR* fish scaler.

—Eureka Fruit-Pitter.

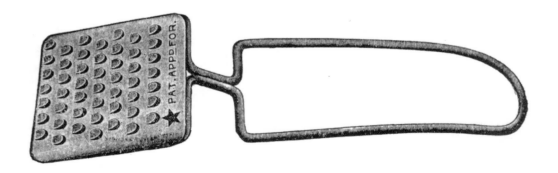

FEDERAL TOOL CO., Everett, MA

Maker of bread knives and ham slicers. *(Illustration at right)*

Pat.d 6-18-1912

FILLGROVE BROS. & CO., Ironton, OH

Maker, in 1898, of a simple vegetable shredder of a type still made today. *(Illustration at left)*

Vegetable Shredder.

FISHER, E.C., New York, NY

Maker of a combination salt shaker and pepper grinder, introduced in 1906. *(Illustration at right)*

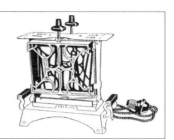

FITZGERALD MFG. CO., Torrington, CT

Maker, beginning about 1920, of the *STAR-RITE* line of electrical kitchen appliances, including waffle irons and toasters. (Illustration at left)

–Salt Shaker and Pepper Grinder Combined.

FOOTE FOUNDRY CO., J.B., Frederickstown, OH

Maker of the *CRYSTAL* ice cream freezer made in ten sizes, from one to 20 quarts, and introduced in 1908. *(Illustration at right)*

The Crystal Ice Cream Freezer.

FORBES CHOCOLATE CO., Cleveland, OH

Operated by Benjamin P. Forbes. Maker of the *TRIUMPH* fruit jar wrench, introduced in 1902. *(Illustration at left)*

Pat'd. 11-3-1903

The Triumph Fruit Can Wrench.

FORSTER & SON, J.C., Pittsburgh, PA

Maker of the 4-in-1 combination can opener and jar opener (Fig.1) and a combination peeler, corer and melon baller (Fig.2).

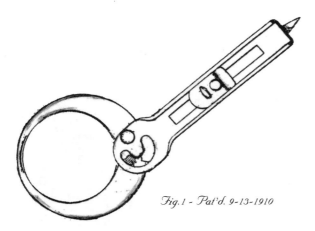

Fig.2 - Pat'd. 12-26-1916

Fig.1 - Pat'd. 9-13-1910

4-S FOOD PRESS CO., New York, NY

Maker of *STOCKING'S* Simplex Straining and Seeding press introduced in 1905. *(Illustration at right)*

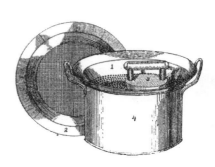

—*Stocking's Straining and Seeding Press.*

Pat'd. 2-10-1903

FOWLER & KEENE, New York, NY

Maker, in 1889, of clam roasters in two sizes; small (Fig.1) for little-neck clams and *UNIVERSAL* (Fig.2) for larger clams.

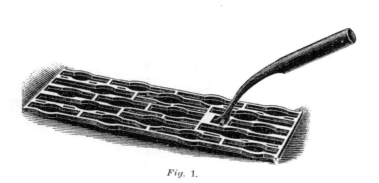

Fig. 1.

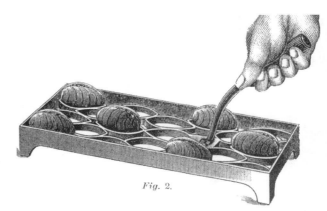

Fig. 2.

The Universal Clam-Roaster.

FRANKLIN SPECIALTY CO., Reading, PA

Maker of the *NEW IDEA* hot cake iron, introduced in 1904. *(Illustration at right)*

New Idea Hot Cake Iron.

FRARY, JAMES D., Meriden, CT

A short lived firm founded in 1888 and operated by James D. Frary (1832-1890) until his death in 1890. Products were made by the Meriden Malleable Iron Co. under contract.

Products include the *SULLIVAN* cork puller (Fig.1); *FIFTH AVENUE* (Fig.2) cork puller; *GIANT* self-extracting corkscrew (Fig.3); corkscrews with a pick, wire stripper and ice breaker (Fig.4); a simple self-extracting corkscrew (Fig.5); a combined corkscrew, can opener and ice-pick (Fig.6); and a combined self-extracting corkscrew, ice-pick, wire stripper and ice breaker (Fig.7). The *SEASIDE* lemon press and stainer (Fig.8) and the *DAISY* lemon squeezer (Fig.9) were introduced in 1889.

(Illustrations continued on next page)

The Sullivan Cork-Puller.

Fig.1 - Pat'd. 8-12-1884

Giant Self-Extracting Corkscrew.

Fig.3

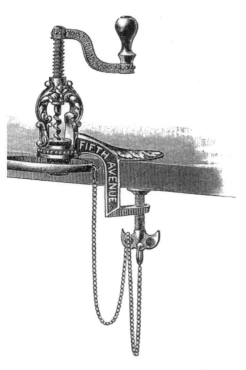

Fifth Avenue Cork Extractor.

Fig.2

Fig.5

—*Self-Extracting Corkscrew.*

Fig.6

Fig.4

—*Corkscrew with Pick or Wire Stripper.*

—*Combined Corkscrew, Can-Opener, Ice-Pick, &c.*

Fig.7

—*Combined Corkscrew, Ice-Pick, Breaker, &c.*

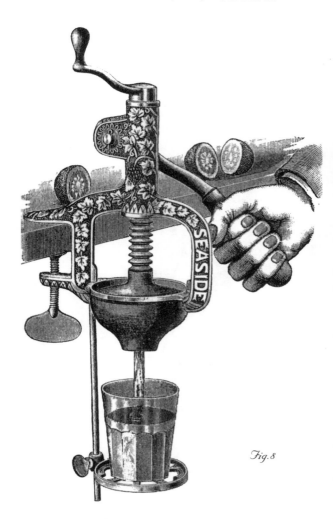

Fig.8

—*The Seaside Lemon Press and Strainer.*

Fig.9

Daisy Lemon and Lime Squeezer.

FREEPORT NOVELTY CO., Freeport, IL

Formed in 1898 by Albert Baumgarten, who had been previously associated with the Arcade Mfg. Co. Maker of the *X-RAY* lemon squeezer (Fig.1); a nut cracker (Fig.2); a horizontal acton lemon squeezer, patented June 12, 1900; a quick-action lemon squeezer (Fig.3); the *SHOMEE* cork puller (Fig.4) introduced in 1900; the *PULLMEE* cork puller, patented May 28, 1901; the *CORKEE* bottle corker, patented February 19, 1901; and a hand bottle corker (Fig.5). By 1902, the *X-RAY* lemon squeezer, the *SHOMEE* and *PULLMEE* cork pullers, and the *CORKEE* bottle corker were products of Manning, Bowman & Co.

Fig.2 - Pat'd. 10-10-1899

X-Ray Lemon Squeezer.

Fig.1 - 12-5-1899 & 7-1-1902

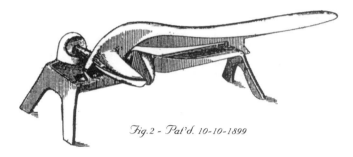

The Shomee Cork Pull.

Fig.4 - Pat'd. 4-1-1902

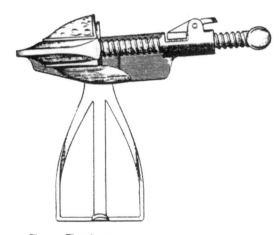

Fig.3 - Pat'd. 7-31-1900

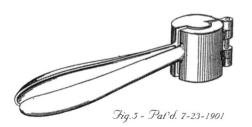

Fig.5 - Pat'd. 7-23-1901

FREIMUTH, JOHN, Sheboygan, WI

Maker of *HOXIES* automatic ice cream freezer, patented February 2, 1892.

FREMONT CRESCENT METAL & MFG. CO., Fremont, OH

Maker, in 1910, of a variety of kitchen utensils such as shown in the ad at right.

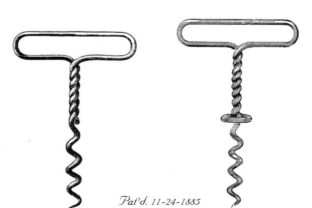

Pat'd. 11-24-1885

FRIEDMANN, ALBERT, Milwaukee, WI

Inventor and probably maker of twisted wire corkscrews.
(Illustration at left)

FRISBIE, R., Middletown, CT

Inventor and maker of a nut cracker. The illustration below is from the 1861 Pratt & Co. catalog.

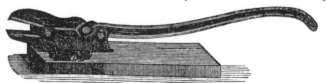

Pat'd. 5-17-1859

Japanned, Iron, Nut Crack, for Small and Large Nuts, or Walnuts,

GAUMER CO., JOHN L., Philadelphia, PA

Maker of the *MUDGE* canner (Fig.1) and an adustable jar holder (Fig.2), both introduced in 1897.

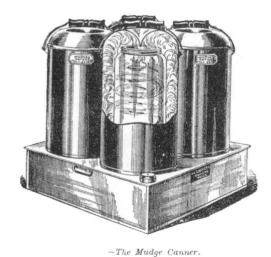

—The Mudge Canner.

Fig.1 - Pat'd. 7-27-1886

Adjustable Jar Holder.

Fig.2

GAYNOR & MITCHELL MFG. CO., Bridgeport, CT

Maker of *GRANT'S* patent orange and lemon peeler introduced in 1891.

Pat'd. 1-5-1892   —Grant's Patent Orange and Lemon Peeler.

GEE, CHARLES E., Lowell, MA

Maker of the *GEE* potato, apple, and turnip peeler, introduced in 1900. *(Illustration at right)*

The Gee Potato Parer.

Pat'd. 4-9-1867

GEER & HUTCHINSON, Peoria, IL

Maker of a cast iron and wood cherry stoner. The stoner is clearly the prototype for the *FAMILY* cherry stoner made for many years by the Goodell Co. *(Illustration at left)*

The Knead-Full Bread Maker.

GEM MFG. CO., Boston, MA

Maker of the *KNEAD-FULL* bread and cake mixer introduced in 1908. *(Illustration at left)*

GEUDER, PAESCHKE & CO., Milwaukee, later
GEUDER & PAESCHKE MFG. CO., Milwaukee, WI, later
GEUDER, PAESCHKE & FREY CO., Milwaukee, WI

Formed in June, 1880, as a partnership of William Geuder and Charles A. Paeschke. Reorganized as the Geuder & Paeschke Mfg. Co. in 1882 and as Geuder, Paeschke & Frey Co. by 1909. The firm was a large maker of several lines of metal ware, such as the *CREAM CITY* line, and four lines of enameled ware: *VIOLET* (turquoise blue with white spray), *GARNET* (brown and white mottled), *TULIP* (turquoise blue with marblized mottling), and *MOTTLED GRAY* (dark gray, nicely mottled).

Offerings in 1889 included a combination grater and slicer in hand (Fig.1) and revolving (Fig.2) models. In 1892, the firm introduced the *CREAM CITY* flour bin and sifter (Fig.3). A fireless cooker was introduced in 1909 (Fig.4).

Products offered in 1910 included *QUEEN* flour sifters (Fig.5); *EVER-READY* nutmeg graters (Fig.6); box graters (Fig.7); *CREAM CITY* graters (Fig.8); apple corers (Fig.9); *CREAM CITY* spring cake pans (Fig.10); *CREAM CITY* roasting pans (Fig.11); and lunch pails (Fig.12).

Later products included *CREAM CITY* spring pans in more elaborate styles (Figs.13-14); a checker board cake pan set (Fig.15); and the *SCOOPS ALL* ladle with a flattened front (Fig.16). *(Illustrations on next two pages)*

—Front View
of Grater.

—View of
Slicer.

Fig. 1

—Revolving Grater and Slicer

Fig. 2

The Cream City Flour Bin and Sifter.

Fig. 3 - Pat'd. 4-26-1892

Fireless Cooker Vessel.

Fig. 4

QUEEN.

EVER-READY NUTMEG.

Fig. 5

EXTERIOR

INTERIOR

Fig. 6

Fig. 7

Fig. 8

Fig. 9

WITHOUT TUBE, LOOSE BOTTOM.

Fig. 10

CREAM CITY.

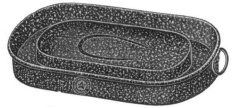

Fig. 11

Fig. 12

Fig. 13

Fig. 14

Fig. 15

Fig. 16

GIBBS MFG. CO., Canton, OH

Maker of the *QUICK CUT* can opener and *QUICK CUT* mincing knife, both introduced in 1895.

Quick Cut Can Opener.

Quick Cut Mincing Knife.

Pat'd. 7-16-1895

GILCHRIST CO., Newark, NJ

Founded in 1902 by Raymond B. Gilchrist. Maker of the *YANKEE* cork puller introduced in 1903 (Figs.1-2); the *YANKEE* lemon squeezer (Fig.3); and *YANKEE NO. 7* cork puller (Fig.4) introduced in 1904.

Gilchrist also made table top machines for driving corks into bottles, patented September 29, 1908; cork compressors, patented September 28, 1909; lemon squeezers (Fig.5) and (Fig.6) were offered by 1910.

In 1908, Gilchrist introduced a line of ice cream dishers which included the No. 30 (Fig.7); the No. 31 (Fig.8); and the No. 33 (Fig.9). The firm had 38 employees in 1910, but became a victim of the depression and was absorbed by the Hamilton Beach Co. in 1931. *(Illustrations continued on next page)*

Fig.1

Pat'd. 6-5-1907 (filed in 1901)

—Yankee Cork Puller, First Operation.

Fig.2

·Yankee Cork Puller to Clamp on Counter.

Fig.3 - Pat'd. 3-28-1905

—Yankee Lemon Squeezer.

Fig.4 - Pat'd. 4-25-1905, 6-19-1906 & 4-8-1913 (filed in 1904)

Fig.5 - Pat'd. 3-22-1910

Fig.6 - Pat'd. 1-3-1911

Fig.7 - Pat'd. 9-1-1914

BRONZE METAL, POLISHED

No. 30—8, 10, 12, 16 or 20 Dishes to the Quart..

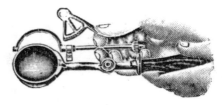

No. 31 — Nickel plated bronze metal frame, nickel silver bowl and scraper, varnished wood handle; has thumb piece to rotate the scraper. Can be quickly taken apart for cleaning.

Dishes to Quart..... 8   12   16   20   24   30

Fig.8 - Pat'd. 3-23-1915

Fig.9 - Pat'd. 9-1-1914

GILCHRIST MFG. CO., Chicago, IL, <u>later</u>
GILCHRIST & MEANS, Chicago, IL

Operated by Raymond B. Gilchrist. Maker, in 1889, of the *LIGHTNING* cork puller (Fig.1), patented June 19, 1888, and October 30, 1888. By 1901, when the *MODERN* lemon squeezer (Fig.2), *MODERN* cork puller (Fig.3) and *MODERN* ice pick (Fig.4) were introduced, the firm name had changed to Gilchrist & Means. Gilchrist left by 1902 and founded the Gilchrist Co. in Newark, NJ.

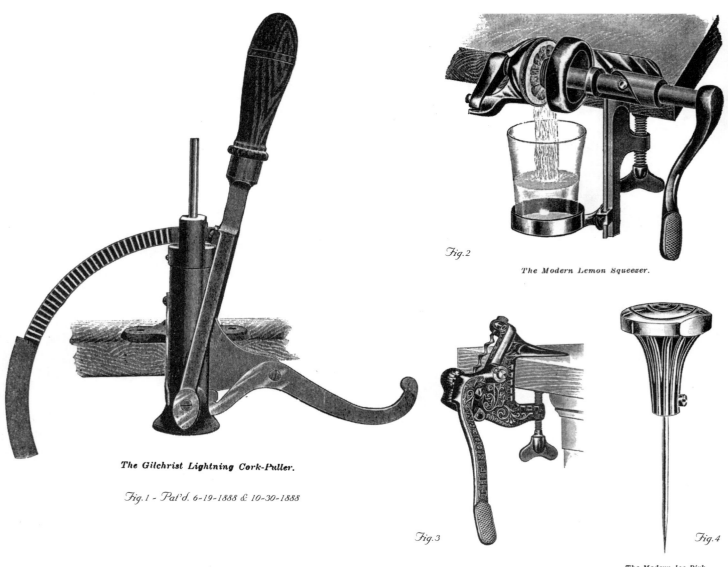

Fig.2

The Modern Lemon Squeezer.

The Gilchrist Lightning Cork-Puller.

Fig.1 - Pat'd. 6-19-1888 & 10-30-1888

Fig.3

Fig.4

The Modern Ice Pick.

GILES & NIELSEN NICKEL WORKS, Troy, NY

Maker of the *CLIPPER* ice cream spoon, introduced in 1904, patented by Rasmus Neilsen. The firm was taken over by, or was reorganized as, the Geer Mfg. Co. about 1906.

Pat'd. 2-7-1905

The Clipper Improved Sanitary Ice Cream Spoon.

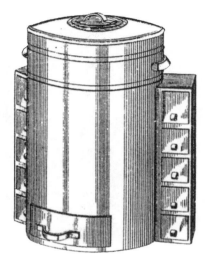

GLASCOCK BROS. MFG. CO., Muncie, IN

Maker, in 1899, of combination flour bin, sifter, and spice cabinet, patented December 27, 1898. *(Illustration at right)*

GLOVER, J. ALLEN, Ardsley, NY

Maker of the *LIGHTNING* mixing spoon introduced in 1903. The teeth were intended to "cut up the shortening and mix it with the flour."

The Glover Lightning Mixing Spoon.

GOOCH, CHARLES, Cincinnati, OH, later
GOOCH FREEZER CO., Cincinnati, OH

Inventor and maker of Gooch's *IXL* ice cream freezer and made in twelve sizes from two quarts to 10 gallons (Fig.1). The *PEERLESS* ice cream and fruit-cream freezer (Fig.2) was added by 1888. In 1889, the firm name changed to Gooch Freezer Co., which continued to make the *PEERLESS* freezer. Later in 1889, the firm introduced the *ZERO* (Fig.3), *PET* (Fig.4) and *BOSS* (Fig.5) models, all made in 2, 3, 4, and 6 quart sizes. Gooch's last freezer patent was issued September 4, 1894, about the time when the firm reorganized as the Peerless Freezer Co. *(Illustrations on next page)*

GOOCH'S I-XL
ICE CREAM FREEZER,

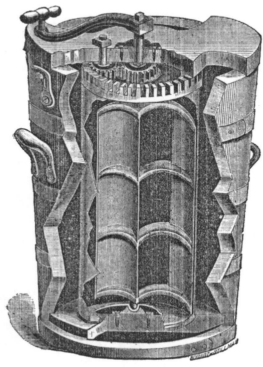

Fig.1 - Pat'd. 6-11-1867, 1-21-1868, & 7-4-1871

Fig.2

Fig.3

Fig.4

Fig.5

GOODELL CO., Antrim, NH

Founded in 1864 as a partnership of David H. Goodell (1834-1915) and George R. Carter to make apple parers of Goodell's design, later patented June 18, 1867. Goodell bought out Carter in 1871 and incorporated the firm in 1875 as the Goodell Co.

Products included the *CLIMAX* apple corer and slicer, patented February 16, 1869; the *FAMILY* apple parer (Fig.1); the *LIGHTNING* peach parer, patented May 10, 1870; a peach stoner, patented December 10, 1872; the *DANDY* paring, coring and slicing machine, introduced in 1889 for high volume use (Fig.2); the *EUREKA* parer, corer and slicer (Fig.3); the *BONANZA* parer and corer, introduced in 1890 (Fig.4); the *TURN TABLE '98* parer (Fig.5); the *BAY STATE* (Fig.6); and *IMPROVED BAY STATE* (Fig.7) parers, corers and slicers marketed in 1899; and the *WHITE MOUNTAIN* potato parer (Fig.8) and apple parer (Fig.9), introduced about 1900. *(continued on next five pages)*

Fig. 1 - Pat'd. 8-10-1869

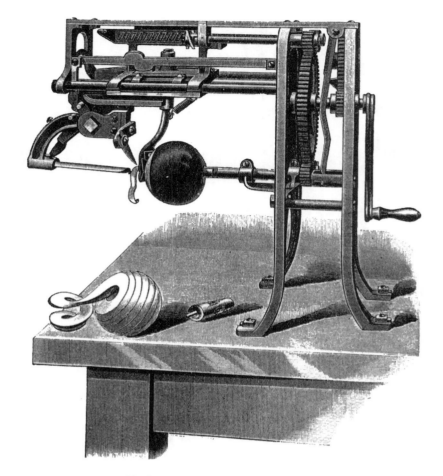

The Dandy Apple Parer, Corer and Slicer.

Fig. 2 - Pat'd. 11-16-1886, 3-13-1888, & 5-8-1888

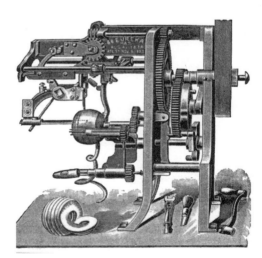

Fig. 3 - Pat'd. 8-4-1874, 4-27-1886, & 11-6-1886

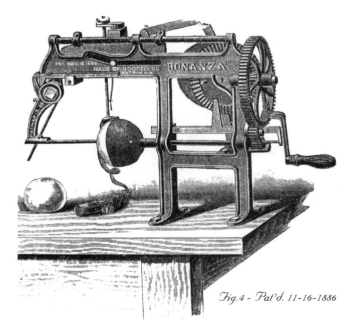

Fig. 4 - Pat'd. 11-16-1886

The Bonanza Parer and Corer.

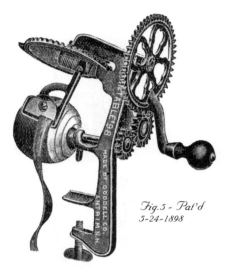

Fig. 5 - Pat'd
5-24-1898

The Turn Table '98 Apple Parer.

Fig. 6

Fig. 7

WHITE MOUNTAIN POTATO PARER.

Fig. 8

Apple Parers.
WHITE MOUNTAIN.

AUTOMATIC PUSH-OFF.

Fig. 9

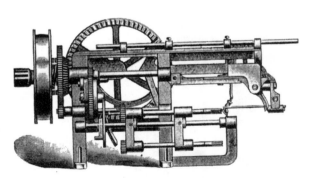

The Right Hand Power Apple Parer.

Fig. 10 - Pat'd. 9-30-1902

Power operated apple parers for high volume use were the *RIGHT HAND* (Fig.10); the *EVAPORATOR* also introduced in 1902 (Fig.11) and the *NEW CENTURY* introduced in 1907 (Fig.12).

Other products included the *VICTOR* vegetable parer (Fig.13); the *SARATOGA* potato parer and slicer (Fig.14); the *SUCCESS* orange parer (Fig.15) introduced in 1908; and the *FAMILY* cherry stoner (Fig.16), introduced before 1895; the *ACME* can opener (Fig.17) introduced in 1890; the *CALIFORNIA* can opener (Fig.18) introduced in 1897; a peach pitting knife (Fig.19) introduced in 1903; and the *PEERLESS* knife sharpener and steel (Fig.20), introduced in 1905.

The firm also made table and kitchen cutlery, including *STAR* butcher knives (Fig.21) and bread knives (Fig.22); fruit knives, patented August 5, 1902; carving forks, patented May 14, 1901, and April 7, 1903; and bird carvers (Fig.23).

Fig.11 - Pat'd. 1-20-1903

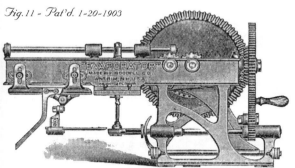

The Evaporator Hand Apple Parer.

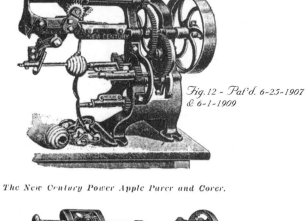

Fig.12 - Pat'd. 6-25-1907 & 6-1-1909

The New Century Power Apple Parer and Corer.

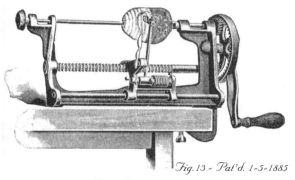

SARATOGA.

Fig.14

Fig.13 - Pat'd. 1-5-1885

Victor Vegetable Parer.

Fig.15 - Pat'd. 11-14-1911

Success Orange Parer.

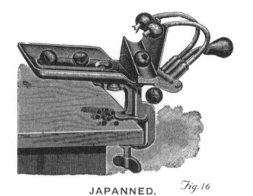

JAPANNED.   *Fig.16*

Fig.17   The Acme Can Opener.

Fig.18

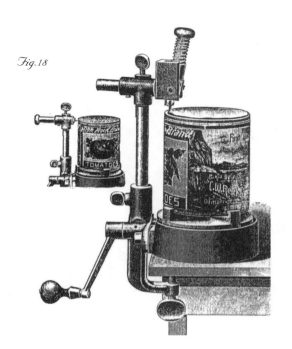

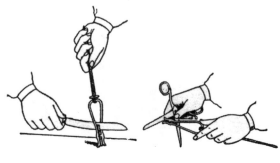

—*Peerless Sharpener and Steel Combined.*

Figs. 21-22 - Pat'd. 10-6-1868 — Fig. 23 - Pat'd. 9-6-1904

—*First Operation in Sharpening Carver.*   —*Sharpening Scissors.*

Fig. 20

Peach Pitting Knife.   *Fig. 19*

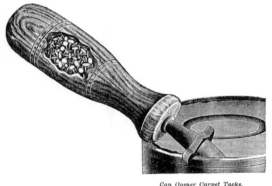

Can Opener Carpet Tacks.

GRAND CROSSING TACK CO., Chicago, IL

As a sales incentive in 1895, the firm marketed 200 of their tacks enclosed in the handle of a can opener and priced at five cents. *(Illustration at left)*

GRAND RAPIDS GRATER CO., Grand Rapids, MI

Maker of the *YANKEE* rapid nutmeg grater introduced in 1904. *(Illustration at right)*

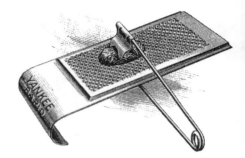

The Yankee Rapid Grater.

BARDEN'S COMBINATION.

GRANVILLE MFG. CO., Granville, IL

Maker, c1910, of *BARDEN'S* combination ice pick, tenderer, hand axe and cleaver. *(Illustration at left)*

GRAVITY TWINE BOX CO., Cleveland, OH

Maker, beginning in 1892, of the *HOUSEHOLD JEWEL* beater, patented by Henry Juergens. The beater was offered as an egg beater, cream whipper, cake beater, and drink mixer. *(Illustration at right)*

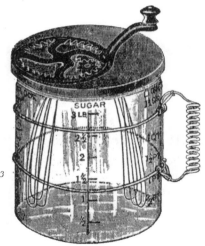

Pat'd. 6-20-1893

The Household Jewel.

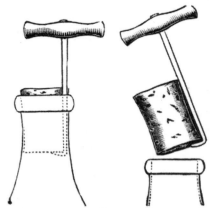

GREELY'S CORK EXTRACTOR.

CORKS LIFTED OUT WHOLE.

Pat'd. 3-6-1888

GREELY, B.J., Boston, MA

Inventor and maker of *GREELY'S* cork extractor. *(Illustration at left)*

GREEN & NOBLE BROTHERS, Brooklyn, NY

Maker of the *PEERLESS* bread cutter, introduced in 1901. A gauge allowed cuts from 1/32" to 4". *(Illustration at right)*

The Peerless Bread Cutter

GREY IRON CASTING CO., Mount Joy, PA

Maker of a combination meat tenderer and ice pick, introduced in 1892.

Meat Tenderer and Ice Pick.

GRISWOLD, ASHBEL, Meriden, CT

Maker of "tea-pots and other articles out of block tin" from 1810 to 1842.

MAGIC.

GRISWOLD, CHARLES L., Chester, CT
Inventor and maker of the *MAGIC* "self-raising" corkscrew. *(Illustration at right)*

Pat'd. 7-22-1884

GRISWOLD MFG. CO., Erie, PA

Formed in 1884 as a reorganization of Selden & Griswold Mfg. Co. Products included a line of *ERIE* cast iron hollow ware (Figs.1-6); the *AMERICAN* waffle iron, introduced about 1885 (Fig.7); and an improved version (Fig.8); the *ERIE* coffee mill, introduced in 1895 (Fig.9) and a wall mount coffee mill, patented December 13, 1898, and December 27, 1898; cast aluminum coffee pots introduced in 1895 (Fig.10); the *AMERICAN* deep ring waffle iron (Fig.11) and the *ERIE* double broiler (Fig.12), both introduced in 1897. The *CLASSIC* rotary food chopper was introduced in 1902 (Fig.13) and in an improved version in 1904 (Fig.14). Coal tongs (Fig.15) were offered in 1908.

Later offerings included the *SAFETY FILL* cast aluminum tea kettle (Fig.16); a percolator coffee pot, patented August 15, 1911; and further improved *AMERICAN* waffle irons (Fig.17). The "heart and star" pattern waffle iron (Fig.18) was covered by a design patent (Fig.19). *(Illustrations continued on next two pages)*

Fig.1

LOW KETTLES.

Fig.2

REGULAR KETTLES.

Fig.3

FLAT BOTTOM KETTLES.

Fig.4

REGULAR POTS.

Fig.5

TEA KETTLES.

Fig.6

SPIDERS.

Fig.7

Fig.8 - Pat'd. 5-14-1901

—*Improved American Waffle Iron.*

Fig. 9

The Griswold Coffee Mill.

The Erie Cast Aluminum Coffee Pot.

Fig. 10

Fig. 11 - Pat'd. 3-23-1897

American Deep Ring Waffle Iron

Fig. 12

Erie Double Broiler.

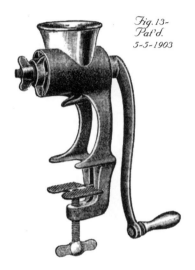

*Fig. 13-
Pat'd.
5-5-1903*

Classic Food Chopper.

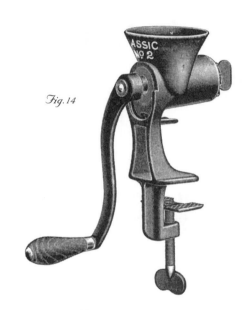

Fig. 14

Classic Food Chopper.

Fig. 15

*Fig. 17 - Pat'd.
7-11-1922*

**Cast
Aluminum**

**Colonial,
Safety
Fill**

Fig. 16 - Pat'd. 9-9-1913

Fig. 18 - Pat'd. 5-18-1920

55,188. COOKING-RECEPTACLE. CHARLES A. MASSING, Millcreek township, Erie county, Pa., assignor to Griswold Manufacturing Company, Erie, Pa., a Corporation of Pennsylvania. Filed Jan. 27, 1919. Serial No. 273,496. Term of patent 14 years.

The ornamental design for a cooking receptacle as shown.

Fig. 19 - Design Patent 5-18-1920

GUNDELACH & CO., Chicago, IL

Maker of the Gundelach Continous Automatic Alarm Catch Basin, for use as a drip pan under an ice box. In use, water was piped from the main section, when full, into a small cup which tipped when full and rang a bell. The bell would ring every few seconds as water would continue to fill and tilt the cup. *(Illustration at right)*

The Gundelach Automatic Alarm Catch Basin.

Gurney Alarm Catch Basin.

GURNEY REFRIGERATOR CO., Fond du Lac, WI

A major maker of ice boxes and refrigerators. In 1893, the firm introduced an alarm catch basin which acted as a drip pan. When full, a float caused a wind- up bell to sound a warning. *(Illustration at left)*

GWINNER MFG. CO., Hamilton, OH

Maker, in 1893, of the *MATADOR* meat slicer. *(Illustration at right)*

The Matador Meat Slicer.

HABERMAN MFG. CO., Berlin Village, L.I., NY

Became part of the National Enameling & Stamping Co. when the latter was formed in 1899.

Hailes' Odorless Frying Pan.

HAILES, WILLIAM Albany, NY

Maker of kettles, patented December 18, 1866, and December 17, 1867. In 1891 he introduced *HAILES*' odorless frying pan. *(Illustration at left)*

HALL CANNER CO., Grand Rapids, MI

Maker, beginning in 1918, of "a complete device for cold pack canning and preserving" with a capacity of 12 jars, either pints or quarts. Priced at $5.50, it was 21" tall and 12" diameter. *(Illustration at right)*

HALL & CARPENTER, Philadelphia, PA

Maker of the CROWN asbestos griddle, introduced in 1894 (Fig.1) and a frying pan with deep frying basket (Fig.2), patented by Zachary T. Hall.

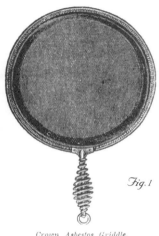

Fig.1

Crown Asbestos Griddle.

Fig.2 - Pat'd. 4-28-1896

HALL, F.W., New York, NY

Maker of the *UNIQUE* skewer puller introduced in 1894.

HALL MFG. CO., Wallingford, CT

Maker of the *KLONDIKE* combination can opener and tack puller. The firm sold out to C. Rogers & Bros. in 1898. *(Illustration at right)*

The Klondike Combination Can Opener

Pat'd. 4-18-1905

The Halsey Ice Pick and Chipper.

HALSEY, C.W., Evansville, IN

Maker of the *HALSEY* ice pick and chopper, introduced in 1904. *(Illustration at left)*

HAMBLIN & RUSSELL MFG. CO., Worcester, MA

Operated by Frank H. Hamblin. Maker of a variety of kitchen items including; a rotary corn popper introduced in 1891 (Fig.1); the *YANKEE* strawberry huller (Fig.2) introduced in 1897; cooking pots with non-scorch inserts, patented November 9, 1909; bread slicers (Fig.3); egg whips (Fig.4); flour sifters, patented October 15, 1918; and strainers (Fig.5). *(continued on next page)*

Fig.1   *Rotary Corn Popper.*

Fig.2   *Yankee Strawberry Huller.*

Fig.4 - Pat'd. 6-4-1918

Fig.3 - Pat'd. 9-9-1912

Fig.5 - Pat'd. 12-3-1918

Fig.6

"Hold-Fast Lifter."

In 1917 the firm introduced a line of home canning items including the *HOLD-FAST* lifter (Fig.6); the *HELPING HAND* (Fig.7) for handling hot fruit and vegetables; the *JENNIE MAY* tray, a wire evaporator (Fig.8); the *MILLER* (Fig.9), *PERCY* (Fig.10) and *FLANDERS* (Fig.11) jar holders; and a jelly strainer (Fig.12).

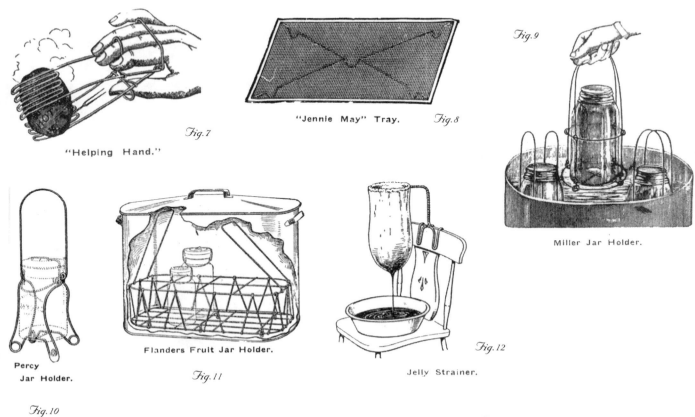

"Helping Hand." Fig.7

"Jennie May" Tray. Fig.8

Fig.9

Miller Jar Holder.

Percy Jar Holder.
Fig.10

Flanders Fruit Jar Holder.
Fig.11

Jelly Strainer.
Fig.12

for a busy housewife

(Cut away showing inside)

Grates flakily —does not crush or chop —Cocoanut, horseradish, potatoes, cheese, bread, etc. etc. Can't cut fingers—A time saver.
At stores or $1.40 postpaid.
Hamilton Metal Products Co. Hamilton, Ohio

CLIMAX FOODGRATER ★

HAMILTON METAL PRODUCTS CO., Hamilton, OH

Maker, in 1924, of the *CLIMAX* food grater shown at right.

HANDY THINGS MFG. CO., Ludington, MI

Maker, c1895-1912, of the *HANDY* can opener.

HANDY.

Pat'd. 6-11-1895

HARKER & CO., JOHN B., Minneapolis, MN

Maker of the *HARKER* waffle iron (Fig.1) *HARKER* egg baker (Fig.2), and *HARKER* griddle (Fig.3), all introduced in 1893.

Fig. 1.—The Harker Waffle Iron.

Fig. 2.—The Harker Egg Baker.

Fig. 3.—The Harker Griddle.

JIM'S

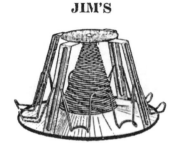

HARKIN & WILLIS, Ann Arbor, MI

Maker, in the 1920's, of *JIM'S* stovetop toasters. *(Illustration at right)*

The Kitchen Jewel.

HARKINS FOUNDRY CO., Bristol, PA

Maker, in 1889, of the KITCHEN JEWEL device which was to be placed in a stove hole to lower the pot closer to the fire. It was claimed to be "a great coal saver". *(Illustration at left)*

HARPER SUPPLY CO., Chicago, IL

Operated by James M. Harper. Maker of *HARPER'S* nut cracker, introduced in 1911. Harper claimed that "the jaws are wider than any other, and the nut resting against the plate brings it in line with the jaws, hence the nut is cracked all over evenly." *(Illustration at right)*

Pat'd. 4-6-1914

The Cleveland Rapid Grinder.

HARRIS MFG. CO., Cleveland, OH

Maker, in 1902, of the *CLEVELAND RAPID* coffee and spice mill. *(Illustration at right)*

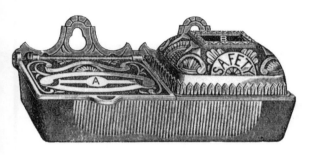

Combined Match-Safe and Match-Receiver.

HASBROUCK, E.P., Syracuse, NY

Maker, in 1889, of the *SAFETY* combination match-safe and match-receiver. *(Illustration at left)*

HAVELL, GEORGE, Newark, NJ

Maker of a line of crockery pots with metal lids and trim, introduced in 1888. Items included the *OXFORD* sauce pan (Fig.1), *VENICE* tea pot (Fig.2), and *DRESDEN* kettle (Fig.3).

Fig. 1.—Oxford Sauce Pan.

Fig.1

Fig. 2.—Venice Tea Pot.

Fig.2

Fig. 3.—Dresden Kettle.

Fig.3

HAWKS, MOSES L., New York, NY

Inventor, and probably maker, of the *HERCULES* can opener.

A GIANT OF STRENGTH

Pat'd. 8-12-1902

113

HEEKIN & CO., JAMES, Cincinnati, OH

Maker of the *KIN-HEE* coffee pot. "If you can boil water you can make coffee fit for a king." *(Illustration at right)*

Pat'd. 5-22-1900

Demonstrated at Pan-American Exposition

This shows the coffee pot upside down, the top filled with boiling water and coffee submerged. It stands for one minute, straining cloth is put on, then the bottom. Then the entire pot is turned right side up and the coffee is ready to serve. A child can do it. *Patented May 22, 1900.*

HEFFRON, C.M., Rochester, NY

Maker of the *SUN* apple parer and corer (Fig.1), *SUN* apple slicer (Fig.2), both introduced in 1891; and the *WORLD* parer and corer (Fig.3) introduced in 1893. *(Illustrations continued on next page)*

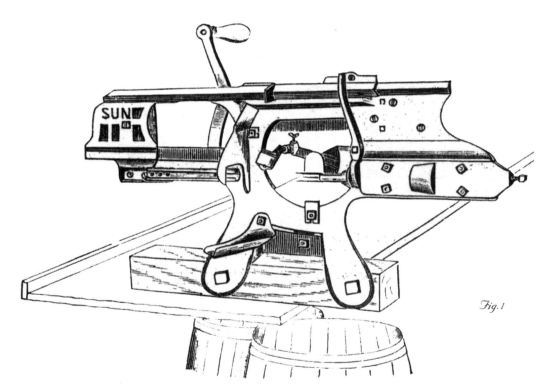

Fig.1

Sun Parer and Corer.

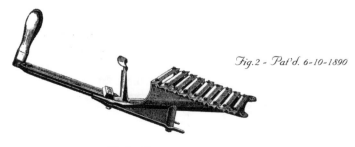

Fig.2 - Pat'd. 6-10-1890

The Sun Slicer.

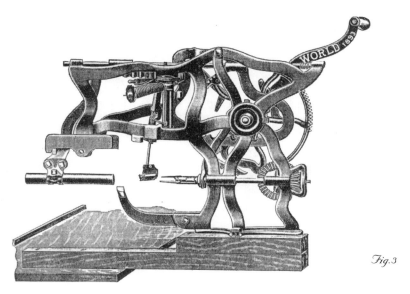

Fig.3

The World Apple Parer.

Pat'd. 10-28-1873

HEINZ & MUNSCHAUER, Buffalo, NY

A partnership of Adam Heinz (1837-1898) and George J. Munschauer. The partners operated the Niagara Stamping & Tool Works formed in 1879 to make sheet metal machines and tools. The firm also made a few specialty items, including an ice chopper. *(Illustration at left)*

HENIS CO., CHARLES F., Philadelphia, PA

Maker of self-basting broilers (Fig.1); the *HENIS* patent vegetable press (Fig.2); and the *SOLITAIRE* one cup coffee maker (Fig.3), introduced in 1888.

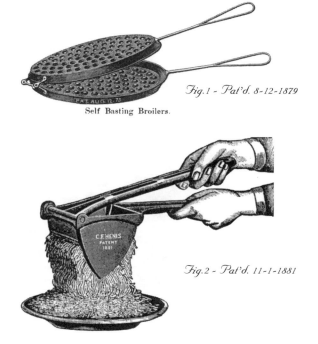

Fig.1 - Pat'd. 8-12-1879

Self Basting Broilers.

Fig.2 - Pat'd. 11-1-1881

*Fig.3 - Pat'd.
11-4-1884*

The Solitaire Coffee Urn.

HENIS' SONS & CO., W.G., Philadelphia, PA

Maker of the *BOVINIZER* meat tenderizer, patented August 20, 1907.

HENN & CO., A.S., New Haven, CT

Maker of the *HENN* can opener introduced in 1893 (Fig.1) and the *SURE GRIP* introduced in 1895 in two styles (Fig.2). In 1895, the firm offered the *DANDY* (Fig.3) and *DAISY* (Fig.4) mincing knives.

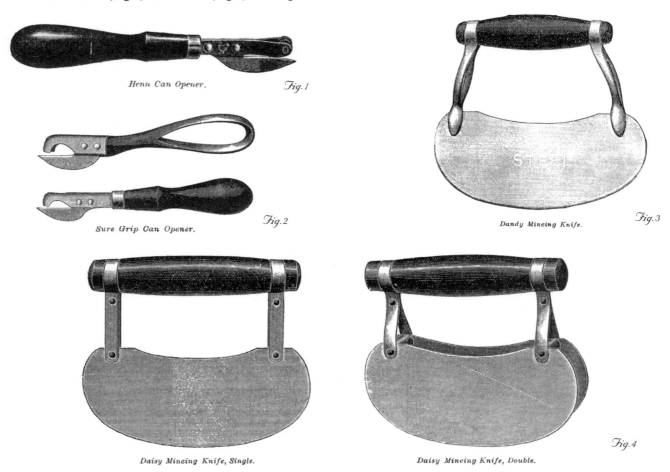

Henn Can Opener. *Fig.1*

Sure Grip Can Opener. *Fig.2*

Dandy Mincing Knife. *Fig.3*

Daisy Mincing Knife, Single.

Daisy Mincing Knife, Double. *Fig.4*

HERO FRUIT JAR CO., Philadelphia, PA

Maker, in 1910, of a variety of stamped aluminum ware as shown below.

LEMON SQUEEZERS.　　　SALT AND PEPPER SHAKERS.　　　MEASURING CUPS.

WILL FIT ANY SIZE TUMBLER.

SELF RIGHTING.

SATIN FINISH.

HERO STAMPING WORKS, Cleveland, OH

Maker, in 1897, of the *HERO* fish scaler (Fig.1) and the *HERO* ice shredder (Fig.2), patented by Henry L. Schwarzenberg..

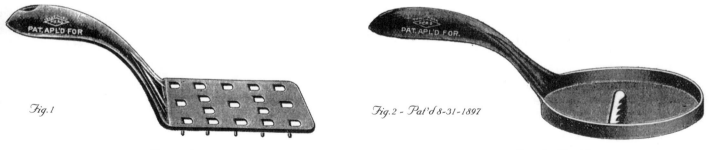

Fig.1

Hero Fish Scaler.

Fig.2 - Pat'd 8-31-1897

Hero Ice Shredder.

HERRING, ANAXAMANDER, Crown Point, NY

Inventor and maker of a patent potato slicer. *(Illustration at right)*

HETZEL MFG. CO., Pittsburgh, PA

Maker of a knife and scissors sharpener introduced in 1901.

*Pat'd.
6-27-1876*

The Hetzel Knife and Scissors Sharpener.

HEY MFG. CO., M., Philadelphia, PA

Maker of a cast iron grape mill (Fig.1) and a fruit press (Fig.2) both introduced in 1897.

Fig.1

Grape Mill.

Fig.2

Wine or Fruit Press.

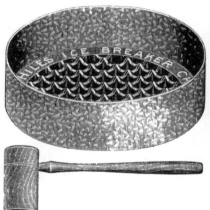

Pat'd. 10-8-1901

HILES & CO., C.A., Chicago, IL

Maker of the *HILES* ice breaker, introduced in 1900. In use, ice was pounded through a cast iron grate. *(Illustration at right)*

The Hiles Ice Breaker.

HILL & WHITNEY MFG. CO., Boston, MA

Maker of the *MATCHLESS* coffee pot (Fig.1), introduced in 1894 and the *BOSTON* self basting roaster and baker (Fig.2), introduced in 1895.

—The Matchless Coffee Pot.

Fig.1 *—Filter in Coffee Pot Raised.*

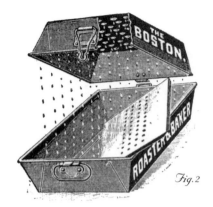

Fig.2

The Boston Self Basting Roaster and Baker.

Hillson's Steam Cooker and Measure

HILLSON, H.M., Boston, MA

Maker of a combination steam cooker and measure, designed to be placed in the top opening of a tea kettle, thus becoming a double boiler. *(Illustration at left)*

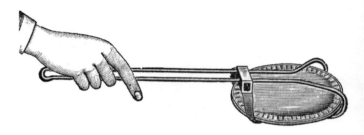

HOBBS, GEORGE W., Charlestown, MA

Maker of the *SAFETY GRIP* hot dish lifter, introduced in 1894. *(Illustration at right)*

The Safety Grip Lifter.

HOFF, Joseph E., Newark, NJ

Inventor and probably maker of a rotary potato parer. Hoff assigned half the patent to George F. Stow. *(Illustration on next page)*

Rotary Potato Parers.

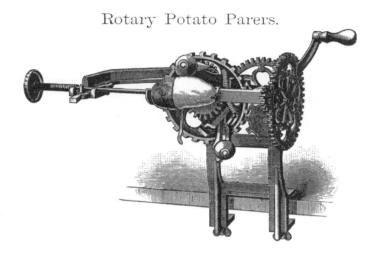

HOLT-LYON CO., Terrytown, NY

Founded in 1903 by Thomas Holt, president, and Nelson Lyon, secretary and treasurer. Nelson had begun making eggbeaters in Albany, NY, in 1898 and this firm is probably a reorganization of Nelson Lyon.

Maker, in 1904 and later, of improved *DOVER* egg beaters with flared dashers (Figs.1-2), patented August 22, 1899, and April 3, 1900. In 1909, the improved *DOVER* egg beater, cream whip and mayonnaise mixer, with an oil dripper attachment, was introduced (Fig.2). The firm also made *HOLT'S JAR CREAM WHIP* (Fig.3) for extending butter. Equal amounts of butter and milk were put in the jar, warm water filled the space between the metal jacket and the beater jar, and the beater was used to blend the mixture.

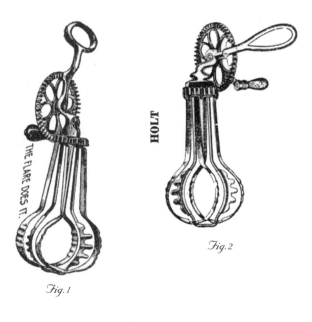

Fig.1

Fig.2

Figs. 1 & 2 pat'd. 8-22-1899 & 4-3-1900

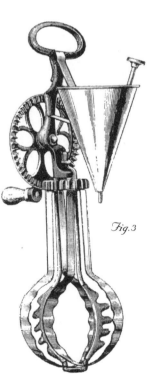

Fig.3

Holt's Improved Egg Beater, Cream
Whip and Mayonnaise Mixer,
with Oil Dripper Attached.

Fig.4

HOME NOVELTY CO., St. Louis, MO

Maker of the *COTNER* dipper and cup handle, introduced in 1892.

-*The Cotner Dipper and Cup Handle.*

HOME SUPPLY MFG. CO., Rockford, IL

Maker of a fruit jar top straightener and truer, introduced in 1906. It was designed to straighten the flange or edge of bent jar tops. *(Illustration at right)*

Pat'd. 4-4-1905

Fruit Jar Top Straightener and Truer.

The Gem Slicing Machine.

HORTON & LINK MFG. CO., Herkimer, NY

Maker of the *GEM* slicing machine, introduced in 1908. *(Illustration at left)*

HOTCHKISS, EDWARD S., Bridgeport, CT

Maker, in 1888, of the *STRAIGHT FLUSH* lemon squeezer and meat press. *(Illustration at right)*

The Hotchkiss Lemon Squeezer.

120

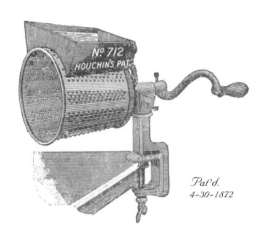

Pat'd.
4-30-1872

HOUCHIN MFG. CO., New York, NY

Operated by T.W. Houchin. Maker of *HOUCHIN'S* revolving grater for "grating cocoanut, horseradish, carrots, bread, crackers and cheese." The grater was offered into the early 20th century. *(Illustration at right)*

PEERLESS.

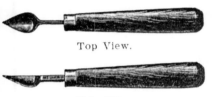

Top View.

Side View.

Pat'd. 1-26-1909

HOUCK, JOHN D., Toledo, OH

Inventor and maker of the *PEERLESS* fruit and vegetable eyer, a hand held cherry pitter, patented December 28, 1909; a coffee percolator patented April 27, 1909; and the *PEERLESS* bottle and can opener, patented October 19, 1912.

HOUSEHOLD NECESSITIES MFG. CO., Philadelphia, PA

Maker of the *ATLAS* can opener, introduced in 1908.

Atlas Can Cutter.

HOUSEHOLD NOVELTY WORKS, Chicago, IL

Maker, in 1900, of the *WONDER* egg beater and cream whip. The firm also claimed to be the largest manufacturers of pure aluminum, scotch granite, and tin ware in the world. *(Illustration at right)*

HOXIE & CLARK, Rochester, NY

Maker of the *LIGHTNING* bread cutter (Fig.1) and the *LIGHTNING* potato slicer (Fig.2), both introduced about 1889.

LIGHTNING POTATO SLICERS.

The Lightning Bread Cutter.

Fig.1

Fig.2

HUDSON, C.E., Leominster, MA, <u>later</u>
HUDSON PARER CO., Leominster, MA

Maker of apple parers, corers and slicers beginning about 1882 with a rocking table model (Fig.1). The *LITTLE STAR* model (Fig.2) was introduced in 1885 and was made, in slightly modified form as late as 1911 (Fig.3). In 1888, the firm introduced the 88 model (Fig.4) claimed to be almost as good as the *LITTLE STAR* and cheaper. *(Illustrations continued on next page)*

Fig.1 - Pat'd. 1-24-1882

Fig.2 - Pat'd. 6-9-1885

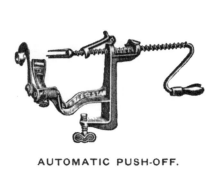

AUTOMATIC PUSH-OFF.
Fig.3

Fig.4

Hudson's New '88 Parer, Corer and Slicer.

-*Perfect Can Opener.*

Pat'd. 2-1-1898

HULL, LUTHER S., Middletown, CT

Maker, beginning in 1897, of the *PERFECT* can opener, patented by Stephen Tallman. *(Illustration at left)*

HULL, M.L., Cleveland, OH

Maker of *HULL'S* one pound coffee roaster, introduced in 1888. *(Illustration at right)*

Hull's Coffee Roaster.

Pat'd. 8-5-1879

HUNTER, J.M., Cincinnati, OH

Inventor and maker of a crank type flour sifter. The *HUNTER* trade name was retained by the Fred J. Meyers Mfg. Co. when it took over production about 1888. *(Illustration at left)*

HUTCHINS CO., C.K., Buffalo, NY

Maker of *MRS. HUTCHINS* strainer spoon, introduced in 1906. It was designed for "skimming the scum which arises on jellies, preserves and soups when cooking."

-*Mrs. Hutchins' Strainer Spoon.*

IDEAL COFFEE POT CO., Philadelphia, PA

Maker, in 1881, of a coffee pot in which the coffee grounds were suspended in a wire cloth sack held by a flange at the top. *(Illustration at right)*

WE GIVE AWAY Combined Grater and Slaw Cutter

(Regular price, **50 cents**), with every purchase of Kitchen Set No. 50 (price **$1.00**), as an advertisement (for April only).

PATENTED AUGUST 15, 1893.

Combined Grater and Slaw Cutter
Regular Price, 50 Cents

The Slicer sheet is made of Apollo galvanized iron, with steel cutting-blades. It will slice cabbage, cucumbers, apples, potatoes, onions, turnips, beets, and everything in the vegetable line. It is used in the kitchen every day. The Grater is detachable.

Kitchen Set No. 50
Regular Price, $1.00

This Set consists of one each, Meat Tenderer (which will actually make tough meat tender), Famous Parer and a Bread Knife, all finely nickel-plated and sharpened. Each Set in beautiful bronze-lined box.

All of the above articles sent, securely packed, by express, all charges prepaid, to any address in the U. S. upon receipt of **$1.00**. (Send Postal Money Order, Express Money Order, or Bank Draft.) AGENTS WANTED.

ILLINOIS CUTLERY COMPANY, Decatur, Ill.

Grater & Slaw Cutter pat'd. 8-15-1893

Ocean Churn.

ILLINOIS CUTLERY CO., Decatur, IL

Maker of a combined grater and slaw cutter, given with the purchase of a $1.00 kitchen set (Fig.1); and the *OCEAN* churn (Fig.2) introduced in 1899.

ILLINOIS PURE ALUMINUM CO., Lemont, IL

Formed in 1892 with a capital of $50,000. Maker of aluminum kitchen ware including a baking dish, introduced in 1895 (Fig.1); griddles (Fig.2) and roasting pans (Fig.3), introduced in 1897; and the *GEM* steam cooker (Fig.4), introduced in 1906.

Fig.1
—*Pure Aluminum Baking Dish.*

Fig.2
—*Aluminum Griddles.*

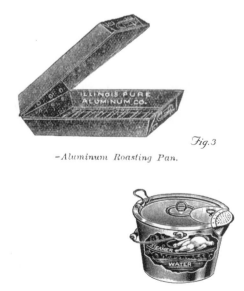

Fig.3
—*Aluminum Roasting Pan.*

Fig.4
Gem Aluminum Steam Cooker and Preserving Kettle.

ILLINOIS STAMPING CO., Chicago, IL

Maker of the *CHICAGO* line of copper utensils, introduced in 1895.

Fig. 1.—Copper Lipped Preserving Kettle.

Fig. 2.—Copper Deep Cooking Pot.

Fig. 3.—Copper Stewpan.

IMPERIAL METAL MFG. CO., New York, NY

Maker, in 1909, of *PERFECTION* hot corn holders. *(Illustration at right)*

Pat. Feb. 9th, 1909.

Isn't it Worth 20 Cents

twice over to enjoy your green corn without soiling and burning your fingers? You can do it with a pair of

"Perfection Hot Corn Holders"

Pat'd. 2-9-1909

They're sanitary and practical; made of solid metal, heavily nickeled, easily cleaned and *will not tarnish.* Ask your dealer. If he hasn't them, send to us direct.

By mail, prepaid, **20 cents a pair**
Or, better still, **3 pairs for 50 cents**

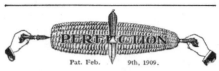

IMPERIAL METAL MFG. CO., 422 East 106th St., New York

Sanitary, Economical,
Convenient, Clean

Here's a New Idea in Salt Shakers

We Want You to Try a Pair

Delivers salt from the bottom, which is the only opening, so that when it is set down the opening is closed, thereby excluding all damp air, dust and dirt. Result — the salt always remains dry and shakes freely.

The salt cannot come out until you shake it, but you can always get salt without delay when you want it.

Made from beautiful cut-glass, Colonial design with non-corrosive aluminum bottom.

A Pair of Meaker Salt and Pepper Shakers Delivered Anywhere For **$1.00**

Money Back if You Are Not Satisfied

No more damp, clogging salt or pepper, or celery salt that has lost its flavor by exposure to the air.

Everyone who tries this shaker wants more of them, destined to be used on every table in the land, so simple and good you'll wonder why someone did not think of it before. Just the thing for a Christmas present, beautiful, inexpensive and sure to be appreciated. Enclose a dollar for a pair today. You will want more.

The Ireland & Matthews Mfg. Co., Iron and Wight Sts., Detroit, Mich.
References: Dun's or Bradstreet's.

IRELAND & MATTHEWS MFG. CO., Detroit, MI

Maker, in 1908, of *MEAKER* bottom delivery salt and pepper shakers. Priced at $1.00, they were quite expensive for the time. *(Illustration at left)*

IRON-CLAD MFG. CO., New York, NY

Maker, 1893-1898, of *SALAMANDER* double-bottom cookware (Figs.1-3) and a boiler for corn or asparagus (Fig.4).

Fig.3

–Second Bottom of Pure Copper.

—Iron Clad Salamander Cook Pot.

Fig.2

Fig.1

Fig.4

Boiler for Asparagus, Corn, &c.

IRONA MFG. CO., New York, NY

Maker of a lemon squeezer, patented August 1, 1905. The squeezer was designed to be clamped on a table or bar top.

IRWIN MFG. CO., New York, NY

Maker of the *SLICK-OPE* can opener. The patented feature was a method of locking the sliding cutter bar in place.

SEE THAT LOCK

Pat'd. 11-1-1910

JACK FROST FREEZER CO., New York, NY

Maker, in 1893, of the *JACK FROST* freezer which had been offered by the American Automatic Vending Machine Mfg. Co. in 1891. The design was unique, with the ice/salt mixture enclosed in a cylinder that was rotated in a pan containing the cream mixture.

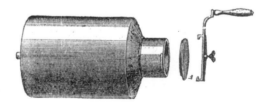

Fig. 2.—Cylinder with Cap and Handle Detached.

Fig. 1.—The Jack Frost Freezer.

Fig. 3.—Pan with Rounded Bottom for Holding Mixture to be Frozen.

JAMIESON CO., R.W., New York, NY

Maker of the *EASY* dough mixer introduced in 1904 (Fig.1); and the *PERFECT* bread mixer (Fig.2), introduced in 1905.

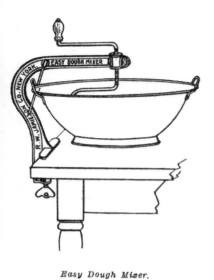

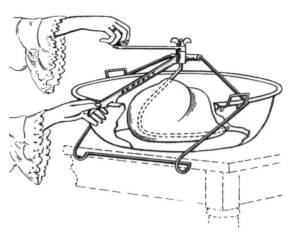

The Perfect Bread Maker.

Easy Dough Mixer.

Fig.2

Fig.1

JANEWAY, W.F., Columbus, OH

Maker of a dinner pail, introduced in 1892. Note the spout which allowed coffee or tea to be poured without removing the upper parts. *(Illustration at right)*

Janeway's Dinner Pail.

JENNINGS-HALL-SPERRY CO., Wallingford, CT

Maker of the *SLY-SIR* meat slicing machine, introduced in 1908. *(Illustration at left)*

The Sly-Sir Meat Slicing Machine.

JEWEL TOOL CO., New York, NY

Maker of the *JEWEL* can opener, introduced in 1894. This is probably one of the first can openers with a rotating cutting wheel. *(Illustration at right)*

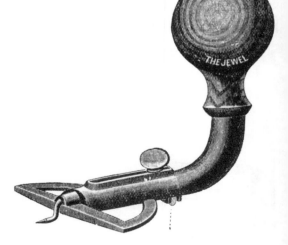

Jewel Can Opener.

JOHNSON FOUNDRY & MACHINE WORKS, Battle Creek, MI

Maker, in 1905, of the *YALE* fruit, lard and tincture press. It was offered in 2, 4, and 8 quart sizes. *(Illustration at left)*

Yale Fruit, Lard and Tincture Pr

JOHNSON, WILLIAM, Newark, NJ

Founded in 1834 by William Johnson, Sr., the firm was taken over by his son William Johnson, Jr. in 1864 and operated until 1909. Primarily a maker of hand tools, the firm made a few kitchen items such as the cabbage corer *shown at right*.

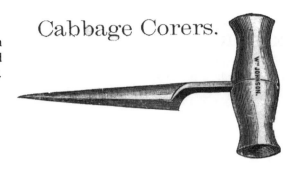

Cabbage Corers.

Pat'd. 3-24-1903

The Marvel Can Opener.

KALISCHER MFG. CO., Cleveland, OH

Maker of the *MARVEL* can opener introduced in 1902 and patented by H. Kalischer. It sold for 10 cents. *(Illustration at left)*

KEEN & HAGERTY MFG. CO., Baltimore, MD

A 500 employee company, capitalized at $250,000. Maker of tinware, galvanized ware, and gray flint enameled ware. In 1901, the firm was absorbed by the National Enameling & Stamping Co. *(Illustration at right)*

Culinary Tea Cup Measure.

KEENO CORPORATION, New York, NY

Maker, in 1924, of the *KEENO* knife sharpener "it's black and white." *(Illustration at left)*

KEINER-WILLIAMS STAMPING CO., Richmond Hill, NY

Maker of ice cream dishers, patented November 7, 1905. The key that rotates to free the ice cream is marked K W.

KELSEA & BOUTELL, Antrim, NH

Formed about 1885 by W.H. Boutell who was previously associated with the Goodell Co. Maker of the *RIVAL* apple paring, coring and slicing machine. By 1890, the firm had moved to Rochester, NY, and reorganized as Abbott & Boutell. *(Illustration at right)*

Pat'd. 10-9-1883, 9-16-1884, & 6-25-1889

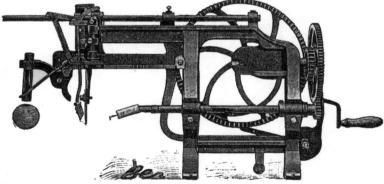

The Rival Apple Paring, Coring and Slicing Machine.

KETCHUM & CO., E., New York, NY

Maker, in 1859, of ice cream freezers, patented by H.B. Masser. Early production had all wood outer tubs; later production was made with iron covers and bottoms. *(Illustration at right)*

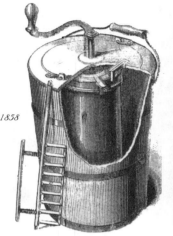

Pat'd. 12-15-1848 & 1-19-1858

KIECKHEFER BROTHERS, Milwaukee, WI, <u>later</u>
KIECKHEFER BROS. CO., Milwaukee, WI

Formed in 1880 as a partnership of William H. and Ferdinand Kieckhefer, the firm incorporated in 1892 with capital of $1,000,000. Maker of *ROYAL GRANITE* enamel ware in a wide variety of types and styles; a few of which are shown below. The firm became part of the National Enameling & Stamping Co. when that company was formed in 1899. *(Illustrations continued next two pages)*

TURBAN CAKE MOULDS.

OCTAGON CAKE MOULDS.

ROUND CAKE MOULDS.

TURK'S HEAD CAKE MOULDS.

CHILDREN'S MUGS.

COMBINATION "DOUBLE" SAUCE PANS.

SALT BOXES.

GRAVY STRAINERS.

BABY FOOD CUPS.

FRUIT JAR FILLERS.

MEASURING CUPS.

WITH HINGED LID.

130

BERLIN SAUCE POTS.

CUP DIPPERS.

COCOA SHAPED DIPPERS.

CUPS AND SAUCERS.

GERMAN MIXING BOWLS.

CAKE TURNERS.

ROUND COFFEE FLASKS.

OBLONG DINNER BUCKETS.

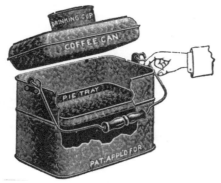

ACME DINNER BUCKETS.

COFFEE FLASKS.

CONVEX SAUCE POTS.

TEA POTS.

COFFEE POTS.

OIL STOVE TEA KETTLES.

TEA KETTLES.

BREAD RAISERS.

SPIT CUPS.

COLANDERS.

GRADUATED MEASURES.

STANDARD MEASURES.

FRUIT PRESERVING KETTLES.

WINDSOR KETTLES.

LIPPED PRESERVING KETTLES.

SOUP STOCK POTS.

KILBOURNE MFG. CO., Fair Haven, VT

Maker of the *EUREKA* toaster, introduced in 1900. (*Illustration at right*)

The Eureka Toaster.

KIT-CHIN-KIT CORP., Evanston, IL

Operated by John H. Lickert. Maker of a line of kitchen cutlery including a combination cleaver, meat tenderer, and ice pick (Fig.1), a bread knife (Fig.2), a grapefruit knife (Fig.3), a garnishing knife (Fig.4), and a combination stirrer and turner (Fig.5).

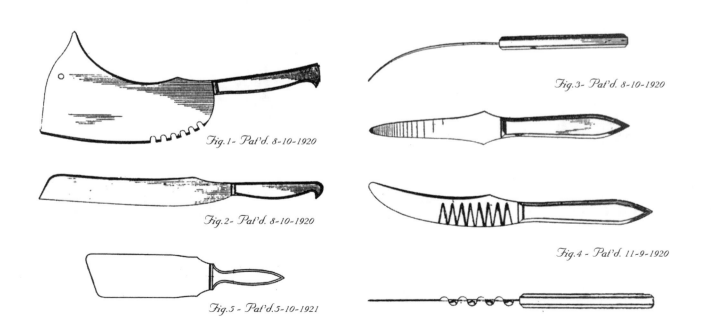

Fig.1- Pat'd. 8-10-1920

Fig.2- Pat'd. 8-10-1920

Fig.5 - Pat'd.5-10-1921

Fig.3- Pat'd. 8-10-1920

Fig.4 - Pat'd. 11-9-1920

KLINE & CO., Florin, PA

Maker, in 1896, of Kline's patent *BOSS* jar holder and top wrench.
(Illustration at right)

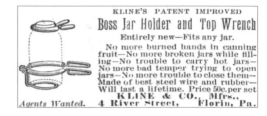

No. 0.   *1908*

KNAPP & COWLES MFG. CO., Bridgeport, CT

Maker of a variety of hardware items, including lemon squeezers and food choppers.
(Illustration at left)

KOENIG & CO., M.F., Hazleton, PA

Maker, in 1890, of the *EXCELSIOR* roaster & baker.
(Illustration at right)

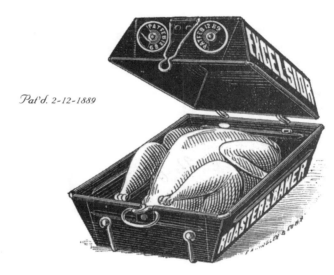

Pat'd. 2-12-1889

Excelsior Baking and Roasting Pan.

KOHLER & CO., F.E., Canton, OH

Maker, beginning in 1893, of the *HOUSEWIVES' DELIGHT* can opener and skewer puller, patented by Frederick E. Kohler.

Fig. 1.—Housewives' Delight Can Opener.   *Fig. 2.—Adapted to Square Cans.*   *Fig. 3.—As Skewer Puller.*

Pat'd. 6-13-1893

—One-Minute Butter-Fly Churn.

LA ROCHE & CO., E.M., New York, NY

Maker of the *BUTTERFLY* churn introduced in 1904.

LALANCE & GROSJEAN MFG. CO., New York, NY

A partnership of Florian G. Lalance (1824-1903) and Charles L. Grosjean, this French company began exporting enamel ware to the U.S. in 1870. In 1876, it opened a plant in Woodhaven, L.I., and claimed to be the first producer of enamel ware in the U.S. Products included double and triple saucepans introduced in 1898 (Fig.1) and seamless tea and coffee pots (Fig.2) introduced in 1899. In 1900, the firm introduced *REGAL* enamel ware, offering it in mottled dark blue and white or green and white. Mottled gray *AGATE* nickel steel enamel ware (Figs.3-5) was offered in 1915. *PARISIAN* coffee mills (Fig.6) were offered in 1886; *IMPERIAL* coffee mills (Fig.7) and spoon type egg beaters (Fig.8) were offered in 1910.

—Double Saucepan.   —Triple Saucepan.

Fig.1

Patent Seamless Tea Pot.   Patent Seamless Coffee Pot.

Fig.2

Agate Nickel-Steel Stewing or Preserving Lipped Kettle.

Fig.3

Agate Nickel Steel Seamless Milk or Rice Boiler.

Fig.4

Three-Piece Roaster Showing Pans and Cover.

Fig.5

Fig.6 - Pat'd. 2-17-1885

Fig.7

Fig.8

LANDERS, FRARY & CLARK, New Britain, CT

Formed in June, 1864, by George M. Landers (1813-1895), James D. Frary (1832-1890) and John W. Clark (1822-1903). By 1895, the firm employed 600 hands and was capitalized at $500,000. Clark left the firm in 1870 and Frary in 1876. Charles S. Landers (1846-1900), son of George M. Landers, headed the firm for a number of years. In 1900, the firm bought out the AMERICAN CUTLERY CO and by 1920 employment had risen to 4,000. Landers, Frary & Clark was absorbed by the GENERAL ELECTRIC CO. in 1965.

Early kitchen products included coffee mills, patented June 11, 1878, December 13, 1881, and February 28, 1882; L.F.& C. lemon squeezers, introduced in 1894 (Fig.1); and a variety of cutlery, patented March 24, 1896, and June 2, 1896.

The firm offered a variety of housewares under the *UNIVERSAL* tradename, including vegetable slicers (Fig.2), introduced in 1901; a bread maker (Fig.3), introduced in 1903, later improved ; a similar cake maker (Fig.4); a lard and fruit press and sausage stuffer (Fig.5); a paring knife with detachable gage, patented February 21, 1905; and a crank driven knife cleaner (Fig.6), introduced in 1908.

(continued on next three pages)

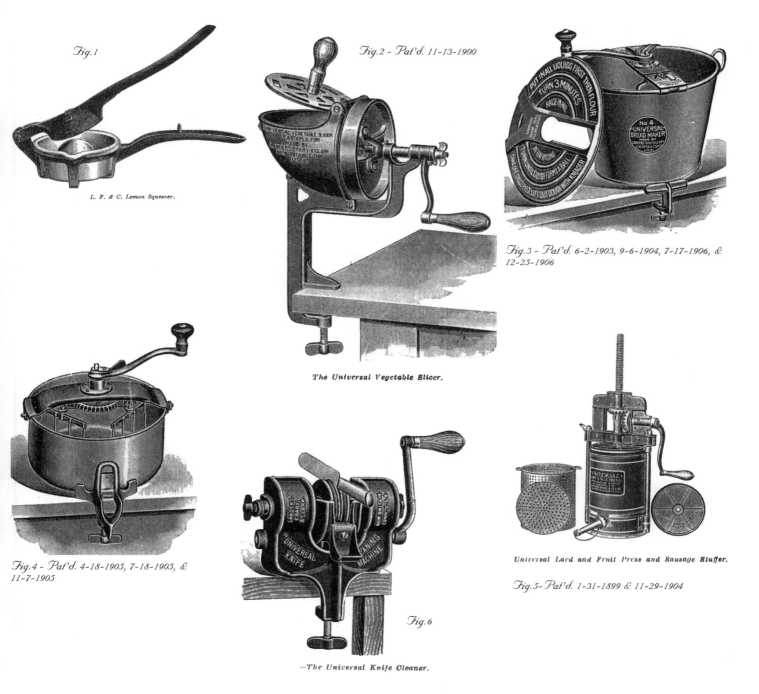

Fig.1

L. F. & C. Lemon Squeezer.

Fig.2 - Pat'd. 11-13-1900

The Universal Vegetable Slicer.

Fig.3 - Pat'd. 6-2-1903, 9-6-1904, 7-17-1906, & 12-25-1906

Fig.4 - Pat'd. 4-18-1905, 7-18-1905, & 11-7-1905

Fig.6

—The Universal Knife Cleaner.

Universal Lard and Fruit Press and Sausage Stuffer.

Fig.5 - Pat'd. 1-31-1899 & 11-29-1904

UNIVERSAL coffee mills were offered in table models (Figs.7-8); wall mount (Fig.9) and clamp-on (Fig.10) models; and a grocery counter model patented March 29, 1910. CROWN mills (Fig.10A) were offered by 1910. REGAL wall mount coffee mills (Fig.11) were available before 1920.

The UNIVERSAL food chopper was offered in three family sizes (Figs.12-14) and several larger sizes for butcher shops, etc. The UNIVERSAL meat chopper (Fig.15) was introduced in 1911.

—*Universal Coffee Mill No. 110.*

Fig. 7 - Pat'd 2-14-1905

—*Universal Coffee Mill No. 109.*

Fig.8 - Pat'd 2-14-1905

Fig. 9 - Pat'd 11-24-1908 & 8-31-1909

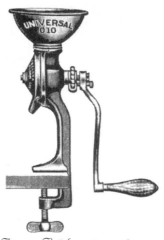

Fig. 10 - Pat'd 11-24-1908 & 8-31-1909

"CROWN," NO. 1
STEEL CASES,
BLACK ENAMEL FINISH,
BRASS SLIDING COVER

Fig. 10A

Fig. 11- Pat'd 7-28-1914, 10-20-1914 & 6-18-1918

Fig. 12 - Pat'd. 10-12-1897, 4-18-1899, 10-1-1901 & 5-29-1906 Same dates for Figs. 13 & 14

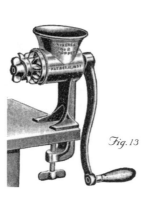

Fig. 13

Fig.14

Fig.15 - Pat'd 2-21-1911 & 1-5-1915

The *UNIVERSAL* meat juice press (Fig.16); mayonnaise mixer, patented April 27, 1915; churn and cream whip (Fig.16A); ice shave (Fig.17); lunch boxes in sliding top model (Fig.18); tilt top model (Fig.19), patented July 3, 1917, and child's model (Fig.20) were available before 1920.

Coffee pots offered in 1910 included the *EMPIRE* (Fig.21), *ELITE* enamel in blue and white (Fig.22), and *UNIVERSAL* in stove top (Fig.23) and alcohol (Fig.24) models. The percolator models were patented May 22, 1906, and July 16, 1907, and an improved percolator top was patented January 3, 1911.

Fig.16

Fig.16A - Pat'd. 4-4-1916

Fig.17 - Pat'd. 10-5-1915

Motor Grey Finish, Furnished with Pint Vacuum Bottle and Aluminum Drinking Cup.

Fig.18 - Pat'd. 2-11-1913, 4-8-1913, & 5-13-1913

CHILDREN'S LUNCH KITS

Fig.20

Hard Black Fibre Case

Heavy Gauge Tin Plate Box 10½ in. Long, 4¾ in. Wide, 7 in. High. Furnished with Pint Vacuum Bottle.

Fig.19 - Pat'd. 7-3-1917

Fig.21

Fig.22

Fig.23

Fig.24

Fig.25- Pat'd. 11-16-1909

Fig.26- Pat'd. 11-16-1909

Tea ball pots, patented November 16, 1909, included a samovar version (Fig.25) and three styles of polished aluminum types (Figs.26-28). Electrical appliances included coffee pots, patented February 11, 1913, April 29, 1913; small ovens, patented February 15, 1915, April 27, 1915, and April 18, 1916; table top ovens (Fig.29); waffle irons (Fig.30); and table top grills in round (Fig.31) and oblong (Fig.32) models. Toasters included the *THERMAX* model, patented February 14, 1922; *UNIVERSAL* in Standard (Fig.33) and De Luxe (Fig.34) models; *REVERSIBLE* model (Fig.35); toast rack model (Fig.36); and a model which loaded through a drawer in the side and toasted both sides of the bread at once (Fig.37).

Fig.27

Fig.28

Fig.29 - Pat'd. 3-12-1918

Fig.30 - Pat'd. 10-25-1921 & 12-26-1922

Fig.31 - Pat'd.1-22-24 & 3-17-1925

Fig.32 - Pat'd.1-22-24 & 3-17-1925

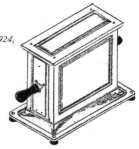

Fig.37 - Pat'd. 1-8-1924, 7-1-1924, & 3-31-1925

UNIVERSAL
Standard Model

Nickel Plated, Cool Fibre Handles and Feet, Complete with 6 ft. Heater Cord and Standard Attachment Plug, Holders with Strong Springs Keep Bread Firmly in Place Insuring Evenly Browned Toast. *Fig. 33*

De Luxe Design

Nickel Plated, Ebonized Handles, Ebonized Ball Feet, Fancy Design Top, Bread Holders and Base, Feed Through Switch in Connecting Cord, Complete with 6 ft. Heater Cord and Standard Attachment Plug. *Fig. 34*

Reversible Model

Nickel Plated, Cool Fibre Handles and Feet, Complete with 6 ft. Heater Cord and Standard Attachment Plug. *Fig. 35*

The patented easy-swinging bread racks —opening like doors—allow the bread to be quickly toasted both sides without being touched by fingers.

Reversible Model

Nickel Plated, Cool Fibre Handles and Feet, Complete with 6 ft. Heater Cord and Standard Attachment Plug. *Fig. 36*

The patented easy-swinging bread racks —opening like doors—allow the bread to be quickly toasted both sides without being touched by fingers.

Pats: Figs.33-34: 12-9-1913, 6-1-1915, 10-5-1915; Fig.35: 11-16-1920, 1-31-22, 2-14-1922; Fig.36: 2-14-1922

LANE, A.J., Glenville, OH

Maker, in 1888, of a suction filter coffee pot, designed to boil coffee with the grounds free in the water and then remove the grounds with the lifting of a filter assembly. *(Illustration at right)*

Suction Filter Coffee-Pot.

LANE BROTHERS, Milbrook, NY

A partnership of John G. and William J. Lane. Maker, in 1877 and earlier, of the *SWIFT* coffee mill (Fig.1). The brothers also offered *LANE'S* coffee roaster (Fig.2), by W.J. Lane. The mills, made in 30 different styles, and the roaster were of larger size, sold primarily to grocers.

No. 16.

THE
SWIFT MILL.
ESTABLISHED 1845.

The annexed cut shows one of the many styles of Coffee Mills of our manufacture, especially adapted to Grocers' use and all retailers of coffee. They are highly ornamental, and workmanship of the very best. Silver Medal awarded at the Great Fair of American Institute last autumn. We make more than 30 styles.

ALSO

Lane's Portable Coffee Roaster

Will roast 30 to 40 lbs. at once, and can be used as a stove at other times.
Send for descriptive list.

GENERAL AGENCY:
S. HAVILAND & SON,
259 Pearl St., N. Y.
LANE BROS.,
Millbrook, N. Y.
Also sold by leading wholesale houses.

Fig.1 - Pat'd 10-16-1866, 1-14-1868, 6-20-1874, & 2-9-1875

Fig.2 - Pat'd 12-16-1873

LASHER MFG. CO., Davenport, IA

Maker, in 1910, of *KITCHEN KUMFORT* trowels "for turning eggs, meat balls, croquettes, cakes, etc.". The *KITCHEN KUMFORT* trade name and most products were taken over by ANDREWS WIRE & IRON WORKS about 1920.

LAVIGNE & SCOTT MFG. CO., New Haven, CT

Formed in 1890 by Joseph P. Lavigne. Maker, in 1893, of the *PEERLESS* meat tenderer, patented by Rose B. Lavigne.

Pat'd. 11-21-1893

—Lavigne's Peerless Meat Tenderer.

LAWRENCE HARDWARE WORKS, New York, NY

Maker, in 1904, of the *DUPLEX* can opener.

Pat'd. 11-24-1903

Duplex Can Opener.

LEACH ROASTER & BAKER CO., Paxton, IL

Maker of the *CHAMPION* roaster or oven, introduced in 1895. *(Illustration at right)*

—Roaster or Oven in Use.

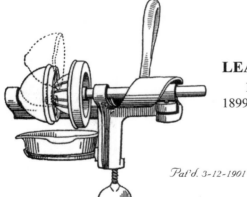

LEADER SPECIALTY CO., Chicago, IL

Maker of the *LEADER* lemon squeezer, patented by James Coomber, and introduced in 1899. Coomber assigned half the patent to Frederick A. Hastings. *(Illustration at left)*

Pat'd. 3-12-1901

The Leader Lemon Squeezer.

LEHMAN, BOLEN & CO., Decatur, IL

Maker of the *LEHMAN* can opener introduced in 1890. *(Illustration at right)*

Pat'd. 5-7-1889

The Lehman Can-Opener.

LEHMANN'S PATENT EGG BEATER.

" Best of All."

LEHMANN, CHARLES, New York, NY

Inventor and maker of the *BEST OF ALL* egg beater
(Illustration at right).

Pat'd. 9-10-1872 & 2-10-1874

ONE THIRD THE SIZE

LELAND MFG. CO., Great Barrington, MA

Maker, in 1904, of the *LELAND* broiler in round and oblong
styles.

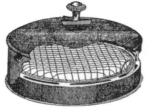

Fig. 1.—Leland Broiler, Round.

Fig. 2.—Oblong Broiler.

LIGHTNING DASHER EGG BEATER CO., Toledo, OH

Maker, in 1893, of the *LIGHTNING* dasher and egg beater. *(Illustration at right)*

Lightning Dish and Kettle Cleaner.

LIGHTNING DISH & KETTLE CLEANER CO., Minneapolis, MN

Maker of the *LIGHTNING* dish and kettle cleaner, introduced
in 1900. Consisting of a simple steel disc with a hinged handle, it
could "also be used to shave ice, clean window glass and polish wooden bowls, kneading boards,
etc." *(Illustration at left)*

LINDEN, N., Chicago, IL

Inventor and maker of a coffee roaster. *(Illustration at right)*

Pat'd. 11-15-1870

LISK MFG. CO., Canadaigua, NY

Maker of enameled steel ware, including an oval dinner pail introduced in 1902 (Fig.1) and coffee pots (Fig.2) offered in 1905. *(Illustrations at right)*

Fig.1

Fig.2

—*Lisk's Oval Dinner Pail.*

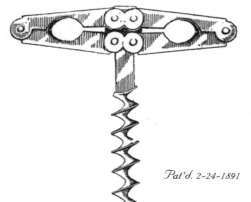

LITTLE GIANT LETTERPRESS CO., New York, NY

Maker, in 1892, of the *HANDY* pocket corkscrew. *(Illustration at left)*

Pat'd. 2-24-1891

—*Handy Pocket Cork Screw, Open.*

Pat'd. 7-1-1890

LLOYD MFG. CO., W.J., Philadelphia, PA

Maker of the *GREAT AMERICAN* meat cutter, patented by Charles F. Leopold and introduced in 1890. *(Illustration at right)*

—*Great American Meat Cutter, with Stuffing Attachment.*

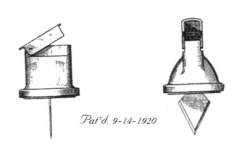

LOEB-STRONGSON CORP., Brooklyn, NY

Maker of a pouring spout for use with condensed milk cans *(Illustration at left)*

Pat'd. 9-14-1920

LOGAN & STROBRIDGE IRON CO., New Brighton, PA

Operated by John H. Logan. Maker, in 1878, of *BRIGHTON* (Fig.1) and *FRANCO-AMERICAN* (Fig.2) coffee mills and "cast iron goods generally." Other coffee mills included a model with a thumb hook, patented March 24, 1891; the *BRIGHTON SPECIAL*, introduced in 1898 (Fig.3); the *BRIGHTON STAR* introduced in 1901 (Fig.4); a wall mill (Fig.5); the *COLONIAL* (Fig.6), introduced in 1904. *(continued on next page)*

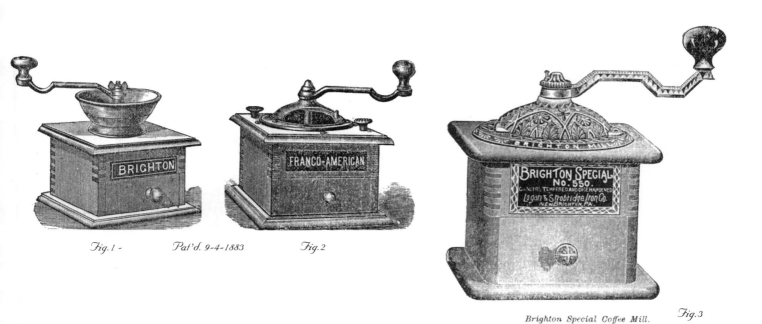

Fig.1 -   *Pat'd. 9-4-1883*   *Fig.2*

Brighton Special Coffee Mill.   *Fig.3*

Brighton Star Coffee Mill
Fig.4

New Wall Coffee Mill.
Fig.5 - Pat'd. 3-28-1905

Colonial Coffee Mills.
Fig.6

Fig.7

Other products included the LIGHTNING mincing knife (Fig.7), introduced in 1877; the *BRIGHTON* fruit and lard press (Fig.8), introduced in 1895; and the *BRIGHTON* ice shredder and snowball maker (Fig.9). In 1899, it offered the *BRIGHTON* meat juice extractor (Fig.10) and in 1902 the *STERLING* (Fig.11) and *AMERICAN QUEEN* (Fig.12) lemon squeezers were added. The *PREMIER* lemon squeezer (Fig.13) and *AMERICAN* (Fig.14) lemon squeeze were introduced in 1905. *(illustrations continued on next two pages)*

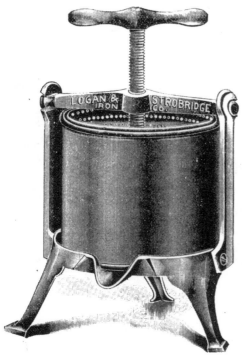

Fig.9 - Pat'd. 12-21-1897

Brighton No. 10 Ice Shredder.

Brighton Fruit and Lard Press.

Fig.8

Fig.10

Brighton Meat Juice Extractor.

Fig. 11   —Sterling Lemon Squeezer No. 16.

Fig. 12   —American Queen Lemon Squeezer No. 18.

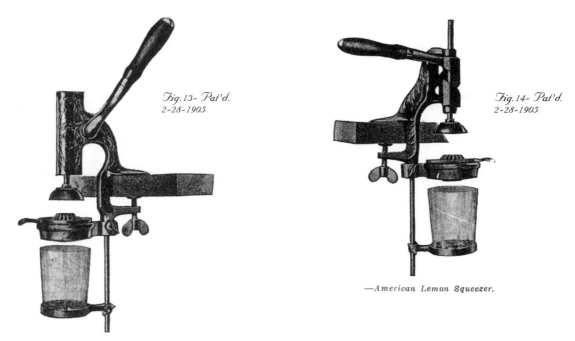

Fig.13- Pat'd.
2-28-1905

Fig.14- Pat'd.
2-28-1905

—American Lemon Squeezer.

—Premier Lemon Squeezer.

LOLL MFG. CO., F.W., Meriden, CT

Maker, in 1906, of the *ONE-MINUTE* egg and cream beater (Fig.1). The *EASY* can opener (Fig.2) was introduced in 1907.

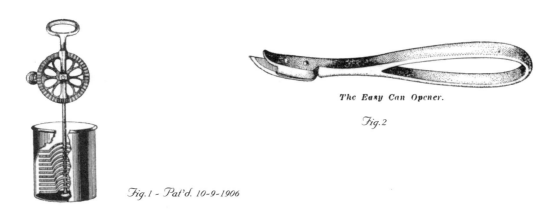

The Easy Can Opener.

Fig.2

Fig.1 - Pat'd. 10-9-1906

The One-Minute Egg and Cream Beater.

LONGSHORE & BRO., Mansfield, OH

Maker of a combination stove handle and household tool.

Pat'd. 10-23-1866

LOSS, FRANCIS H., New York, NY

Maker, in 1893, of the compound lever *RELIABLE* (Fig.1) and *PEERLESS* (Fig.2) corkscrews and a web banding jar holder (Fig.3).

—*Reliable Cork Screw.*

Fig.1

Fig.2

—*Peerless Cork Screw.*

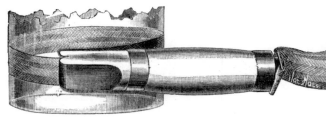

Preserve-Jar Holder.

Fig.3

LUDWIG, C.T., Bucyrus, OH

Maker of the *STAR* chopping knife, patented by Mary Ludwig and introduced in 1891. *(Illustration at right)*

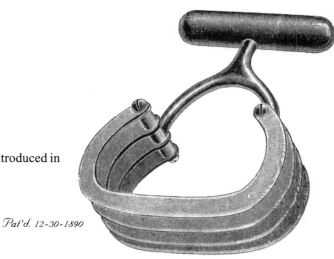

Pat'd. 12-30-1890

The Star Chopping Knife.

World's Best.

Pa'd. 3-7-1882

No. 1.

No. 2.

LYMAN, ARTHUR W., Brooklyn, NY

Inventor and maker of the *WORLD'S BEST* can opener made iron handle (Fig.1) and wood handle (Fig.2) styles. *(Illustration at left)*

LYMAN, W.W., Meriden, CT

Inventor and maker of *LYMAN'S* can opener. He was also granted a second can opener patent, July 12, 1870, but no examples are known.

Pat'd. 7-19-1870

Par'd. 2-22-1898

LYON, NELSON, Albany, NY

Maker, in 1898, of the *PERFECTION* egg beater and cream whip. An earlier, and very similar version was patented September 7, 1897. In 1903, Lyon joined with Thomas Holt to form the HOLT-LYON CO. *(Illustration at right)*

Lyon Egg Beater and Cream Whip.

LYONS SPECIALTY CO., Lyons, IA

Maker, in 1902, of a mason fruit jar wrench. *(Illustration at right)*

Lyons Mason Fruit Jar Wrench.

The Toledo Kitchen Knife,

MAHLER & GROSH, Toledo, OH

Formed in 1878 as a maker of pocket and table cutlery. In 1890, the firm offered the *TOLEDO* kitchen knife "a women's invention used for chopping potatoes while warming, turning griddle cakes, removing cookies from tins, and many other purposes". *(Illustration at left)*

Pat'd. 5-30-1911

MAK-MOR SALES CO., New York, NY

Maker of the *MAK-MOR* butter machine. Although it resembles a churn it is a "butter extender" meant to mix a pound of butter with a pint of milk, resulting in two pounds of "butter". *(Illustration at right)*

MALIN & CO., Cleveland, OH

Maker of *MRS. MALIN* sink strainer, introduced in 1909. It could also be used as a collander. *(Illustration at left)*

Mrs. Malin's Sink Strainer.

MALTBY, HENLEY & CO., Boston, MA

In operation from 1888 to 1899, the firm offered a variety of sporting goods and housewares. Maker of the *TRIUMPH* combined broiler and fry pan in 1890 (Fig.1); *DIAMOND* kitchen knife (Fig.2); *MONARCH* combination broiler and odorless fry pan in 1893 (Fig.3); *BOSTON* can opener (Fig.4); and *RELIABLE* and *PEERLESS* corkscrews. The entire line was taken over by SMITH & HEMENWAY CO. in 1899.

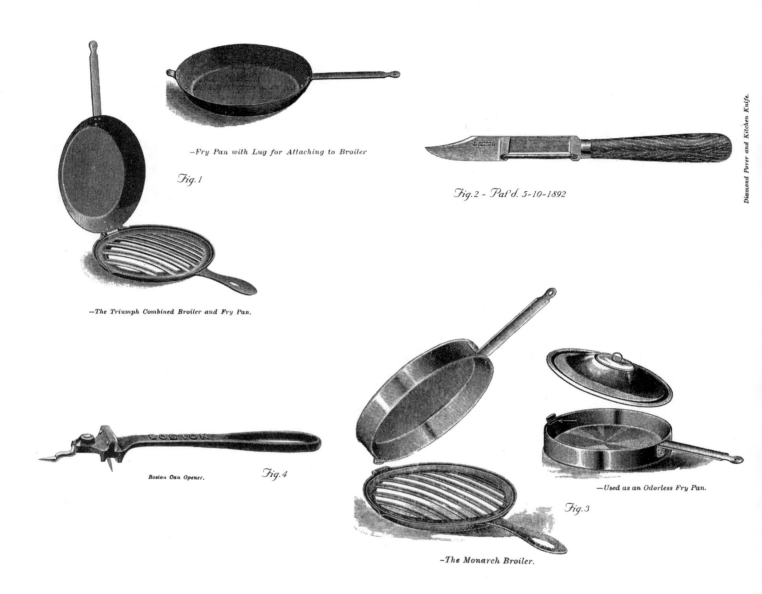

—Fry Pan with Lug for Attaching to Broiler

Fig.1

Fig.2 - Pat'd. 5-10-1892

Diamond Parer and Kitchen Knife.

—The Triumph Combined Broiler and Fry Pan.

Boston Can Opener.   *Fig.4*

—Used as an Odorless Fry Pan.

Fig.3

—The Monarch Broiler.

MANNING, BOWMAN & CO., Meriden, CT

Formed 1859 in Middletown, CT, by Thaddeus Manning and Robert Bowman. The firm moved to Meriden, CT, in 1872 and incorporated with Edward B. Manning as president. In 1878, the firm patented metal trimmed iron ware which became a staple. *(continued on next three pages)*

Early products included tea and coffee pots, patented June 3, 1862, August 18, 1868, and July 19, 1870; molasses pitchers, patented July 1, 1873; a combination lemon squeezer and nutcracker (Fig.1); and the *DRUM* lemon squeezer (Fig.2). Other products included a line of *MIKADO* pearl agate ware (Figs.3-4), and the Draper *PERFECTION* tea pot strainer (Fig.5), introduced in 1892; the *HAWTHORNE* julep strainer (Fig.6); *MERIDEN* cork puller (Fig.7) and *SIMPLEX* cork puller (Fig.8) both introduced in 1894; detachable handle coffee pot "to prevent injury from the heat" (Fig.9), introduced in 1897; and a table mounted lemon squeezer, patented July 4, 1899.

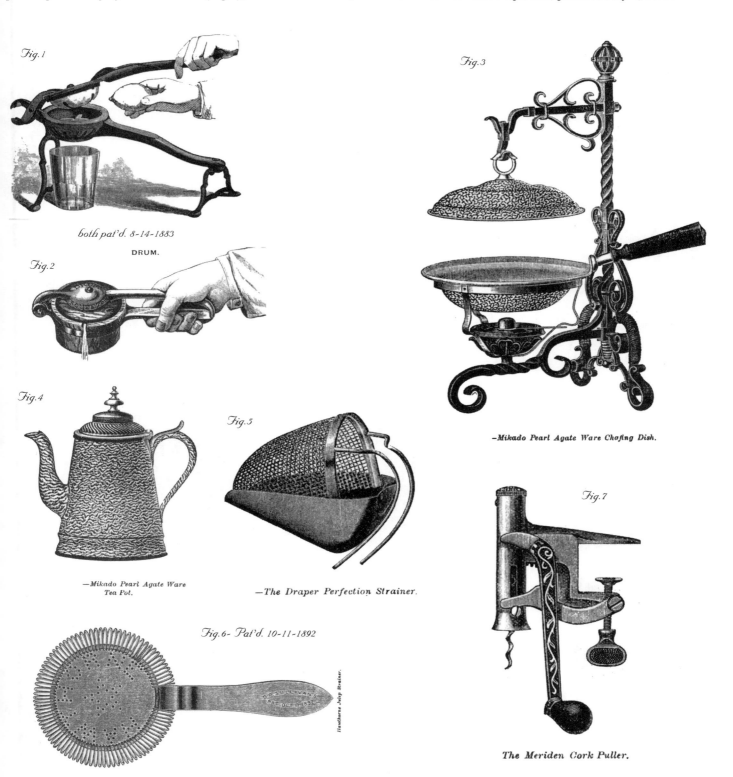

Fig.1

both pat'd. 8-14-1883

DRUM.

Fig.2

Fig.3

—*Mikado Pearl Agate Ware Chafing Dish.*

Fig.4

—*Mikado Pearl Agate Ware Tea Pot.*

Fig.5

—*The Draper Perfection Strainer.*

Fig.6- Pat'd. 10-11-1892

Fig.7

The Meriden Cork Puller.

The *CAPEE* bottle capper (Fig.10), *CORKEE* corking machine (Fig.11), and *SHOMEE* (Fig.12) and *PULLMEE* (Fig.13) cork pullers, previously made by the FREEPORT NOVELTY CO., were introduced in 1902.

Fig.8

Simplex Cork Puller.

Fig.9

Detachable Handle Coffee Pot.

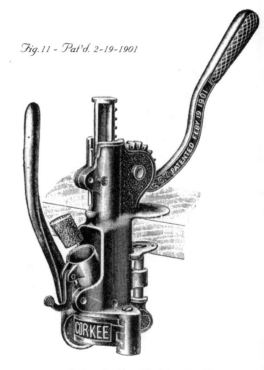

Fig.10

The Capee Bottle Capper No. 83.

Fig.11 - Pat'd. 2-19-1901

Corkee Corking Machine No. 39.

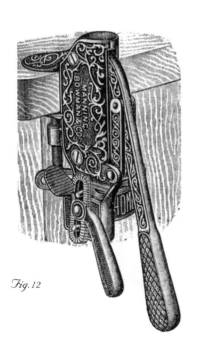

Fig.12

—Shomee Cork Puller No. 30.

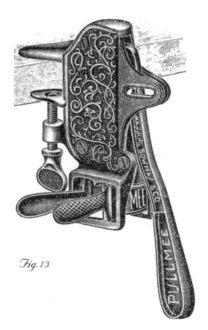

Fig.13

—Pullmee Cork Puller No. 35.

The *ECLIPSE* bread maker, patented January 14, 1902, and September 27, 1904, was introduced in 1905 (Fig.14); the *METEOR* circulating coffee percolator in 1906 (Fig.15); and a mission style chafing dish with an oak base in 1909 (Fig.16).

Later products included percolators (Fig.17) and (Fig.18); and the *REVERSIBLE* electric toaster, patented February 2, 1915, December 28, 1920, and December 4, 1923.

"ECLIPSE" Bread Maker

does more than mix the dough; it **actually kneads it by compression.** The only bread maker which does this. Perfect bread in three minutes.

The hands never touch the dough. Easiest working. Lasts a lifetime, saves its cost in a few bakings. Price **$2.00.** Send for booklet "L-5," and give name of your dealer.

MANNING, BOWMAN & CO., Sole Mfrs., Meriden, Conn.

Price $2.00

Fig.14- Pat'd. 1-14-1902 & 9-27-1904

Fig.15

Meteor Circulating Coffee Percolator.

Fig.16

Alcohol Gas Stove Chafing Dish, Mission Style, Oak Base and Alcolite Burner.

Fig.17- Pat'd. 11-12-1912

Fig.18 - Pat'd. 3-3-1914

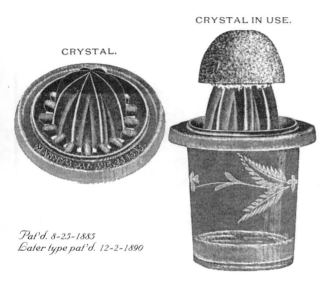

CRYSTAL IN USE.

CRYSTAL.

Pat'd. 8-25-1885
Later type pat'd. 12-2-1890

MANNY LEMON JUICE EXTRACTOR, Rockford, IL

Organized in October, 1890, with capital of $25,000. Wm. A. Talcott was president and Johnathon P. Manny vice-president. Maker of the moulded glass lemon squeezer. *(Illustration at left)*

MATTHAI, INGRAM & CO., Baltimore, MD

Maker of a patented fly fan in 1888 (Fig.1), the *COLUMBIA* fly fan introduced in 1893 (Fig.2), and the *FOWLER* improved model introduced in 1898 (Fig.3) . All three were advertised as "keyless", and were wound by rotating the base.

The firm also made a variety of wire goods such as soap shakers (Fig.4), and handled (Fig.5), and flat-ringed (Fig.6) pot scrubbers offered in 1910. Other products included the *LIGHTNING* cream whip and egg beater (Fig.7) offered in 1886; the *MARYLAND* roaster and baker introduced in 1892 (Fig.8), the *IDEAL* round bread pan, introduced in 1897 (Fig.9), and the egg poacher (Fig.10).   The firm became part of the National Enameling & Stamping Co. when that company was formed in 1899.   *(Illustrations continued on next page)*

THE LATEST IMPROVED FLY FAN.

NO KEY REQUIRED. COMPLETE IN ITSELF.

It winds up like a clock. Runs over one hour. Drives all flies away by shadow of wings while revolving.
Simple, durable, effective.

Invaluable in the dining room, sick room, office, or at the seaside. While running there is entire freedom from the annoyance of flies. It is a great household comfort.

Patented.
Price, $2.50 each, or $3.00 express paid.
If you cannot procure from your Hardware Dealer write to Manufacturers,
MATTHAI, INGRAM & CO., Baltimore, Md.   *Fig.1*

Fig.2

The Columbia Fly Fan.

Fig.3

The Fowler Improved Fly Fan.

Soap Shakers.

Fig.4 - Pat'd. 9-14-1875

Fig.5

RINGED.

Fig.6

LIGHTNING CREAM WHIP & EGG BEATER   *Fig.7*

IMPROVED
ROASTER & BAKER   *Fig.8*

The Maryland Roaster and Baker.

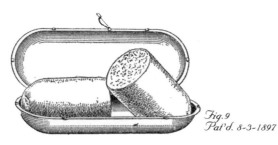

Fig.9
Pat'd. 8-3-1897

Ideal Bread Baker.

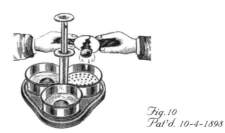

Fig.10
Pat'd. 10-4-1898

Maryland Egg Poacher.

MATTHEWS, JOHN, New York, NY

Maker, in 1868, of the Matthews ice shave. The plane, complete with tongs and tumbler as shown below, sold for $10.00.
(Illustration at right)

McDERMAID, JOHN, Rockford, IL

Formed in 1871. In 1891 the firm employed 30 hands making *BOSS* and *STAR* churns, patented December 14, 1880, October 9, 1888, March 19, 1889, and September 8, 1891. The *BELLE* churn, *shown at left,* was made in six sizes from one to 17 gallons, and as late as 1911.

McGILL, WILLIAM C., Cincinnati, OH

Inventor and maker of a green-corn cutter. McGill also made flour sifters, patented February 20, 1866, April 3, 1866, and May 8, 1866; a combination can opener and pan lifter, patented September 24, 1867; and corkscrews, patented January 8, 1867. *(Illustration at right)*

Pat'd. -10-1866

McGILL'S GREEN-CORN CUTTER.

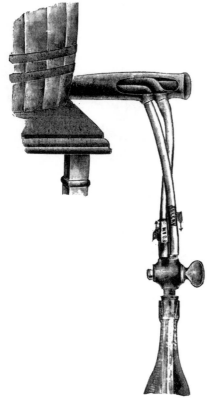

McKenna's Home Bottler.

McKENNA, A.&T., Pittsburgh, PA

Maker of a home beer bottler, introduced in 1898. *(Illustration at left)*

McLOON MFG. CO., Rockland, ME

Maker, in 1895, of McLoon's patent cheese knife. *(Illustration at right)*

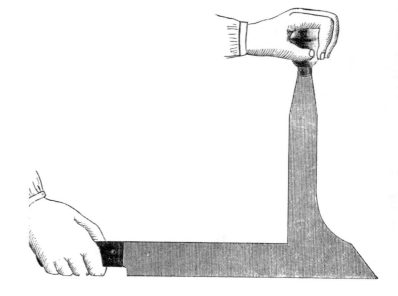

McLoon's Patent Cheese Knife.

McNEIL, JOHN A., Grand Rapids, MI

Inventor and maker of a beefsteak pounder. The circular head could be pivoted 90 degrees for use as a potato masher.

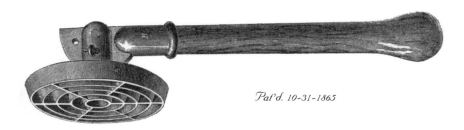

Pat'd. 10-31-1865

MEADVILLE VISE CO., Meadville, PA

Formed about 1890 as a reorganization of the Barrett Vise & Tool Co., the firm became the Barrett Machine Tool Co. in 1905. Maker of the *ALWAYS READY* cheese cutter introduced in 1891. *(Illustration at right)*

The Always Ready Cheese Cutter.

Pat'd. 3-25-1890

Means' No. 55 Coffee Mill.

MEANS MFG. CO., Lancaster, OH

Maker, in 1891, of Means' *IMPROVED* coffee mills. It claimed the long stem provided "a perfect and complete place for holding on to the mill."
(Illustration at left)

MEISSELBACH & BRO., A.F., Newark, NJ

A partnership of August F. Meisselbach and his brother William. Maker, in 1892, of the *COLUMBIA* can opener.

Pat'd. 9-26-1893

Columbia Can Opener.

MERIDEN BRITANNIA CO., Meriden, CT

Formed in 1857 to make a variety of products, most from britannia metal. Britannia metal is a tin-antimony-copper alloy capable of taking a fine polish and very popular for tableware in the 19th century. Products included porcelain lined pitchers (Fig.1); and egg-cookers (Fig.2) equipped with a bell which rang when the eggs reached the selected degree of hardness.

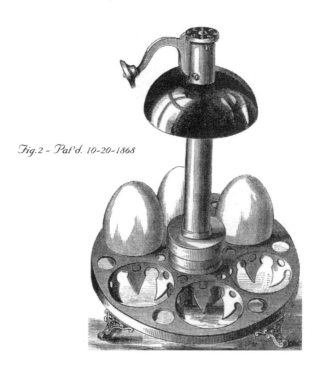

Fig.2 - Pat'd. 10-20-1868

Fig.1 - Pat'd. 6-30-1868

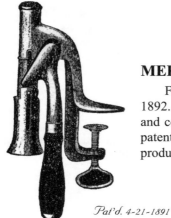

MERIDEN MALLEABLE IRON CO., Meriden, CT

Formed in 1868 with a capital of $75,000. George W. Lyon was president and 350 hands were employed in 1892. The firm made a wide variety of brass and malleable iron household items including lamps, nut crackers, and corkscrews. Cork pullers included the *RAPID* model *shown at left*, introduced in 1890; the *INFANTA* patented January 1, 1895; and other models. Counter top lemon squeezers, patented April 19, 1892, were also produced.

Pat'd. 4-21-1891

The Rapid Cork Puller.

MESSENGER'S

MESSENGER, CHARLES, Cleveland, OH

Inventor and maker of the *COMET* can opener. *(Illustration at right)*

MEYERS MFG. CO., FRED J., Covington, KY

Maker, in 1886, of Sharp's can openers, patented February 7, 1882, January 29, 1884, and August 24, 1886; a patent oval corn popper; mincing knives and hardware specialties (Fig.1). A new revolving corn popper, with round basket (Fig.2) was introduced in 1888. *HUNTER'S* flour sifter, previously made by J.M. Hunter (Fig.3), was offered beginning about 1888.

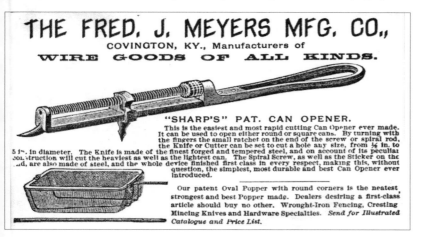

Fig.1

Fig.2   *New Corn Popper.*

Fig.3

Hunter Sifter.

Crary's Patent Bin and Sifter.—
General View.

MIDDLEPORT BIN & SIFTER CO., Middleport, OH

Maker, in 1889, of *CRARY'S* patent flour bin and sifter. *(Illustration at left)*

MILWAUKEE WIRE WORKS, Milwaukee, WI

Maker, in 1876, of the *VICTOR* flour sieve, patented by Oliver Bond. *(Illustration at right)*

Pat'd. 8-17-1875

GOLD MEDAL APPLE PARER.

MONROE BROTHERS, Fitchburg, MA

A partnership of James F. Monroe and Edwin Monroe. Maker of the *GOLD MEDAL* apple parer. *(Illustration at right)*

Pat'd. 8-21-1866

The **Morgan Broiler, $1.00**

Broils steaks, chops, oysters, fish, etc., to perfection, saves all the juices and applies them to basting the meat at each turn, making it palatable as well as tender.

No odor, no smoke, worth its weight in gold, made from wrought steel, will not crack, warp nor break, only one size, suitable for seven, eight or nine griddle hole, adapted for use over coal, gas, oil, gasoline, or wood fire. **For 25 cents** we will deliver a broiler by express to any part of the U.S. You can examine it and if you wish to keep it pay the balance **75 cents** to the express agent. Perfect satisfaction guaranteed or money refunded.

MORGAN MFG. CO., Chicago, Ill.

Agents and canvassers can make money by selling the Morgan Broilers. Write for special terms to Agents.

MORGAN MFG. CO., Chicago, IL

Maker of wrought steel broilers in 1895. In 1891, the same broiler had been offered as the *MORGAN* broiler by the Sun Stamping Co. *(Illustration at left)*

MORTON, JAMES, Philadelphia, PA

Inventor and maker of a cork extractor. It was "adapted to extracting corks on which rings or hooks are already formed" or a special corkscrew, shown below, could be used in conjunction with the lever. *(Illustration at right)*

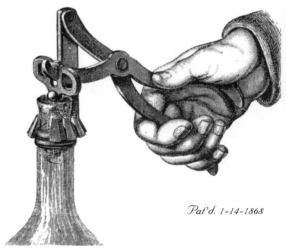

Pat'd. 1-14-1868

MORTON'S DOBULE-LEVER CORK EXTRACTOR.

MOSELEY & STODDARD MFG. CO., Rutland, VT

Maker, c1881-1905, of the *STODDARD* barrel churn, patented by M.O. Stoddard. *(Illustration at left)*

Pat'd. 5-3-1881

MOSSBERG MFG. CO., Attleboro, MA
MOSSBERG WRENCH CO., Attleboro, MA
MOSSBERG CO., FRANK, Attleboro, MA

The MOSSBERG MFG. CO. was formed by Frank Mossberg in 1889 to make hardware items and lasted only until 1896. The firm made the *AMERICAN* knife and scissors sharpener introduced in 1891 (Fig.1).

An improved version (Fig.2) was introduced in 1894 by the Mossberg Wrench Co. also formed by Frank Mossberg in 1889. This firm was reorganized as the Frank Mossberg Co. in 1901 and was maker of a variety of stamped goods, including a combination bottle opener and screwdriver (Fig.3).

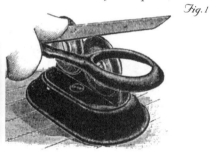

American Knife Sharpener.

—*American Knife Sharpener.*
Fig. 1

—*Used for Sharpening Scissors.*

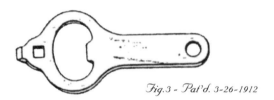

Fig.3 - Pat'd. 3-26-1912

MOSTELLER MFG. CO., Chicago, IL

Founded by Dosier Mosteller about 1906. Maker, in 1908, of an automatic lemon squeezer, which combined a knife, squeezer and strainer (Fig.1). It later offered a simpler type (Fig.2). The *UNIQUE* ice cream disher (Fig.3), made in six sizes, from 6 to 20 to the quart, was introduced in 1908. A new model (Fig.4) was offered in 1909 and a rack and pinion model was patented March 8, 1910.

Other products included a fruit and vegetable pitter, based on its *UNIQUE* ice cream disher ,(Fig.5); a liquid strainer (Fig.6); and a bread and meat slicer.

(Illustrations on next page)

The Mosteller Automatic Lemon Squeezer.

Fig.1 - Pat'd. 1-2-1906

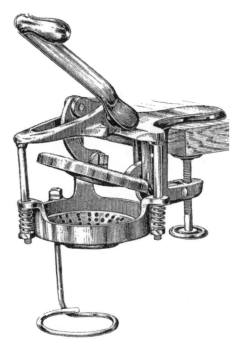

The Mosteller **Orange and Lemon Press.**

Fig.2 - Pat'd. 11-9-1909

The Unique Ice Cream Disher.

Fig.3 - Pat'd. 7-3-1906 & 8-27-1907

—Unique Ice Cream Disher, Full of Cream.

Fig.4

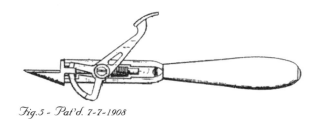

Fig.5 - Pat'd. 7-7-1908

Fig.6 - Pat'd. 8-25-1908

MURRAY IRON WORKS, Burlington, IA

Maker, in 1877, of *DRAW CUT* meat choppers, stuffers, and lard presses. *(Illustration at right)*

NASHUA IRON & BRASS FOUNDRY CO., Nashua, NH

Maker of the *WHITE MOUNTAIN* ice pick, introduced in 1899. The pick was equipped with a sliding ram handle.

White Mountain Ice Pick.

NATIONAL CO., Boston, MA

Maker, beginning in 1919, of Roberts *LIGHTNING* mixer. "Beats eggs, whips cream, churns butter——." The firm offered the mixer in pint and quart sizes, and claimed to have sold 200,000 by 1921. *(Illustration at right)*

NATIONAL ENAMELING & STAMPING CO., Milwaukee, WI

Founded in 1899, the firm used the *NESCO* trade name. Products offered in 1910 included *ACME* flour sifters, patented November 4, 1902; *PERFECTION* self-basting roasting pans in black (Fig.1) and royal granite finish (Fig.2); and a combination roaster and cereal cooker (Fig.3). In later years the firm's electric roasters were so well known that *NESCO* became a generic term for roaster ovens.

PERFECTION.   PERFECTION.

Fig.1   *Fig.2*   ROASTER AND CEREAL COOKER.
                                                      Fig.3

NATIONAL MFG. CO., Worcester, MA

Maker of the *VICTOR* rotary flour sifter, introduced in 1902. *(Illustration at left)*

Special F Victor Rotary Sifter.

NATIONAL MFG. & SUPPLY CO., Pittsburgh, PA

Maker, beginning in 1903, of the *E-Z MIXER*. It was "designed for beating eggs, whipping cream, custards, churning butter and for any kind of batter, etc." *(Illustration at right)*

Pat'd.
6-30-1903

NATIONAL SPECIALTY MFG. CO., Philadelphia, PA

Maker, in 1894 of the *NATIONAL* tobacco cutter (Fig.1) and the *NATIONAL* coffee and spice mill (Fig.2). The *NATIONAL* sausage stuffer and lard press (Fig.3) was introduced in 1897 and an improved version (Fig.4) in 1898. An improved spout for the sausage stuffer was patented June 23, 1908. The *NATIONAL* meat and food chopper (Fig.5) was introduced in 1901.

Offerings in 1903 included coffee mills, fruit, wine and jelly presses, sausage stuffers and lard presses, tobacco cutters, and meat and food choppers. Later coffee mills were covered by patents issued April 30, 1907, and May 28, 1907. *(Illustrations continued on next page)*

Fig.1

National Tobacco Cutter.

Fig.2

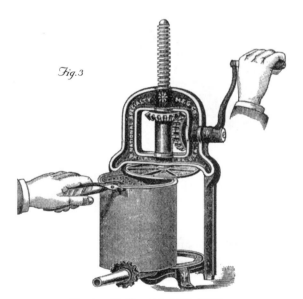

National Coffee, Drug and Spice Mill.

Fig.3

Sausage Stuffer and Lard Press.

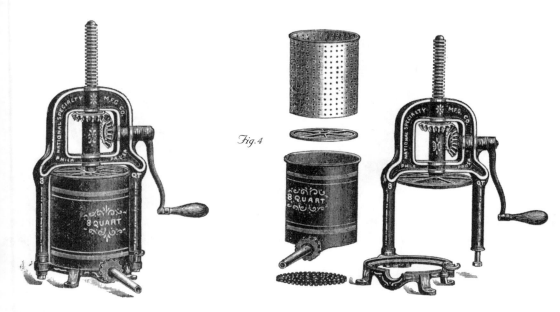

·*The* 1898 *National Sausage Stuffer and Lard Press.*

Fig.4

—*Various Parts of Sausage Stuffer and Lard Press.*

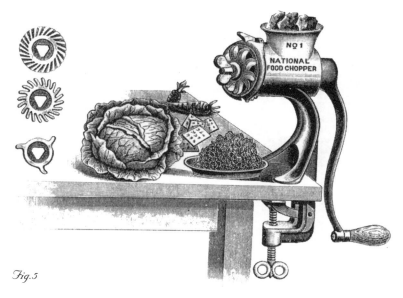

Fig.5

National Meat and Food Chopper.

NEW ENGLAND ENAMELING CO., Middletown, CT

Maker, in 1908, of the *IDEAL* coffee percolator (Fig.1). In 1910, the firm took over the *AUTOSPIN* ice cream freezer line from the Autospin Co., renamed it the *IDEAL*, and offered it as a combination freezer and churn in single (Fig.2) and double (Fig.3) models. Later products included cooking pots with handles patented December 23, 1919. *(Illustrations on next page)*

—Ideal Coffee Percolator.   *Fig.1*

Fig.2

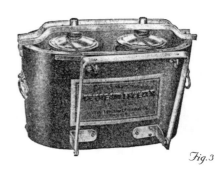

Fig.3

NEW ENGLAND SPECIALTY CO., North Easton, MA

Operated by Augustus J. Leavitt. Maker of Leavitt's *COMMON SENSE* can opener. Leavitt claimed "no joints or adjustable parts and therefore nothing to get out of order."

Pat'd. 12-19-1882

NEW HAVEN WIRE GOODS CO.,
New Haven, CT

Maker of a broiler and toaster introduced in 1888.

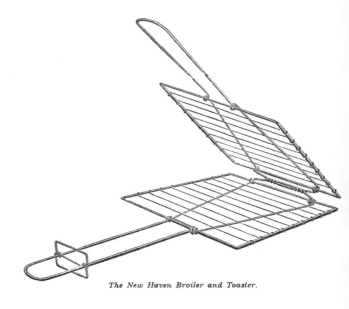

The New Haven Broiler and Toaster.

NEW STANDARD HARDWARE WORKS, Mount Joy, PA

Formed about 1915 as a reorganization of the Universal Hardware Works. The firm continued manufacture of *NEW STANDARD* rotary food choppers, *DANDY* cherry stoners in rotary (Fig.1) and plunger (Fig.2) types, and *ALL STEEL* ice cream freezers (Fig.3). New products included a fruit and lard press (Fig.4) and a crank operated cherry stoner (Fig.5), both introduced in 1915.

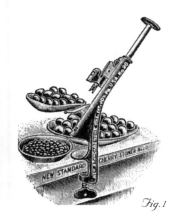

Fig.1

New Standard Cherry Stoner.

Fig.2

NEW STANDARD "ALL STEEL"

Double Motion, Spiral Mixer, All Steel Construction

A heavy, durable, all steel, double action Ice Cream Freezer that clamps to the table and cannot slip.

Makes a smooth, velvety ice cream in less time and with less effort than heretofore thought possible, saves energy and ice, and about half the price of the ordinary freezer.

It is two quart size— serving twelve persons.

Fig.3

New Standard Fruit and Lard Press and Sausage Stuffer.

Fig.4

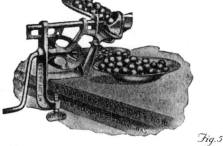

New Standard Cherry Stoner.

Fig.5

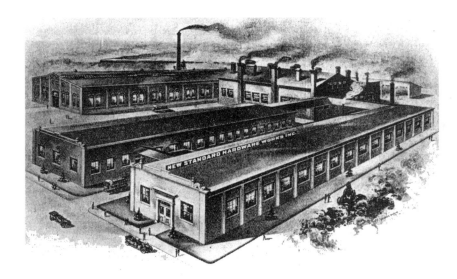

Plant of the New Standard Hardware Works, Incorporated, Mount Joy, Pennsylvania.

NEW UNION MFG. CO., Freeport, IL

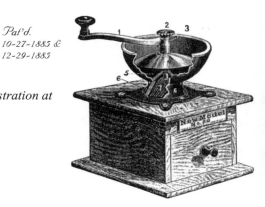

Pat'd.
10-27-1885 &
12-29-1885

Maker, in 1886, of the *NEW MODEL* coffee mill, patented by Edgar H. and Charles Morgan. Charles Morgan was one of the owners of the Arcade Mfg. Co. *(Illustration at right)*

NEW YORK GLASS ENAMELING CO., New York, NY

Maker of the *MAGIC* vegetable parer, corer, slicer and scraper, introduced in 1888. *(Illustration at left)*

NEW YORK STAMPING CO., Brooklyn, NY

Maker, as late as 1920, of *BROOKLYN, EMPIRE* and *ACME* fry pans. The firm also offered a copper and glass *EMPRESS WARE* coffee maker, patented March 2, 1893 and September 17, 1895.

FRY PANS.

SKILLETS.

ACME, COLD HANDLE.

ACME.

Pat'd. 11-14-1876

EMPIRE.

NEW YORK TEXTILE FILTER CO., New York, NY

Maker, in 1883, of filter assembly for use with existing coffee pots. The filter consisted of a cloth bag held between two cones. In use, boiling water was poured into the cone and allowed to seep through the cloth filter which held the coffee grounds. The firm claimed it could also be used for filtering drugs, liquor, jellies, milk and lemonade, and offered cones of glass and porcelain for use with liquids other than coffee. *(Illustrations on next page)*

NEWARK STAMPING CO., Newark, NJ

Formed in 1876 by Henry C. Milligan (1851-1940) who had been previously associated with Lalance & Grosjean. The firm claimed to be the first American maker of enamel ware.

NEWCOMER, J.L., Baltimore, MD

Inventor and maker of an unusual egg beater. The horizontal beaters were driven by a chain from a separate crank mounted above the wood base and metal bowl. *(Illustration at right)*

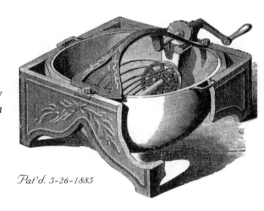

Pat'd. 5-26-1885

NEWMAN'S PATENT MINCERS.

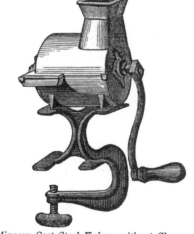

Pat'd. 9-13-1858

NEWMAN, M., Oak Hill, NY

Inventor and maker of *NEWMAN'S* patent mincers. The illustration below is from the 1861 Pratt & Co. catalog. *(Illustration at left)*

		per doz.
No. 1. — Patent, Iron, Mincers, Cast Steel Knives, without Clamp,	. .	$ 15.00
No. 2.— " " " " " " with Clamp,	. .	$ 20.00
No. 3.— " " " Extra Large, without Clamp,	. . .	$ 24.00
No. 4.— " " " " " with Clamp,	. . .	$ 30.00

The Newsam Cooker.

NEWSAM, WILLIAM, Peoria, IL

Maker of the *NEWSAM* cooker, introduced in 1908. *(Illustration at right)*

NICHOLSON, WILLIAM T., Providence, RI

Founded in 1859 by William T. Nicholson (1834-1893) to make a variety of cast iron goods. Products included levels, vises, and kitchen tools such as egg beaters, patented by Nicholson and T. Earle. The egg beater was offered in three styles as shown in the below illustrations from the Pratt & Co. 1861 catalog.

Nicholson also patented a similar egg beater on July 23, 1861. In 1864 he closed this firm and founded the Nicholson File Co.

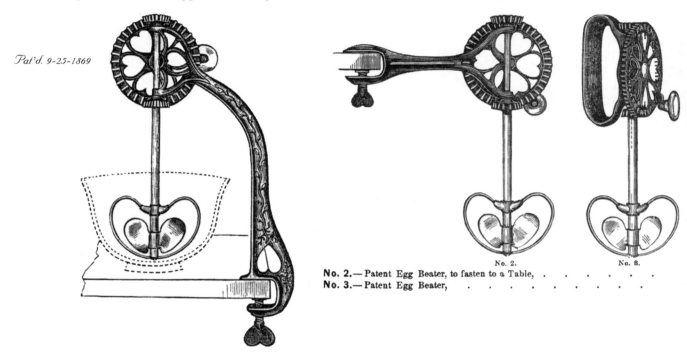

Pat'd. 9-25-1869

No. 1.— Patent, Improved Egg Beater, to fasten to a table,

No. 2. — Patent Egg Beater, to fasten to a Table, ...
No. 3.— Patent Egg Beater, ...

NICHOLSON FILE CO., Providence, RI

Founded in 1864 by William T. Nicholson (1834-1893), the firm became the largest file maker in the U.S. One of its lesser known products was a bread rasp offered about 1889.

Bread Rasp

NICOL & CO., Chicago, IL

Maker of the *DELMONICO* lemon squeezer (Fig.1), introduced in 1899; *DELMONICO* ice cream disher (Fig.2); and the *STAR* meat pounder, ice pick and shave (Fig.3).

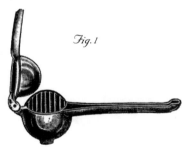

Fig.1

—*Delmonico Lemon Squeezer, Open.*

DELMONICO DISHER.

Fig.2

Pounder, Ice Pick and Shave.

Fig.3

NILES MFG. CO., Niles, OH

Maker of *CRUSTY* bread pans in 1895. *(Illustration at right)*

NITTINGER, AUGUST, Philadelphia, PA

Maker of a feeding attchment for meat choppers (Fig.1), introduced in 1892; and a combination candle holder and match safe (Fig.2), introduced in 1903.

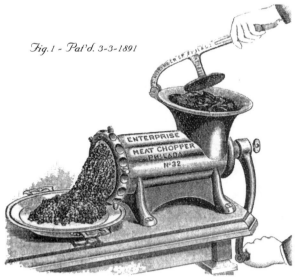

Fig.1 - Pat'd. 3-3-1891

The Nittinger Patent Attachment for Meat Choppers.

Fig.2

Combination Candle Holder and Match Safe.

NORTH BROTHERS MFG. CO., Philadelphia, PA

Founded by Selden G. North (1843-1916) and his brother R.H. North in 1880 and incorporated in 1887. In 1892 the business of the American Machine Co. was purchased and the line of ice shaves, ice chippers, tobacco cutters, fluting machines and meat cutters were continued under the North name. In 1893, the ice cream freezer business of the Shepard Hardware Co. was purchased and added to the North line. *(continued on next two pages)*

Maker of the *KEYSTONE* beater (Fig.1) beginning in 1892 when they bought the Keystone Beater Co. Products offered in 1893, previously made by the American Machine Co., included the *GEM* cake pan (Fig.2); *PERFECTION* meat cutter (Fig.3); *GEM* cake and batter mixer (Fig.4); *AMERICAN* tobacco shave (Fig.5) and cutter (Fig.6); *LIGHTNING* (Fig.7) and *CROWN* (Fig.8) ice chippers; and the *GEM* ice shave (Fig.9).

The New Keystone Beater.
Fig.1 - Pat'd. 12-15-1885

Fig.2
Pat'd.
7-29-1890
—Gem Cake Pan.

-Layer Pan and Measuring Cup.

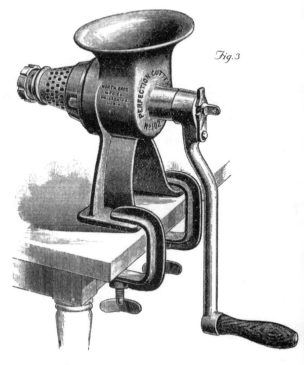

Fig.3

Fig. 1.—The New Perfection Cutter.

The Gem Cake and Batter Mixer.

Fig.4

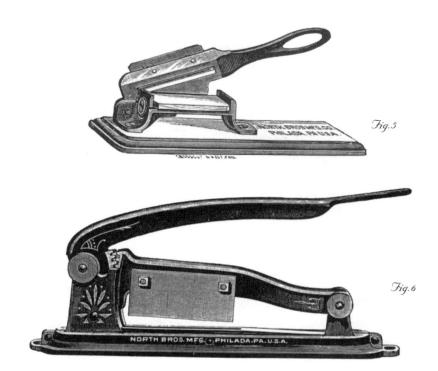

Fig.5

Fig.6

Ice cream freezers included the *LIGHTNING* (Fig.10), previously made by the Shepard Hardware Co.; *GEM* (Fig.11), previously made by American Machine Co.; and *BLIZZARD* (Fig.12), offered in 1895. All were made in nine sizes from one to 14 quarts and later included features patented October 15, 1895. Toy, one pint, models of the *LIGHTNING* and *GEM* freezers (Fig.13) were introduced in 1900. The *AMERICAN TWIN* freezer which could make two flavors at once (Fig.14) was offered by 1912.

Fig.7

Fig.8

Fig.9

Fig.10

Fig.11

Fig.12

Toy Freezers

Fig.14

"LIGHTNING"

"GEM"   *Fig.13*

NORTHERN STEEL & IRON WORKS, Eau Claire, WI

Maker, in 1920, of some of the earlier pressure cookers for home use. *(Illustration at right)*

Hudson's Double or Divided Skillet.

NORTHWESTERN CONSOLIDATED IRON & STEEL MFG. CO., Burlington, IA

Maker of *HUDSON'S* double or divided skillet, introduced in 1908. *(Illustration at left)*

NORTHWESTERN KITCHENWARE MFG. CO., Minneapolis, MN

Maker of the *ECONOMY* colander and fruit press, introduced in 1909. *(Illustration at right)*

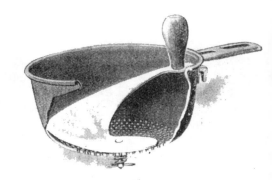

—Interior of Press.

CREASEY'S ICE BREAKER.

Pat'd. 10-29-1878

NOVELTY MACHINE WORKS, Philadelphia, PA

Maker of *CREASEY'S* ice breaker. The breaker was made in several sizes, from a small family type to power driven units that took 100 pound ice blocks.

OHIO STATE STOVE CO., Columbus, OH

Maker, in 1913, of the *OSSCO* portable, glass-door oven for use on oil, gas and gasoline stoves. *(Illustration at right)*

OHIO TIN & COPPER CO., Findlay, OH

Maker of the *PICNIC* dinner pail, introduced in 1888.

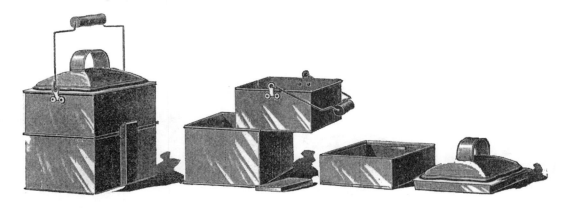

The Picnic Dinner Pail.

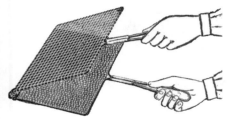

ONONDAGA MFG. & PROMOTING CO., Syracuse, NY

Maker of the *SCIENTIFIC* toaster, introduced in 1904. *(Illustration at left)*

The Scientific Toaster.

OSBORNE & CO., C.S., Newark, NJ

A partnership of Charles S. Osborne (1818-1896), his brother Henry F. Osborne, and brother-in-law william Dodd, formed in 1861 to continue the leather tool business formerly operated by Dodd. Henry F. Osborne left the firm in 1876 to form his own business which was merged back into this firm in 1905.

Leather tools continued as the primary line but the firm also made a variety of kitchen tools. Offerings in their 1911 catalog included: nutcrackers (Fig.1); *WHITE'S* sliding ice picks (Fig.2); several styles of plain ice picks (Figs.3-5); can openers (Fig.6); sardine scissors (Figs.7-8); a combination ice hammer and ice pick (Fig.9); and *OSBORNE'S* patent meat juice presses in several styles (Figs.10-12). The meat juice presses were previously made by H.F. Osborne. *(illustrations continued on next page)*

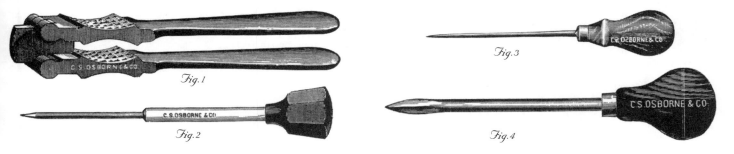

Fig.1 *Fig.2* *Fig.3* *Fig.4*

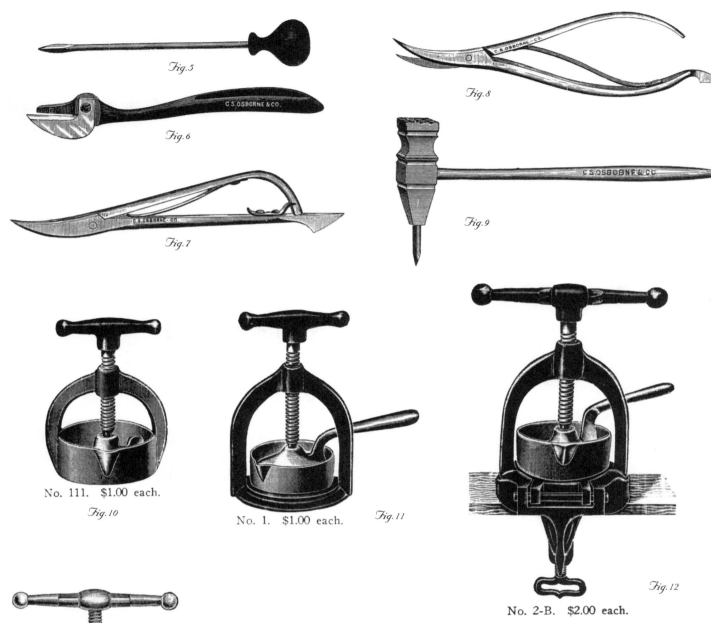

Fig.5

Fig.6

Fig.7

Fig.8

Fig.9

No. 111. $1.00 each.
Fig.10

No. 1. $1.00 each.   *Fig.11*

Fig.12

No. 2-B. $2.00 each.

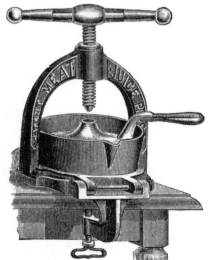

Meat Juice Press.

OSBORNE & CO., H.F., Newark, NJ

Formed in 1876 when Henry Osborne left C.S. Osborne & Co. where he had been a partner with his brother. The firm was merged back into C.S. Osborne & Co. in 1905. Maker of a meat juice press, introduced in 1890 and offered in individual, family, and hospital sizes. An improved version was patented September 10, 1901.
(Illustration at left)

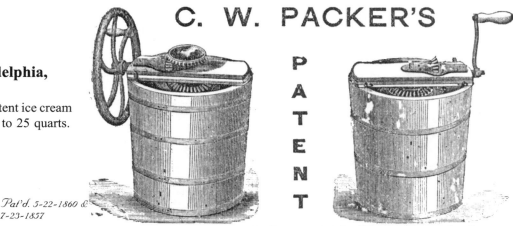

PACKER, CHAS. W., Philadelphia, PA

Maker, in 1872, of *PACKER'S* patent ice cream freezer. Sizes were offered from two to 25 quarts. *(Illustration at right)*

Pat'd. 5-22-1860 & 7-23-1857

PAINE, DIEHL & CO., Philadelphia, PA

Maker, beginning in 1886, of *BRYANT'S* patent egg beaters (Fig.1), and *BRYANT'S* patent soap holder (Fig.2), patented by Charles A. Bryant. Both tools were rotated by Archimedian screw action, driven by the up and down motion of a wooden thimble. The resulting alternating rotation was claimed to "beat eggs quickly and thoroughly" and be "most effective in dissolving soap." Other egg beater offerings included a varient of the Bryant design, patented by G.H. Paine (Fig.3); a model with P D & CO cast as part of the gear spokes (Fig.4); and a model with the letters E A S Y cast as part of the gear spokes (Fig.5). *(continued on next page)*

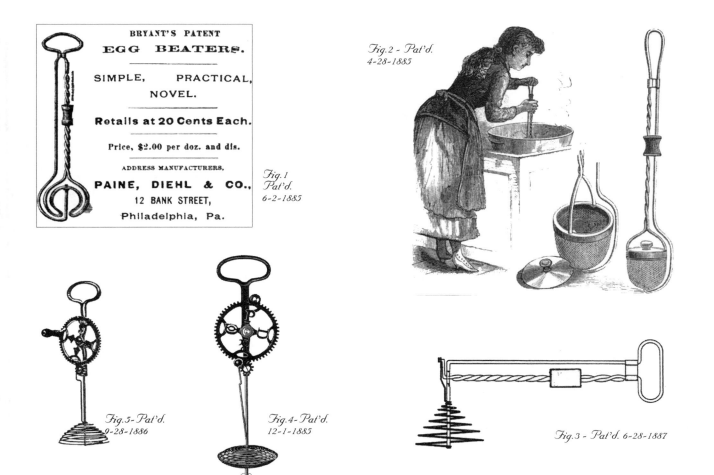

BRYANT'S PATENT
EGG BEATERS.

SIMPLE, PRACTICAL, NOVEL.

Retails at 20 Cents Each.

Price, $2.00 per doz. and dis.

ADDRESS MANUFACTURERS,

PAINE, DIEHL & CO.,
12 BANK STREET,
Philadelphia, Pa.

Fig.1
Pat'd.
6-2-1885

Fig.2 - Pat'd. 4-28-1885

Fig.5- Pat'd. 9-28-1886

Fig.4-Pat'd. 12-1-1885

Fig.3 - Pat'd. 6-28-1887

In 1888, the firm introduced a cast aluminum egg poacher and fryer (Fig.6) and the *DIEHL* fruit press and strainer (Fig.7). The *KEYSTONE* ice cream freezer (Fig.8), an adaptation of its *KEYSTONE* beater, was introduced in 1889.

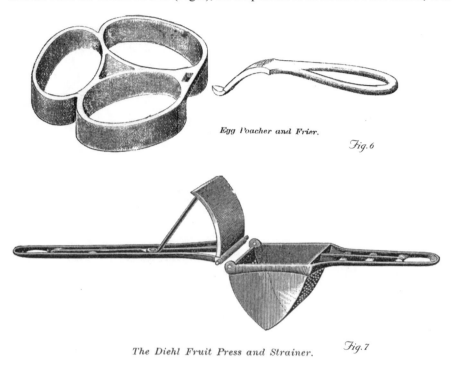

Egg Poacher and Frier.

Fig.6

The Keystone Ice-Cream Freezer.

Fig.8

The Diehl Fruit Press and Strainer.

Fig.7

PALMER & CO., Rockford, IL

Formed in 1879 by H.H. Palmer. In 1891, the firm employed 70 hands in making churns, cooperage, and other dairy products.

PALMER HARDWARE CO., Troy, NY

Maker, in 1892, of the *ACME* ice cream freezer which featured a stationary dasher and rotating cylinder. It was offered in either single or duplex models, the duplex for making two flavors at once. *(Illustration at right)*

—The Acme Freezer.

PARKER & CO., CHARLES, Meriden, CT, <u>later</u>
PARKER CO., CHARLES, Meriden, CT

Formed in 1833 as a partnership of Charles Parker (1809-1902) and his brothers John Parker (1805-1892) and Edmund Parker (1810-1866) to make coffee mills and other hardware items. Patents were granted to one or more of the brothers on June 22, 1832, February 7, 1860, October 29, 1861, and May 5, 1868. The 1860 date is found on wall mounted mills marked J.& E. PARKER. In 1877 the firm incorporated as the Charles Parker Co. *(continued on next page)*

Other coffee mill offerings included the *VICTOR* (Figs.1-3); *NATIONAL (Fig.4); UNION* (Figs.5-6); and *EAGLE* (Fig.7); table top models. Wall mounted types included a model (Figs.8-9), made in several styles; a wall mounted spice mill (Fig.10); and a cannister model patented August 1, 1911.   Free standing coffee mills, made for grocers' use, were introduced in 1898. Adjustable for grind size, they were offered with a single grinder (Fig.11) and double grinders (Fig.12) for grinding two types of coffee at once. *(Illustrations continued on next page)*

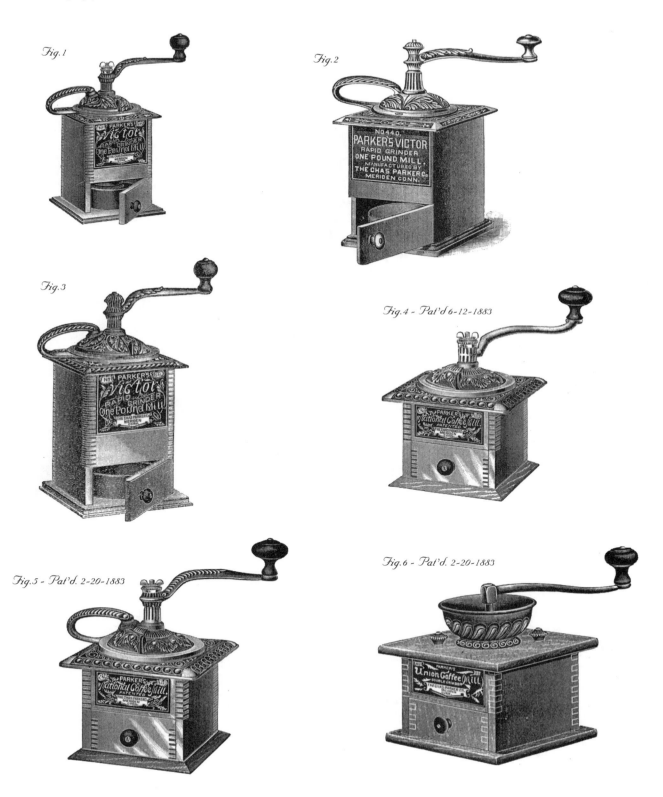

Fig.1

Fig.2

Fig.3

Fig.4 - Pat'd 6-12-1883

Fig.5 - Pat'd. 2-20-1883

Fig.6 - Pat'd. 2-20-1883

Fig.7 - Pat'd. 2-7-1882

Fig.8 - Pat'd. 4-1876

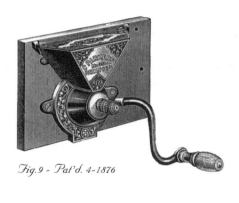

Fig.9 - Pat'd. 4-1876

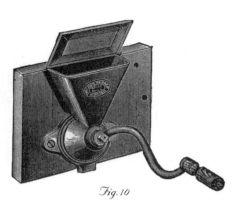

Fig.10

Fig.11 - Pat'd.
3-9-1897

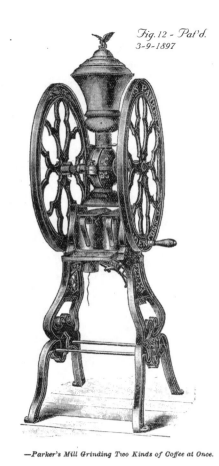

Fig.12 - Pat'd.
3-9-1897

—*Parker's Mill Grinding Two Kinds of Coffee at Once.*

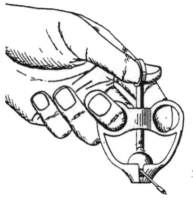

PARKER, EDWIN D., Springfield, OH

Inventor and maker of the *PERFECTION*, hand-held, cherry stoner. Examples are marked only PAT. *(Illustration at left)*

Pat'd. 1-27-1903

PARKER ICE TOOL CO., Worcester, MA

Maker of the *PARKER* ice crushing tool, introduced in 1897.

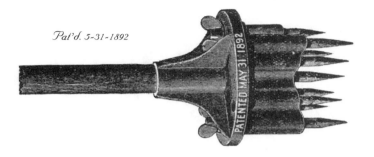

Pat'd. 5-31-1892

PARKER WIRE GOODS CO., Worcester, MA

Maker, in 1902 of the *STAR* meat tenderer (Fig.1); and, in 1907, a wire fruit jar wrench (Fig.2).

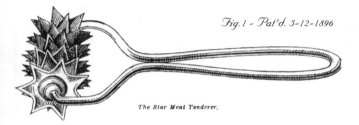

Fig.1 - Pat'd. 5-12-1896

The Star Meat Tenderer.

Fig.2

Fruit Jar Wrench.

PATCH, A.H., Clarksville, TN

Maker, in 1901, of the *TENNESSEE* hand grinding mill, "designed for family or farm use." *(Illustration at right)*

—The Tennessee Hand Grinding Mill, Front View.

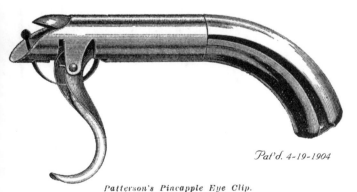

PATTERSON & CO., Rochester, NY

Maker of a Pineapple eye clip, patented by Robert Patterson. *(Illustration at left)*

Pat'd. 4-19-1904

Patterson's Pineapple Eye Clip.

PATTON MFG. CO., Columbus, OH

Maker, in 1890, of the *TRIUMPH* line of cast iron hollow ware (Figs. 1-2) and, in 1899, a line of cast aluminum hollow ware (Figs.3-4).

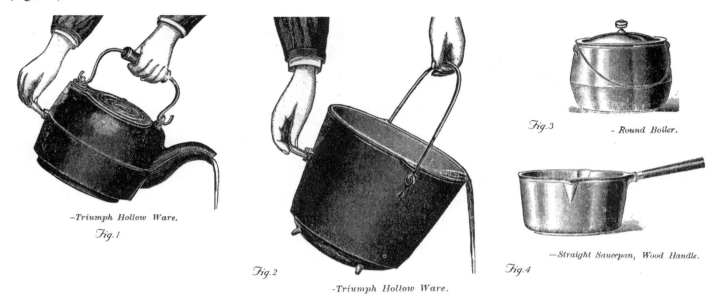

Fig.3

- Round Boiler.

-Triumph Hollow Ware.
Fig.1

Fig.2

-Triumph Hollow Ware.

—Straight Saucepan, Wood Handle.
Fig.4

PAXTON HARDWARE MFG. CO., Paxton, IL

Maker of the *NEVER-SLIP* fruit jar wrench, introduced in 1901.
(Illustration at right)

Fig. 1.—Never-Slip Fruit Jar Wrench.

PECK, STOW & WILCOX CO., Southington, CT

Formed November 1, 1870, by the merger of Peck, Smith Mfg. Co., S. Stow Mfg. Co., and the Roys & Wilcox Co. Products included a variety of hardware items and hand tools.

Early kitchen products included: *WOODRUFF'S* patent meat chopper and sausage stuffer (Fig.1); coffee mills patented April 30, 1878, March 9, 1880, and September 14, 1886; sausage stuffers, patented July 4, 1865; and apple parers, patented October 5, 1880.
(continued on next page)

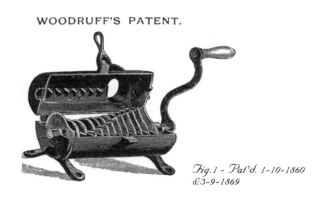

WOODRUFF'S PATENT.

Fig.1 - Pat'd. 1-10-1860
&3-9-1869

Fig.2

Success Can Opener.

Later kitchen products included: the *SUCCESS* can opener (Fig.2), introduced in 1891; the *LITTLE GIANT* meat cutter and sausage stuffer (Fig.3); the *TRIUMPH* meat cutter (Fig.4); can opener (Fig.5); an almond and peanut sheller (Fig.6), introduced in 1894; stove lid lifters, patented June 19, 1894; the *SURPRISE* meat chopper (Fig.7) and the *NEW TRIUMPH* meat cutter (Fig.8), both introduced in 1897; the *IDEAL* meat chopper (Fig.9); an improved cherry seeder (Fig.10) and a vegetable slicer with grater attachment (Fig.11), both introduced in 1900; and *PERRY'S* sausage stuffer (Fig.12) made into the 1920's. *(illustrations continued on next page)*

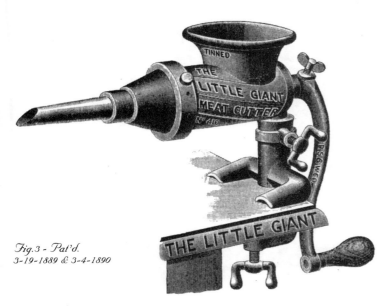

Fig.3 - Pat'd.
3-19-1889 & 3-4-1890

—*Little Giant Meat Cutter.*

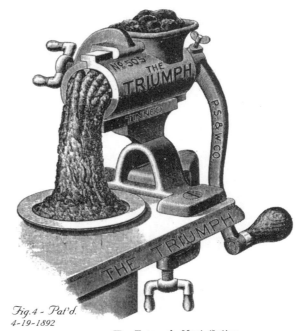

Fig.4 - Pat'd.
4-19-1892

The Triumph Meat Cutter.

Fig.5 - Pat'd.
4-11-1893

Fig.6

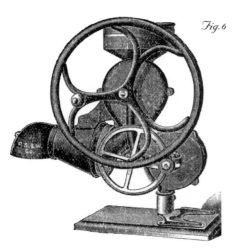

Apparatus for Shelling Peanuts,
Almonds, &c.

Fig.7 - Pat'd.
4-19-1892

—*Surprise Meat Chopper or Food Cutter.*

Fig.8 - Pat'd.
4-19-1892 & 9-3-1895

-*New Triumph Meat Cutter with Fly Wheel.*

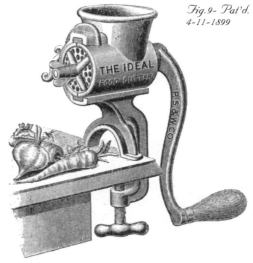

Fig.9- Pat'd.
4-11-1899

-*Ideal Meat Chopper and Food Cutter No. 25*

Fig.10

Improved Cherry Seeder.

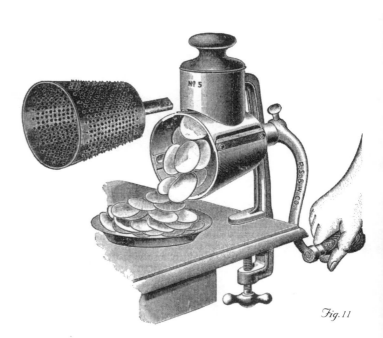

Fig.11

Saratoga Potato and Vegetable Slicer, with Grater Attachment.

PERRY'S.

Fig.12

PEERLESS COOKER CO., Buffalo, NY

Maker, in 1900, of the *PEERLESS* steam coffee pot. It claimed that steam generated by boiling water would gently "draw the strength of the grounds."
(Illustration at right)

The Peerless Steam Coffee Pot.

PEERLESS FREEZER CO., Cincinnati, OH

Formed as a reorganization of the Gooch Freezer Co. Maker, in 1895, of the *ICELAND* ice cream freezer. It was offered in ten sizes, from 2 to 25 quarts. The line was a product of Dana & Co. by 1899.

New Peerless Iceland Freezer.

BUYING A
Peerless Freezer
WITH THE
Vacuum Screw Dasher
Write us for information ; it costs nothing and may save you money.

Our recently published booklet, "**Fifty Ices**," gives full description of the Peerless, with illustrations and price list.

PEERLESS FREEZER CO., Cincinnati, O.

PELOUZE SCALE & MFG. CO., Chicago, IL

Maker of the *PELOUZE* coffee percolator (Fig.1), an attachment for old style coffee pots, introduced in 1902 and an electric toaster (Fig.2).

Fig.1

—The Pelouze Coffee Percolator.

—Pelouze Percolator in Coffee Pot.

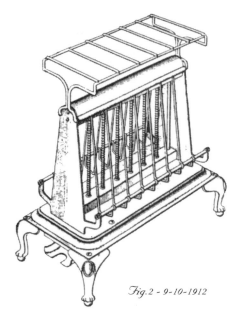

Fig.2 - 9-10-1912

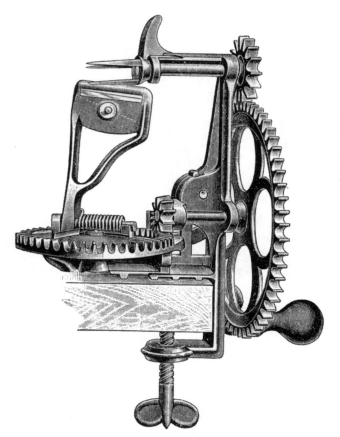

Expert Apple Parer.

PENN HARDWARE CO., Reading, PA

Formed in 1877 by C. Raymond Heizmann (1835-1923) and his brother Albert A. Heizmann (1848-1909). Maker of several styles of apple parers, including the improved *EXPERT* introduced in 1897.
(Illustration at left)

PERCO-WARE CO., Milwaukee, WI

Maker, beginning in 1920, of the *PERCO-POT* which was claimed to "cook by percolation". The aluminum pot, fitted with a removeable steel bottom, was designed to boil the liquid up through perforations around the outer edge of the cover and drain the liquid back into the pot through a hole in the center of the concave lid. The lid locked in place and could be used as a drainer. *(Illustration at right)*

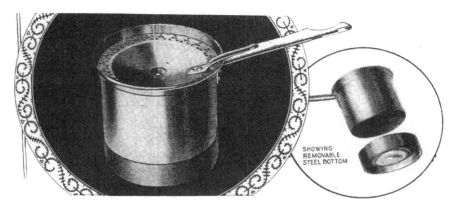

EXCELSIOR TWIN REVERSIBLE

High Grade Cold Rolled Steel, Nickel Plated Over Copper and Highly Polished, Complete with 6 ft. Heater Cord with 70-50 Feed Through Switch and Detachable Plug.

PERFECTION ELECTRIC PRODUCTS CO., New Washington, OH

Maker of the *EXCELSIOR TWIN REVERSIBLE* electric toaster. *(Illustration at left)*

Pat'd. 1-16-1920 & 5-23-1922

PFLEGHAR & SON, F.P., New Haven, CT

Maker, in 1902, of *PERFECTION* corn forks. The corn could be rotated with the forks in place "so that it may be seasoned." *(Illustration at right)*

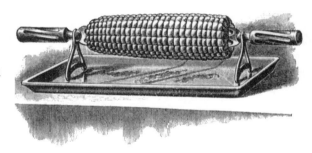

Perfection Corn Forks.

Pat'd. 10-5-1869

PHILADELPHIA PATENT AND NOVELTY CO., Philadelphia, PA

Maker, in 1869, of *GOODES'* detachable knife guard. *(Illustration at left)*

PHILLIPS LAFFITTE CO., Philadelphia, PA

Maker, in 1924, of the *ZIP* "knife sharpener with a handle." *(Illustration at right)*

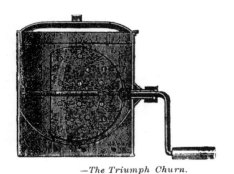

PHYNOTT, J., Louisana, MO

Maker, in 1891, of the *TRIUMPH* churn. *(Illustration at left)*

—*The Triumph Churn.*

PICK & CO., ALBERT, Chicago, IL

Possibly maker, beginning in 1899, of *DEWEY'S SLUGS* folding corkscrews. The firm operated as a jobber, so it may have been an agent rather than the maker. *(Illustration at right)*

PIKE MFG. CO., Pike Station NH

Founded in 1884 by A.F. Pike and his brother Edwin B. Pike, to make scythe stones, oil stones and other items for sharpening tools. Kitchen items included the *TWENTIETH CENTURY* grinder introduced in 1898 (Fig.1) and the *KANTBREAK* knife sharpener (Fig.2) offered in 1913.

Fig. 1

Twentieth Century Shear Grinder.

Fig. 2

For putting a keen-cutting edge on bread and paring knives, kitchen and carving knives, there is nothing to beat this sharpener. Better than a steel because it sharpens so much faster and keener. Handsomely finished and rubber-mounted— practically unbreakable

Price 35 cents at your hardware dealer's or sent prepaid. "Pick a Pike."

PIKE INDIA KANTBREAK KNIFE SHARPENER

A Scissors Sharpener Given Away

Send your dealer's name and 4 cts. for packing and mailing and we'll send our Pike India Sample Stone for scissors, pen knives, ink erasers, needles, etc., also our famous book "How to Sharpen." You'll be pleased. Write today.

PIKE MFG. CO.
103 Main Street, Pike, N. H.

PLUMB NOVELTY CO., W.H., Ansonia, CT

Maker of the *DERBY* can opener, introduced in 1902.
(Illustration at right)

Pat'd. 6-18-1901

The Derby Twentieth Century Can Opener.

POLAR STAR CO., Philadelphia, PA

Maker of the *POLAR STAR* ice cream freezer, patented February 15, 1910, and sold through Smith & Hemenway Co. By 1912, the freezer was a product of the Acme Freezer Co.

POND CO., L.C., Los Angeles, CA

Maker of the *KLEAN-EM* plate and kettle scraper, introduced in 1909.
(Illustration at left)

Klean-em Plate and Kettle Scraper.—Can Also Be Used for Cleaning Sinks, Window Panes, China, Pots, Fry Pans, &c.

POOLE, SAMUEL, Boston, MA

Inventor and maker of *POOLE'S* can opener (Fig.1) and *POOLE'S* nut cracker (Fig.2).

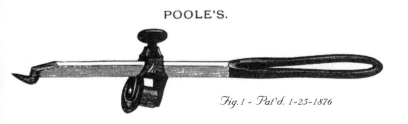

POOLE'S.

Fig.1 - Pat'd. 1-25-1876

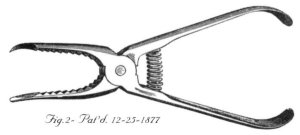

Fig.2- Pat'd. 12-25-1877

The U. S. Mason Jar Wrench.

POWELL, C.A., Cleveland, OH
Maker of the *U.S.* mason jar wrench, introduced in 1901.
(Illustration at right)

PREMIER MFG. CO., Detroit, MI
Maker, in 1923, of the *PREMIER* hand held knife and scissors sharpener.
(Illustration at left)

Pat'd. 7-7-1903

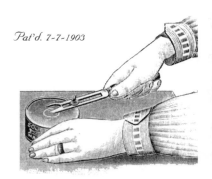

The Twentieth Century Can Opener.

PREMO-HALL MFG. CO., Newark, NJ
Maker of the *TWENTIETH CENTURY* can opener, patented by George F. Hall.
(Illustration at right)

Bread Mixer and Kneader.

PRESCOTT, EDWIN, Boston, MA
Maker of the *PRESCOTT-STANYAN* bread mixer and kneader, introduced in 1893.
(Illustration at left)

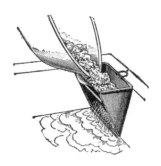

Prisco Movable Front Sink Strainer.

PRITCHARD-STRONG CO., Rochester, NY
Maker of the *PRISCO* moveable front sink strainer, introduced in 1905.
(Illustration at right)

PULLMAN SASH BALANCE CO., Rochester, NY

Maker of the *DELMONICO* meat tenderer introduced in 1893. The tool could be taken apart for cleaning.

Fig. 1.—The Delmonico Meat Tenderer.

Fig. 2.—Plunger and Key.

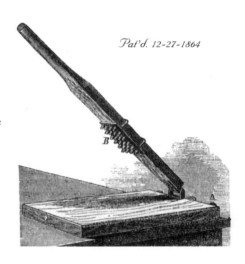

Pat'd. 12-27-1864

PUTNAM, G.W., Peterboro, NY

Inventor and maker of a "beefsteak breaker". Of simple construction, it could also be used "to break ice, press fruit for jelly, or to crack loaf sugar." *(Illustration at right)*

QUACKENBUSH, H.M., Herkimer, NY

Formed in 1871 by Henry M. Quackenbush (1847-1933) to make air rifles. Nut crackers and nut picks later became the primary products, including the *NEW PATTERN (Fig.1) ; SPRING* model, introduced in 1903 (Fig.2); *LINK* style, introduced in 1908 (Fig.3); and a concealed spring type, introduced in 1909 (Fig.4).

New Pattern Nut-Crack.

Fig.1 - Pat'd. 1-29-1889

The Quackenbush Link Nut Cracker.

Fig.3 - Pat'd. 8-11-1908

Quackenbush Spring Nut Crack.

Fig.2 - Pat'd. 4-29-1902

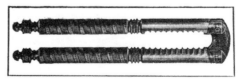

Concealed Spring Nut Crack.

Fig.4 - Pat'd. 8-10-1909

QUAKER NOVELTY CO., Salem, OH

Maker of the *FAULTLESS* hand cranked dish washer in 1895.
(Illustration at right)

QUICKSAFE MFG. CO., Nashville, TN

Maker, in 1923, of the *QUICKSAFE, JR.* can opener, designed to clamp to a table or counter top. A larger *QUICKSAFE* model for hotels and institutions was also available. *(Illustration at left)*

QUINCY HARDWARE MFG. CO., Quincy, IL

Maker of the *QUINCY* corn popper (Fig.1), introduced in 1895 and the *ACME* corn popper (Fig.2), introduced in 1897.

Fig.1

The Quincy Corn Popper.

Fig.2 - Pat'd. 5-24-1892

The Acme Corn Popper.

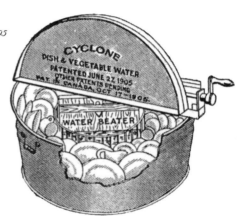

Pat'd. 6-27-1905

RANDLEMAN, Z.S. & C.L., Des Moines, IA

Maker of the *CYCLONE* dish and vegetable washer, introduced in 1905. *(Illustration at right)*

READING HARDWARE CO., Reading, PA

Formed in 1872 by William Harbster (1823-1885) and Matthan Harbster (1831-1912) to make *READING* apple parers under patents ranging from May 5, 1868 to May 22, 1877. Products included the 78 model (Fig.1), introduced in 1878, and the *TWO KNIFE* turn table parer, offered in 1884 (Fig.2).

Fig.1

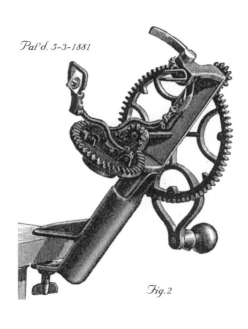

Pat'd. 5-3-1881

Fig.2

REDLINGER, MATT, Freeport, IL

Operator of a bicycle repair shop in 1898, Redlinger began to produce hardware novelties in 1900, but was no longer listed in the Freeport City Directory after 1904. Maker of the *NATIONAL* lemon squeezer (Fig.1), introduced in 1903, and the *NEW CENTURY* nut cracker (Fig.2) introduced in 1904.

Pat'd. 3-17-1903

Fig.1

—The National Lemon Squeezer.

Fig.2

The New Century Nut Cracker.

191

REDTOP ELECTRIC CO., New York, NY

Maker, in 1924, of the *REDTOP* "Electric Duplex Kitchenktte", combination hot-plate and toaster; and a small upright toaster. *(Illustration at right)*

REID-EDELMUTH MFG. CO., Brooklyn, NY

Maker of the *CHAMPION* egg beater (Fig.1) and the *CHAMPION* ice cream freezer (Fig.2), both introduced in 1908.

Two Views of Champion Egg Beater.

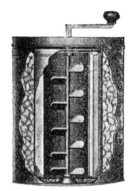

Champion Triple Action Ice Cream Freezer.

REISINGER, HUGO, New York, NY

Maker of the *INVINCIBLE* cork puller, patented by James Coomber and introduced in 1904. *(Illustration at right)*

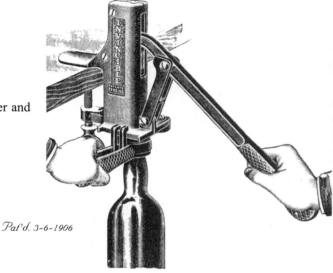

Pat'd. 3-6-1906

Invincible Cork Puller.

REPUBLIC METAL WARE CO., Buffalo, NY

Maker, from about 1908, of a line of *SAVORY* self-basting roasters made in oval shape, blue steel (Fig.1); oblong shape, blue steel (Fig.2); oblong shape, dark blue porcelain enamel (Fig.3); and oval shape, white peppered enamel with dark blue trim (Fig.4).

About 1920 the firm expanded by taking over the plant and business of Sidney Shepard & Co. The product line was enlarged and included *SAVORY* bread boxes (Fig.5); *SAVORY* bread savers complete with wire rack, bread board, bread knife, and crumb tray (Fig.6); and *SAVORY* "steam" double boilers (Fig.7). The roaster line was continued and, by 1923, it claimed to have made 3,000,000.

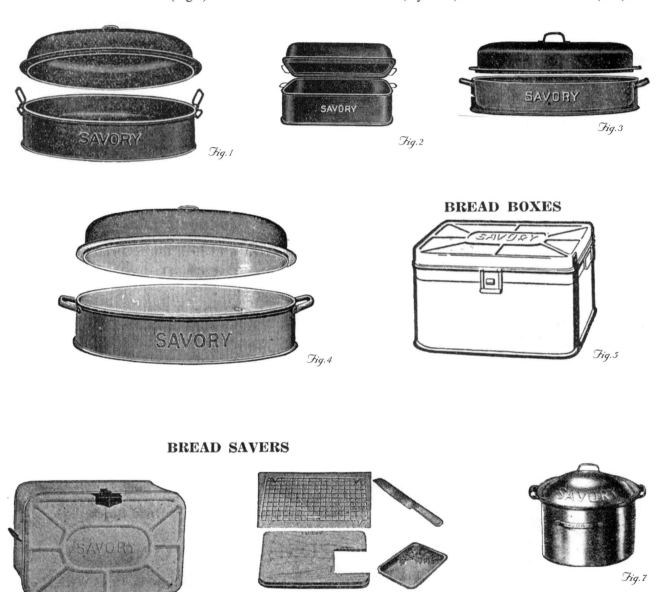

Fig.1

Fig.2

Fig.3

BREAD BOXES

Fig.4

Fig.5

BREAD SAVERS

Fig.6

Fig.7

REPUBLIC STAMPING & ENAMELING CO., Canton, OH

Formed in 1901 by Henry C. Milligan (1851-1940) who served as president until his death in 1940. The firm claimed to be the largest maker of enamel ware in the U.S., with 700 workmen turning out 150,000 pieces daily.

REPUBLIC SUPPLY CO., Pittsburgh, PA

Maker of the *ARMITAGE* fruit jar holder, introduced in 1906. *(Illustration at right)*

The Armitage Fruit Jar Holder.

REX & CO., ALFRED C., Philadelphia, PA

Operator of the Variety Iron Works, the firm offered *KING* egg beaters, patented May 13, 1884, lemon squeezers and other household items in 1886 (Fig.1). Other products included ice choppers, patented July 17, 1883; the *KING* table model lemon squeezer with glass insert (Fig.2); and the *KING* hand model lemon squeezer with glass insert (Fig.3).

Fig.1

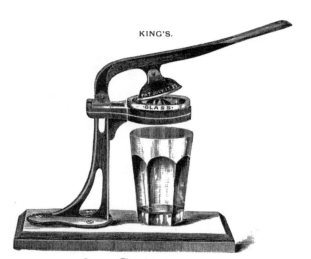

Fig.2 - Pat'd. 7-17-1883

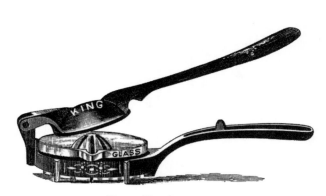

Fig.3 - Pat'd. 4-11-1882

REYMOND & GOTTLOB, New York, NY

Maker, in 1897, of an aluminum "fountain" coffee pot. *(Illustration at right)*

Aluminum Fountain Coffee Pot.

RICHARDSON MFG. CO., Bath, NY .

Maker, in 1896, of *PERFECTION* cake tins which had previously been made by Sidney Shepard & Co.

RICHMOND CEDAR WORKS, Richmond, IN

Maker of *STEEL FRAME* ice cream freezers (Fig.1), introduced in 1909 and *SNOW BALL* ice freezers (Fig.2), introduced in 1910.

Fig.1

Fig.2

RIPLEY, EDWARD, Troy, NY

Best known as a maker of small tools, Ripley also made tea kettles, patented March 14, 1846, July 9, 1867, and July 14, 1868; and sheet metal hollow ware, patented January 1, 1861.

RIPPLEY HARDWARE CO., Grafton, IL

Maker, in 1904, of *20TH CENTURY* granite churns. Made in five sizes, from two to eight gallons, the metal body was covered with blue and white enamel. *(Illustration at right)*

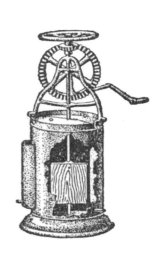

ROCKFORD CAN CO., Rockford, IL

Maker of the *ROSELAND* bread toaster, introduced in 1904. *(Illustration at right)*

The Roseland Bread Toaster.

Pat'd. 2-10-1920

ROCKFORD METAL SPECIALTY CO., Rockford, IL

Maker of the *VANTAGE* can opener. *(Illustration at left)*

ROGERS & BROS., C., Meriden, CT

Formed in 1866 by Cephas B., Gilbert and Wilbur R. Rogers. Employment in 1892 stood at 300 hands, primarily making silver plated table ware and items such as orange and lemon peelers. In 1898, the firm began making the *KLONDIKE* combination can opener and tack puller previously made by the Hall Mfg. Co.

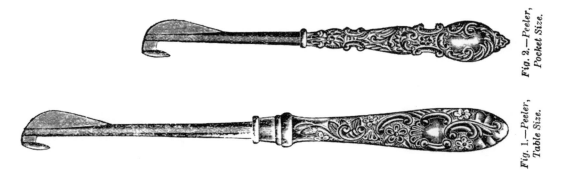

Fig. 2.—Peeler, Pocket Size.

Fig. 1.—Peeler, Table Size.

ROLLMAN MFG. CO., Mount Joy, PA

Operated by Michael A. Rollman. Maker of a variety of cast iron kitchen tools including a potato and apple cutter with changable cutters (Fig.1) and a combination apple corer and slicer (Fig.2), both introduced in 1899; a hand peach stoner (Fig.3) and a potato cutter (Fig.4) introduced in 1900; and a cherry stoner (Fig.5). The *ROLLMAN* food chopper was introduced in 1902 (Fig.6) with a modified version in 1904 (Fig.7). An improved clamp for the food chopper was patented October 30, 1906. The firm appears to have reorganized as the Universal Hardware Works in 1909.

(illustrations continued on next page)

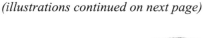

—The Rollman Potato and Apple Cutter.

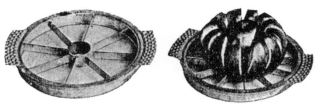

—Hand Apple Slicer and Corer.   *Fig.2*

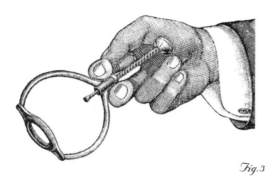

—*The Rollman Peach Stoner*

Fig.3

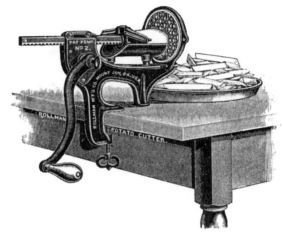

—*The Rollman Potato Cutter.*

Fig.5 - Pat'd. 11-5-1901

TINNED.

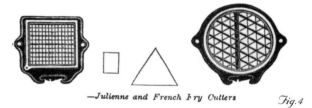

—*Julienne and French Fry Cutters*

Fig.4

Fig.7

Rollman Food Chopper No. 15.

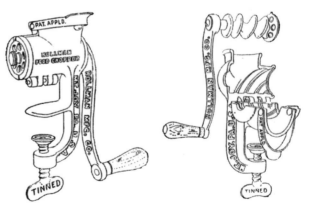

Fig. 1.—*Rollman Food Chopper.*   **Fig. 2.**—**Chopper Open.**

Fig.6 - Pat'd. 5-5-1903

ROME MFG. CO., Rome, NY

Formed about 1892 to make a line of nickel-plated and plain copper tea and coffee pots. Fig.1 shows the new models introduced in 1903. By 1920 the line had expanded to include sauce pans tea kettles (Fig.2) and other copper ware.

Fig.1

2100 Series.

2200 Series.

1200 Series.

Fig.2

-Rome Nickel Plated Copper Tea and Coffee Pots.

The Rose Automatic Grinder.

ROSE & CO., I.M., Philadelphia, PA

Maker of the *ROSE* automatic knife sharpener, introduced in 1904. *(Illustration at left)*

ROSENBLATT, BRYON S., Chicago, IL

Inventor and maker of a cast iron nutcracker. *(Illustration at right)*

Pat'd. 9-14-1915

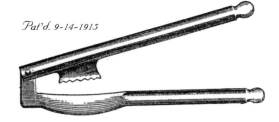

Fig. 1.—The Royal Knife Polisher.   *Fig. 2.—Manner of Using Polisher.*

ROYAL MFG. CO., Lancaster, PA

Maker of the *ROYAL* knife polisher, introduced in 1908.

ROYAL MFG. CO., Philadelphia, PA

Maker of the *HENIS* broiler (Fig.1), introduced in 1902 and the *ROYAL* cherry stoner (Fig.2), introduced in 1903. The stoner could be operated in the hand or clamped to a table.

Fig.1

The Improved Henis Broiler.

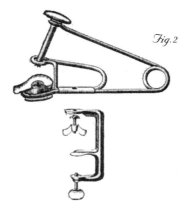

Fig.2

The Improved Royal Cherry Stoner.

RUSS & EDDY, Worcester, MA

Maker of sissors sharpeners (Fig.1) and combination knife and sissors sharpeners (Fig.2).

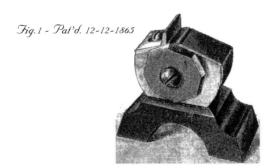

Fig.1 - Pat'd. 12-12-1865

Fig.2 - Pat'd. 7-24-1866

RUSSELL & ERWIN MFG. CO., New Britain, CT

Organized in 1851 by Henry E. Russell (1815-1893) and Cornelius B. Erwin (?-1885) to make hardware items. Kitchen goods included *WATERMAN* waffle irons, patented July 5, 1853; *AMERICAN* waffle irons offered in 1865 (Fig.1); the *HALE* meat cutter and stuffer (Fig.2); *(continued next page)*

cast   Waffle Irons   *Fig.1*

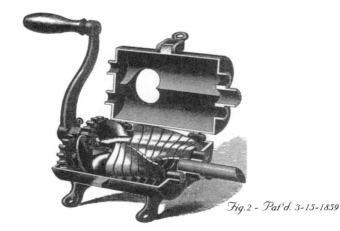

Fig.2 - Pat'd. 3-15-1859

ironware (Fig.3); sausage stuffers, patented July 6, 1858; the *RUSSWIN* food cutter, introduced in 1902 (Fig.4) and an improved model in 1908 (Fig.5).

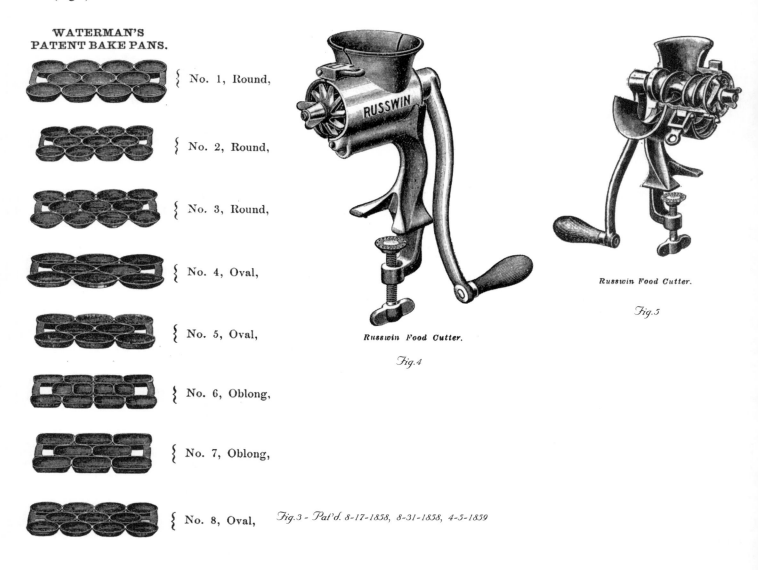

WATERMAN'S PATENT BAKE PANS.

No. 1, Round,

No. 2, Round,

No. 3, Round,

No. 4, Oval,

No. 5, Oval,

No. 6, Oblong,

No. 7, Oblong,

No. 8, Oval,

Fig.3 - Pat'd. 8-17-1858, 8-31-1858, 4-5-1859

Russwin Food Cutter.

Fig.4

Russwin Food Cutter.

Fig.5

ST. LOUIS STAMPING CO., St. Louis, MO

Founded in 1856 by William F. Niedringhaus and his brother, F.G. Niedringhaus. Maker, by 1877, of *GRANITE* iron ware, including baking dishes, tea and coffee pots. The firm became part of the National Enameling & Stamping Co. when the latter was formed in 1899.

Granite Iron Ware Baking Dish, with Nickel Receptacle.

All pat'd. 5-30-1876 & 7-3-1877

·Granite Iron Tea Pot.

-Granite Iron Coffee Pot.

SALEM TOOL CO., Salem, OH

Maker of the *WAGNER* sausage stuffer (Fig.1) and lard presses (Fig.2). The sausage stuffers were made well into the 20th century.

WAGNER'S.

Pat'd. 3-29-1859

LARD PRESS.

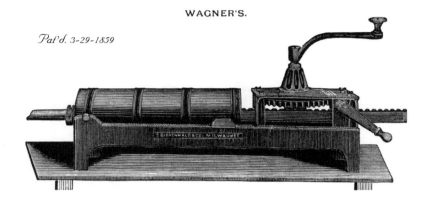

SALOMON, L., New York, NY

Maker of the *ACME* bean cutter, introduced in 1890. *(Illustration at left)*

The Acme Bean Cutter or Splitter.

SARGENT & CO., New Britain, CT

Formed in 1864 as the incorporation of J.B. Sargent & Co. Joseph B. Sargent was president until his death in 1907. Primary products were hand tools and hardware, but some household items were also made.

Kitchen products included the *SPRAGUE* can opener made with metal (Fig.1) and wooden (Fig.2) handles and offered as late as 1926; the No. 5 can opener introduced by 1884 (Fig.3) and offered, in slightly different form (Fig.4) as late as 1926. The No. 16 can opener (Fig.5) was offered by 1905. By 1926 combination can and bottle openers with wooden (Fig.6) or metal (Fig.7) handles were available. *(continued on next two pages)*

Figs. 1 & 2 - Pat'd. 7-21-1874

CLIPPER tobacco cutters (Fig.8), ornamental match safes (Fig.9), and pastry jaggers (Fig.10) were offered in 1884. The *PHENIX* meat cutter (Fig.11) was introduced in 1894, and the *GEM* food chopper (Fig.12) by 1900. Later products included ice picks with wooden (Fig.13) and metal handles (Fig.14), and the *ANGER* cake filler (Fig.15).

No. 5, Can Openers.

Fig.3

Can Openers.

Nos. 5 and 7   *Fig.4*

Steel Blade.

Length over all,
5½ Inches.

Fig.6

Steel Blade.
Length over all,
6 Inches

No. 22

No. 22, Polished White Birch Handle, Nickel Plated Blade

Fig.5

Fig.7

No. 27

Steel Blade.

Length over all,
5½ Inches.

No. 27, Nickel Plated all over   .   .   .   .   . per hundred, $12 60

"CLIPPER" Tobacco Cutters.

Fig.8

Ornamental Match Safes.

Fig.9

Pastry Jaggers.

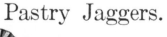

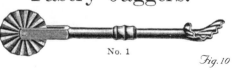

No. 1

Fig.10

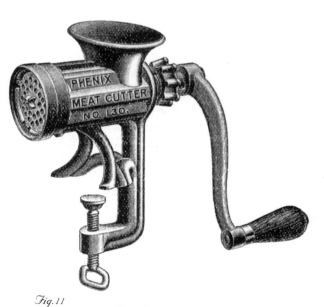

Fig.11

—Meat Cutter with Clamp.

Anger Perfect Cake Fillers.

For filling doughnuts and cakes with jelly, cream, etc.

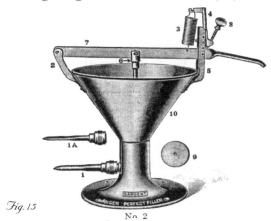

Fig. 12 - Pat'd.
3-8-1892

Fig. 15

No. 2

Fig. 13

One-third Size of No. 21

Hardened and Tempered Steel Point.

Fig. 14

One-third Size of No. 20

Heavy. Hardened and Tempered Steel Point.

SAYRE & CO., L.A., Newark, NJ

Founded by Louis A. Sayre (1842-1915). Maker of apple and peach parers . The improved *MONARCH* peach and apple parer *(below)*, with an additional patent date of June 9, 1891, was introduced in 1891.

Pat'd. 9-11-1883, 4-26-1886, & 6-9-1891

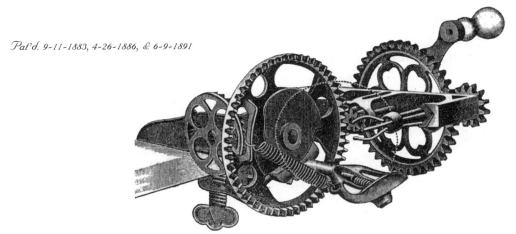

Monarch Peach and Apple Parer, Improved.

SAYRES, CHARLES W., New York, NY

Maker, in 1902, of a corn sheller for fresh corn. *(Illustration at right)*

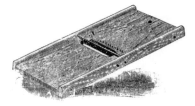

—*The Sayres Corn Grater.*

SCHMIDT, L.H., Cincinnati, OH

Maker of the *STAR* fruit jar holder, introduced in 1889. It was designed to hold the lid in place as it was sealed with wax. *(Illustration at right)*

Star Fruit-Can Holder.

SCHOCH, M.L., Philadelphia, PA

Maker of the *COLUMBIA* kitchen spoon, introduced in 1895. The spoon contained a built-in scraper for use with "preparations having a tendency to stick to a spoon."

Fig. 1.—Columbia Kitchen Spoon.   *Pat'd. 2-6-1894*

Fig. 2.—Columbia Kitchen Spoon, Showing Scraper.

SCHOFIELD, ALBERT B., Brooklyn, NY

Inventor, and probably maker, of the *PEERLESS* can opener (Fig.1); the *DOUBLE ACTION* chopping knife (Fig.2); and a meat pounder, patented February 2, 1897. A *DELMONICO* can opener, marked with the same patent date as the *PEERLESS* has also been reported.

PEERLESS.

Fig.2 - Pat'd. 12-20-1892

Fig.1 - Pat'd. 2-11-1890

SCHRIVER & CO., O.P., Cincinnati, OH

Maker, c1900-1925 and later, of fruit and wine presses, including the *JUICY FRUIT* kitchen size made in three and six quart sizes and offered in 1922. *(Illustration at left)*

SCHROETER BROTHERS HDW. CO., St. Louis, MO

Maker of a variety of graters, including the *PERK'S* combination horseradish grater and cutter (Fig.1) introduced in 1894; an improved style (Fig.2); and a food grater introduced in 1905 (Fig.3). Potato graters (Fig.4) and almond and vegetable graters (Fig.5) were introduced in 1915. The *HOME* nut cracker (Fig.6) was also introduced in 1915 and the *HOME* cherry stoner (Fig.7) in 1918.

—*Perk's Combination Horse-radish Grater and Cutter.*
Fig.1

—*An Improved Horseradish Grater.*
Fig.2 - Pat'd. 11-17-1903

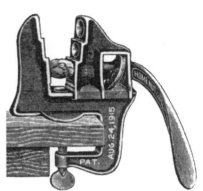

Fig.3   *Schroeter Food Grater.*

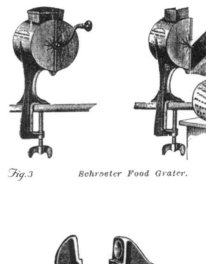

Fig.6 - Pat'd. 8-24-1915

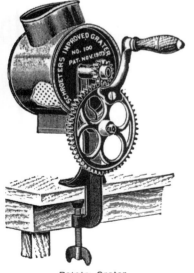

Potato Grater.
Fig.4

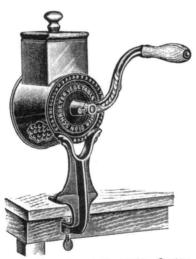

New Almond and Vegetable Grater.
Fig.5

Fig.7 - Pat'd. 8-17-1917

COMMON SENSE

Pat'd. 12-28-1909

SCHUYLER, FRANK B., San Francisco, CA

Inventor and maker of the *COMMON SENSE* stove top toaster. *(Illustration at right)*

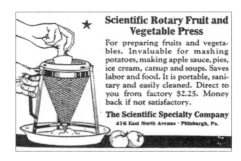

SCIENTIFIC SPECIALTY CO., Pittsburgh, PA

Maker, in 1921, of the *KITCHEN PAL* rotary fruit and vegetable press. *(Illustration at left)*

SCOTT MFG. CO., Baltimore, MD

Maker, in 1883, of *SCOTT'S* rotary knife peach parer, *GOLD MEDAL* apple parer, *VICTOR* and *ORIOLE* apple parers, corers and slicers, *WALKER'S* pineapple slicer, rotary pea assorter, *FELTHAUSEN'S* pea assorter, peach pitting machines, *UNIVERSAL* can opener, *NEW IDEA* can opener, *MEDALLION* egg beater, *VICTORIA* egg beater, *DIAMOND* vegetable grater. Samuel G.B. Cook, was president; employment was 130 hands.

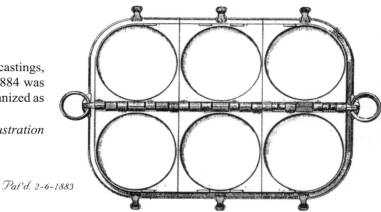

SELDEN & GRISWOLD MFG. CO., Erie, PA

Founded in 1868 by Samuel Selden. Maker of small castings, hollow ware, house furnishing utensils, etc. Employment in 1884 was 100 hands producing $75,000 in goods per year. The firm reorganized as the Griswold Mfg. Co. in 1884.

Kitchen products included a three cake folding griddle. *(Illustration at right)*.

Pat'd. 2-6-1883

SELFSEAL PRESSURE COOKER CO., Jamaica, NY

Maker, in 1924, of the *SELFSEAL* pressure cooker. "No thumbscrews." *(Illustration at left)*

SELTZER SPECIALTY CO., Lebanon, PA

Maker, in 1892, of the *LEBANON* combination egg beater and potato masher (Fig.1). *LEBANON* cake cutters, in three styles, (Fig.2) were introduced in 1893 and the *LEBANON* stove top broilers in 1894 (Fig.3

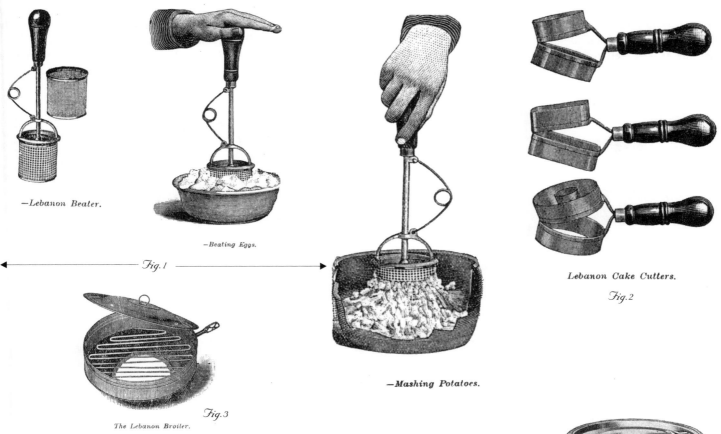

—Lebanon Beater.

—Beating Eggs.

Fig. 1

—Mashing Potatoes.

Lebanon Cake Cutters.

Fig. 2

Fig. 3

The Lebanon Broiler.

SEXTON CO., WM. A., New York, NY

Maker, in 1916, of the EASY ice cream freezer. It was offered in one and two quart sizes. *(Illustration at right)*

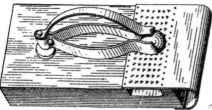

SEXTON, MICHAEL H., Utica, NY

Inventor and maker of a nutmeg grater. *(Illustration at left)*

Pat'd. 5-5-1896

SHEPARD & CO., SIDNEY, Buffalo, NY

Founded by Sidney Shepard (1814-1893) in 1837 as a hardware store. A few years later the firm began making stamped cookware and, by the time of Shepard's death, was one of the largest manufacturers of stamped metal ware in the U.S. The firm's assets were bought by the Republic Metal Ware Co. about 1920.

Products included the *BUFFALO* mincing knife (Fig.1); *BUFFALO* egg poacher (Fig.2) and *PERFECTION* cake and pie tin (Figs.3-4) introduced in 1888; seamless ware introduced in 1889 (Fig.5); *COLUMBIAN* roasting pans introduced in 1892 (Fig.6); the *COMMON SENSE* tea kettle introduced in 1896 (Fig.7); a dinner pail (Fig.8); the *HANDY* sifter and strainer introduced in 1901 (Fig.9); and the *MAGIC* self-righting toothpick or match holder introduced in 1904 (Fig.10). The *BARLER* flour sifter was offered in 1886 (Fig.11) and, slightly modified, as the *SHAKER* flour shifter in 1911 (Fig.12). *(Illustrations continued on next page)*

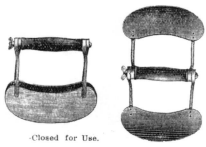

-Closed for Use.

—Open for Cleaning and Sharpening.

The Buffalo Mincing Knife.   *Fig1 - Pat'd.*
12-27-1887

-The Buffalo Steam Egg Poacher.   *Fig.2*

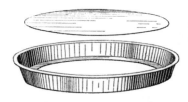

Perfection Cake and Pie Tin.
Fig.3

Fig.4   Use of the Perfection Pie Tin, Showing How a Pie May be Cooled.

Stamped Sheet-Metal Goods.— —Seamless Marking-Cup.

—Seamless Cup.

—Seamless Straight Cup, Extra Depth.

—Seamless Covered Saucepan.

Fig.5

The S. S. & Co. Columbian Roasting and Baking Pans

Fig.7

—Filling the Common Sense Tea Kettle.

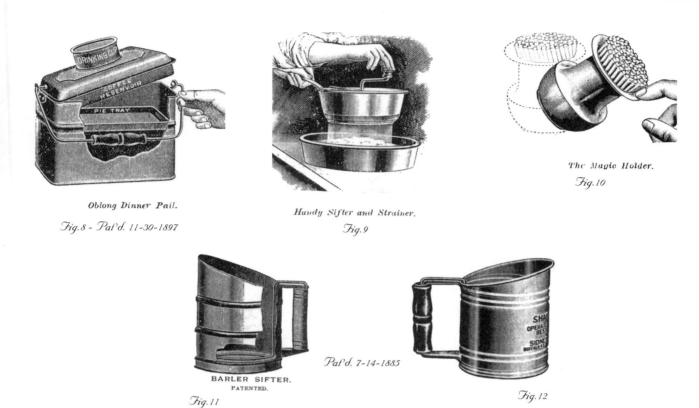

Oblong Dinner Pail.

Fig. 8 - Pat'd. 11-30-1897

Handy Sifter and Strainer.

Fig. 9

The Magic Holder.

Fig. 10

BARLER SIFTER.
PATENTED.

Fig. 11

Pat'd. 7-14-1885

Fig. 12

SHEPHARD HARDWARE CO., Buffalo, NY

Formed in 1866 to make a variety of hardware items. Charles G. Shepard and Walter J. Shepard, sons of the founder, became the sole proprietors in January, 1878.

The *LIGHTNING* ice cream freezer in 2, 3, 4, 6, 8, 10 and 14 quart sizes (Fig. 1) and the *QUEEN CITY* fruit and meat press (Fig. 2) were introduced in 1888. The *GIANT LIGHTNING* ice cream freezer (Fig. 3), made in 14 and 20 quart sizes was introduced in 1889. Also made an improved version of the *QUEEN CITY* press (Fig. 4) and a stove lid lifter (Fig. 5). The ice cream freezer and other hardware lines were bought by North Brothers Mfg. Co. in 1893. *(Illustrations continued on next page)*

Fig. 1- Pat'd.
9-25-1888

—The Lightning Freezer.

Fig. 2- Pat'd.
4-22-1886 &
6-26-1888

—The Queen City Press.

Fig. 3- Pat'd.
9-10-1889,
3-17-1891 &
2-13-1892

The Giant Lightning Ice-Cream Freezer.

Fig.4 - Pat'd. 2-2-1892

Fig.5 - Pat'd. 2-14-1893

—*Shepard's Improved Queen City Press.*

SHERMAN, TANGENBERG & CO., Chicago, IL

Maker of the *PERFECTION* flour bin and sieve, introduced in 1889. *(Illustration at right)*

Perfection Flour Bin and Sieve.

Pat'd. 5-22-1876, 6-27-1876, & 7-10-1877

SHERWOOD, WILLIS H., St. Joseph, MO

Inventor and maker of an "automatic" tea and coffee pot. The pot was a percolater with a flannel cloth filter stretched below the upper compartment and held by a ring. *(Illustration at left)*

SILEX CO., New York, NY

Maker, beginning about 1914, of the well known *SILEX* coffee makers. The first type, shown below, looks much like a piece of laboratory equipment. *(Illustration at right)*

Pat'd. 10-13-1914

SILVER & CO., Brooklyn, NY

Operated by William H. Silver. Maker, in 1886, of *SILVER'S* egg beater and measuring glass (Fig.1); an egg poacher in three- (Fig.2) and six-hole models (Fig.3); a combination egg poacher and fryer, patented November 8, 1886; and *SILVER'S* patent egg timer (Fig.4). Products introduced in 1889 included the *FAMILY* beef tea press (Fig.5), a lemon reamer and strainer (Fig.6) and a potato masher, press and strainer (Fig.7). An improved version of the potato masher (Fig.8) was made as late as 1911. *(continued on next two pages)*

SILVER'S EGG BEATER AND
MEASURING GLASS.

Fig.1 - Pat'd. 5-11-1886

Three Hole.
Fig.2 - Pat'd. 11-3-1885

Six Hole.
Fig.3 - Pat'd. 11-3-1885

SILVER'S PATENT EGG TIMER.

Fig.4

Fig.5
Beef-Tea Press.

Lemon Reamer and Strainer.
Fig.6

Silver & Co.'s Improved Potato Masher, Fruit Press, &c.
Fig.7 - Pat'd. 10-18-1887

Fig.8 - Pat'd. 6-23-1903

Lemon Reamer.
Fig.9

New Beef-Tea Press.
Fig.10

Products introduced in 1889 included a lemon reamer (Fig.9); an improved beef tea press (Fig.10); combination flour bin and sifter (Fig.11); *STAR* coffee pot (Fig.12); *ROYAL* roaster and baker (Fig.13); and the *LITTLE HUSTLER* potato peeler (Fig.14). The Marion Harland process, one cup tea and coffee maker (Fig.15) was introduced in 1893.

New 1894 products included a roasting pan cover, patented December 6, 1892; the *NEW* beater and dessert maker (Fig.16); a juice extractor, shaker, strainer and mixer (Fig.17); an aluminum shaker, strainer and mixer (Fig.18); the *ALUMINUM CUP* juice extractor (Fig.19); the *SANITARY* sink basket (Fig.20); an improved flour bin and sifter (Fig.21); and the *SILVER* porcelain cooking crock, designed to be placed in a larger metal pot with boiling water (Fig.22).

Fig. 11

Combination Flour Bin and Sifter.

Fig. 12

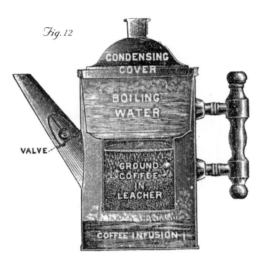

The Star Coffee-Pot.

Fig. 13

—Royal Roaster and Baker.

Fig. 14   Potato-Peeler.

—One Cup Tea and Coffee Urn.

Fig. 15

New Beater and Dessert Maker.

Fig. 16

—Juice Extractor, Shaker, Strainer and Mixer.

Fig. 17

212

An aluminum egg boiler (Fig.23); egg fryer (Fig.24); and a round loaf baking pan (Fig.25); were introduced in 1895. The *BROOKLYN* fruit press and masher (Fig.26); the *BROOKLYN* toaster (Fig.27); a baking pan, patented July 11, 1905; and a filter for the kitchen faucet, patented May 16, 1905, were offered in 1905.

Fig.18

—*Aluminum Shaker, Strainer and Mixer.*

Fig.19

—*Aluminum Cup Juice Extractor*

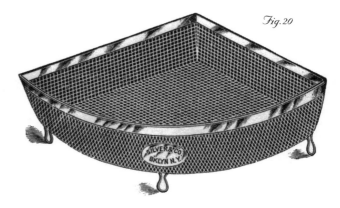

Fig.20

Sanitary Sink Basket.

Fig.21

Flour Bin and Sifter.

—*Cooking Crock.*

Fig.22

—*Cooking Crock in Use.*

Fig.23

—*Aluminum Egg Boiler.*

Aluminum Egg Fryer.

Fig.24

-*Round Loaf Baking Pan.*

Fig.25- Pat'd. 4-20-1897

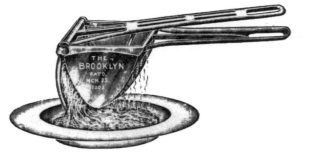

Brooklyn Fruit Press and Masher.

Fig.26 - Pat'd. 3-25-1902

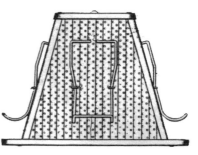

Fig.27- Pat'd. 10-28-1902

SILVER & DEMING MFG. CO, Salem, OH, <u>later</u>
SILVER MFG. CO., Salem, OH

Formed in 1874 by A.R. Silver and John Deming, the company reorganized as the Silver Mfg. Co. about 1890. Maker, c1880-1920, of *SILVER'S RAILROAD* sausage stuffers (Fig.1) and *SILVER'S* sausage stuffer in eight (Fig.2) and twelve (Fig.3) pound sizes. Both types operated on the rack and pinion principle. A.R. Silver also patented food choppers on August 30, 1870, July 11, 1871, and August 12, 1873.

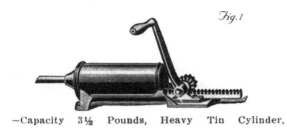

SILVER'S RAILROAD.

Fig.1

—Capacity 3½ Pounds, Heavy Tin Cylinder,

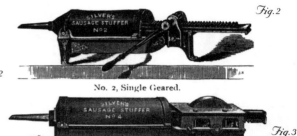

SILVER'S PATENT.

Fig.2

All pat'd. 11-26-1872

No. 2, Single Geared.

Fig.3

No. 3, Double Geared.

Pat'd. 7-20-1909

SIMMONS, BRO. & CO., Philadelphia, PA

Maker, in 1909, of a teapot shaped tea-ball. *(Illustration at left)*

SIMMONS HARDWARE CO., St. Louis, MO

Founded in 1872 by Edward C. Simmons (1839-1902) as E.C. Simmons & Co., the firm incorporated in 1874 as the Simmons Hardware Co. Simmons operated as a hardware jobber, selling to hardware stores throughout the midwest. Products included a wide variety of kitchen items, marked with the *KEEN KUTTER* tradename, which were made under contract by a number of manufacturers.

SKIMIT MFG. CO., Oskaloosa, IA

Maker, in 1923, of the *SKIMIT* cream separator. The device was simply a syphon which sucked the cream off the top of non-homogenized milk. *(Illustration at right)*

SLOAN MFG. CO., Kansas City, MO

Maker of the *SLOAN* aluminum griddle (Fig.1), the *SLOAN* oven (Fig.2), a toaster and stove mat (Fig.3), and a cooling can for cooling water in the ice section of the ice-box (Fig.4), all introduced in 1908.

Fig.1

—*Sloan's Aluminum Griddle.*

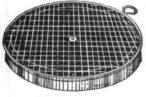

Fig.2

—*The Sloan Toaster and Stove Mat.*

Fig.3

—*The Sloan Cooling Can.*

Fig.4

—*The Sloan Oven.*

SMITH CO., H.D., Plantsville, CT

Established in 1855 by Henry D. Smith as a contract foundry and drop forger. The firm reorganized in 1900 when Lucius V. Walkley bought control and thereafter offered a variety of tools and small household items.

Maker, in 1909, of the *DOUBLE DELIGHT* ice cream freezer designed to simultaneously make one quart each of two flavors. *(Illustration at right)*

Double Delight Freezer.

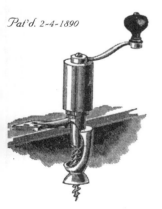

Pat'd. 2-4-1890

The Edie Cork Extractor.

SMITH & EGGE MFG. CO., Bridgeport, CT

Organized in 1873 by F.W. Smith (1829-?) to manufacture a variety of hardware items. Maker, in 1890, of the EDIE cork extractor *(illustration at left)*. In 1900, a table top churn with an odd worm and wheel drive, patented June 12, 1900, was offered.

SMITH & HEMENWAY CO., New York, NY

Incorporated in 1898 with Landon P. Smith, president and J.F. Hemenway, secretary and treasurer. In 1899, the company bought the hardware line previously made by Maltby, Henley & Co., including the *RELIABLE* and *PEERLESS* corkscrews.

Maker, in 1900, of the *WALDORF-ASTORIA* can opener (Fig.1). The *NEW ENGLAND* food chopper (Fig.2) was introduced in 1902 and the *POLAR STAR* ice cream freezer (Fig.3) in 1908.

—Waldorf-Astoria One-Piece Can Opener.   *Fig.1*

FINE

MEDIUM

COARSE

The New England Food Chopper.   *Fig.2*

Fig.3

Polar Star Ice Cream Freezer.

SMITH MFG. CO., F.H., Chicago, IL

Maker of the *BEST YET* knife sharpener, introduced in 1904. *(Illustration at right)*

Best Yet Knife Sharpener.

Pat'd. 5-15-1860

SMITH, S.J., New York, NY

Inventor and maker of an eagle head nutcracker. *(Illustration at left)*

Pat'd. 4-7-1868

SMITH, T.C., New York, NY

Inventor and maker of porcelain-lined lemon squeezers. *(Illustration at right)*

SNOW, GEORGE H., New Haven, CT

Inventor and maker of a match-safe. The safe would feed a single match when the plunger was depressed. *(Illustration at left)*

Pat'd. 4-19-1864

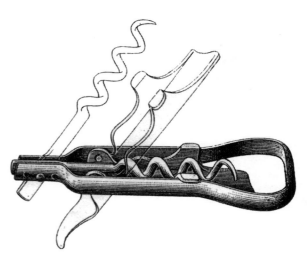

SNOW & PETRELLI MFG. CO., New Haven, CT

Maker of the *UNIVERSAL* folding cork extractor, introduced in 1906. *(Illustration at right)*

—*Universal Lever Cork Extractor.*

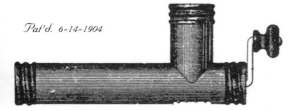

Pat'd. 6-14-1904

SNYDER, F.E., Massillion, OH

Inventor and maker of the *HANDY* nutmeg grater. *(Illustration at left)*

SOMMER'S SON, JOHN, Newark, NJ, <u>later</u>
SOMMER MFG. CO., J.L., Newark, NJ

Maker, in 1895, of the *BOSS* lemon squeezer made of sugar maple with bowls of rosewood, lignum-vitae, or porcelain (Fig.1). The *NEW BOSS,* offered in 1911, was made of malleable iron (Fig.2). *(continued on next page)*

By 1907, the firm was operating as the J.L. Sommer Mfg. Co. and began to specialize in items made of stampings and formed wire such as can openers (Fig.3). In 1911, the firm began offering a variety of figural bottle openers (Figs. 4-9) under design patents granted to John L. Sommer.

Sommer also offered several types of combination bottle openers, including a combined bottle opener and milk bottle lid lifter (Fig.10); combined bottle opener and ice pick (Fig.11); two types of combined bottle openers and cake turners (Figs.12-13); and combined bottle opener and mixing spoon (Fig.14). Other items included a milk bottle cap lifter (Fig.15), and an ice pick (Fig.16).

Sommer's products were very popular as advertising items for dairies, breweries, hotels, grocery stores, etc. and are nearly always found with such markings. *(Illustrations continued on next page)*

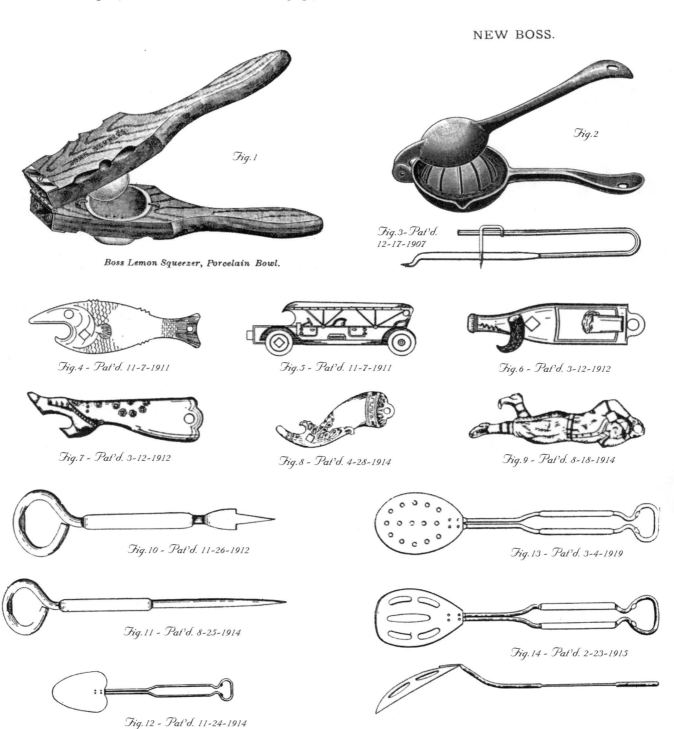

NEW BOSS.

Fig.1

Boss Lemon Squeezer, Porcelain Bowl.

Fig.2

Fig.3 - Pat'd. 12-17-1907

Fig.4 - Pat'd. 11-7-1911

Fig.5 - Pat'd. 11-7-1911

Fig.6 - Pat'd. 3-12-1912

Fig.7 - Pat'd. 3-12-1912

Fig.8 - Pat'd. 4-28-1914

Fig.9 - Pat'd. 8-18-1914

Fig.10 - Pat'd. 11-26-1912

Fig.13 - Pat'd. 3-4-1919

Fig.11 - Pat'd. 8-25-1914

Fig.14 - Pat'd. 2-23-1915

Fig.12 - Pat'd. 11-24-1914

Fig. 15 - Pat'd. 10-20-1921

Fig. 16 - Pat'd. 3-24-1914

SPECIALTY NOVELTY CO., Lancaster, PA

Maker, in 1897, of the *CHAMPION* grater (Fig.1), and the *FAMILY* rotary nutmeg grater (Fig.2).

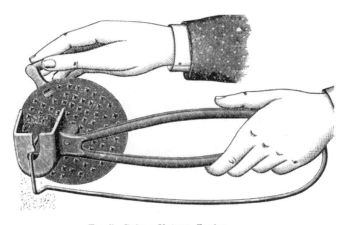

Family Rotary Nutmeg Grater.

Fig. 2 - Pat'd. 8-4-1896

Fig. 1 - Pat'd. 8-17-1897

The Champion Grater.

SPENGLER-LOOMIS MFG. CO., Chicago, IL

Maker, in 1920, of the *KWICKSHARP* knife and scissors grinder. *(Illustration at right)*

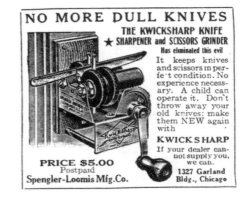

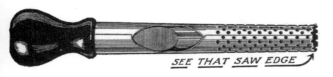

SEE THAT SAW EDGE →

SPENGLER SPECIALTIES, New York, NY

Maker, in 1911, of the *SPENGLER* patent apple corer. The saw edge was claimed to make a clean cut "doing away with hacking and gouging." *(Illustration at left)*

SPERRY, A.W., Wallingford, CT

Inventor and maker of a lever corkscrew.

Sperry's Patent.

Pat'd. 5-28-1878

SPERY, CHARLES F., Herman, MO, later
SPERY & CO., CHARLES F., St. Louis, MO

Charles F. Spery offered the *FAMOUS* parer and slicer (Fig.1) introduced in 1893. In 1894, the firm name was changed to Charles F. Spery & Co. and a line of serrated edge bread, cake and paring knives was introduced (Fig.2). A kitchen set, including a bread knife, meat tenderer, and can opener was introduced in 1895 (Fig.3). The firm was probably absorbed by the Illinois Cutlery Co. which offered nearly identical products in 1898.

Famous Parer and Slicer. *Fig.1*

Spery Serrated Edged Knife. *Fig.2*

Kitchen Set No. 10. *Fig.3*

STANDARD CHURN CO., New York, NY

Maker of the *ONE MINUTE* churn, introduced in 1908.

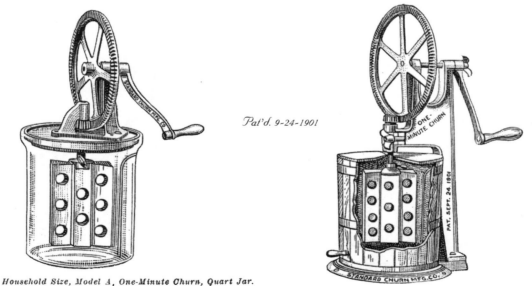

Pat'd. 9-24-1901

Household Size, Model A, One-Minute Churn, Quart Jar.

Special Household Size, Holding a Gallon of Cream.

STANDARD CO., Boston, MA

Maker of a nutmeg grater (Fig.1). An improved style (Fig.2) was introduced in 1890. The *RIVAL* egg beater (Fig.3) was introduced in 1897 and, in 1898, a new patented *DOVER* style egg beater (Fig.4) was offered. A redesigned *RIVAL* egg beater (Fig.5) and a steel handle model (Fig.6) were introduced in 1899 and a new egg beater and cream whip (Fig.7) was added in 1901.

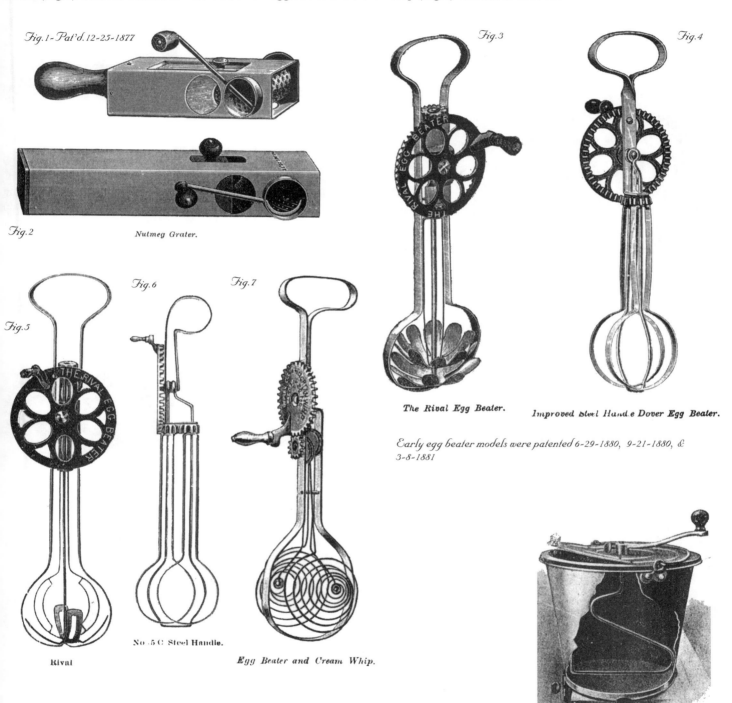

Fig.1 - Pat'd. 12-25-1877

Fig.2

Nutmeg Grater.

Fig.3

Fig.4

Fig.5

Fig.6

Fig.7

The Rival Egg Beater.

Improved Steel Handle Dover Egg Beater.

Early egg beater models were patented 6-29-1880, 9-21-1880, & 3-8-1881

No. 5 C Steel Handle.

Rival

Egg Beater and Cream Whip.

STANDARD STAMPING CO., Albion, NY

Maker of the *DIXIE* improved bread maker, introduced in 1906. *(Illustration at right)*

—Dixie Improved Bread Maker.

221

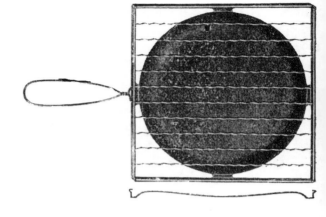

STANDARD STAMPING CO., Marysville, OH

Maker of a bread toaster introduced in 1905. *(Illustration at right)*

STEARNS & CO., E.C., Syracuse, NY

A partnership of Edward C. Stearns and Avis Stearns Mead formed in 1877 and incorporated in 1889. Primary products were a variety of hand tools which continued in production until the factory burned in 1945. Maker, in 1897, of an ice cream freezer claimed to freeze six quarts in two minutes. *(Illustration at left)*

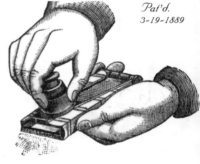

Pat'd. 3-19-1889

STEEL EDGE STAMPING & RETINNING CO., Boston, MA

Maker of the *UNIQUE* nutmeg grater, introduced in 1890. *(Illustration at right)*

The Unique Nutmeg Grater.

Pat'd. 11-1908

STEINFELD BROS., New York, NY

Maker of rotary food choppers, introduced in 1909.

—Steinfeld Food Chopper.

STEPHENS & CO., WINDSOR, Waltham, MA

Maker of the *NIP-IT* strawberry huller, introduced in 1907. *(Illustration at right)*

Pat'd. 12-18-1906

—The Nip-It Strawberry Huller.

Pat'd. 4-28-1914

STERLING MACHINE & STAMPING CO., Wellington, OH

Maker of a variety of stamped cookware, including the tea kettle shown at right.

The Diamond Ice Shaver.

STEVENS, CHARLES B., Minneapolis, MN

Maker of the *DIAMOND* ice shave, introduced in 1891.
(Illustration at left)

Pat'd. 6-7-1859

STEVENS, DeWITT, Newark, NJ

Inventor and maker of a cheese-cutter. Designed for grocers' use, it measured the amount of rotation of the table which equaled the weight of cheese to be cut.
(Illustration at right)

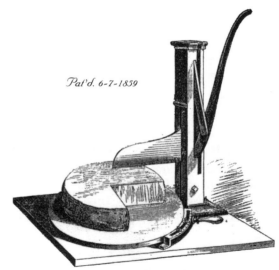

STEVENS' CHEESE-CUTTER.

STEVENS, WOODMAN & CO., Portland, ME

Maker of the *DAISY* milk shake and lemonade shaker, introduced in 1891.
(Illustration at left)

Daisy Shaker.

STILLWELL, E.R., Dayton, OH

Inventor and maker of stove tongs, patented October 2, 1866. The tongs featured two sets of jaws, straight and angled.

Pat'd. 10-2-1866

STILLWELL'S STOVE TONGS.

STORK MFG. CO., Dayton, OH

Maker, in 1904, of the *STORK* can opener and jar sealer.

Pat'd. 12-8-1903

-The Stork Can Opener and Jar Sealer.

STORTZ & SON, JOHN, Philadelphia, PA

Maker of the *CONVENIENT* chopper and mincing knife *(Fig.1)*, and the *PHILADELPHIA* ice chisel (Fig.2), both introduced in 1896.

Fig.1

The Convenient Chopper.

Fig.2

The Philadelphia Ice Chisel.

STOVER MFG. & ENGINE CO., Freeport, IL

One of several Freeport firms founded by Daniel C. Stover (1839-1907). Its primary product was a line of gasoline and kerosene farm engines, but about 1910 it introduced a line of cast iron housewares including *STOVER* waffle irons (Figs.1-2), *IDEAL* nutcrackers (Fig.3), *IDEAL* stove lid lifters (Figs.4-5), *IDEAL* lemon squeezers (Fig.6), *IDEAL* ice picks and shaves, *IDEAL* cornbread pans (Fig.7), and the *IDEAL* combination steak hammer and ice hatchet (Fig.8).

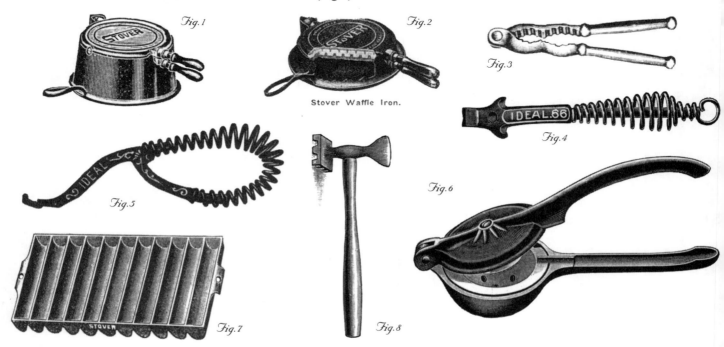

Fig.1　*Fig.2*　*Fig.3*

Stover Waffle Iron.

Fig.4

Fig.5　*Fig.6*

Fig.7　*Fig.8*

STOW MFG. CO., S., Plantsville, CT

Formed in 1852 by Solomon Stow and his sons Enos E. Stow and Orson W. Stow. The firm was absorbed into Peck, Stow & Wilcox when the latter was formed in November, 1870. Maker of sheet-metal working machinery and some kitchen items, including sausage stuffers, patented July 4, 1865, and tea and coffee pots, patented December 10, 1867.

STRANSKY & CO., M., New York, NY

Maker, in 1893, of enameled ware including the *ROYAL* coffee pot. *(Illustration at right)*

Royal Coffee Pot.

STREETER & CO., N.R., Rochester, NY

Operated by Nelson R. Streeter. Maker of the *SENSIBLE* can opener offered in 1886 (Fig.1); the *SENSIBLE* ice tool (Fig.2); *STREETER'S* pot scraper (Fig.3); a combination nutcracker and nutpick (Fig.4); *STREETER'S* mincing knife (Fig.5); the *DUPLEX* mincing knife (Fig.6); and the *SENSIBLE* mincing knife (Fig.7) all introduced in 1893.
(continued on next page)

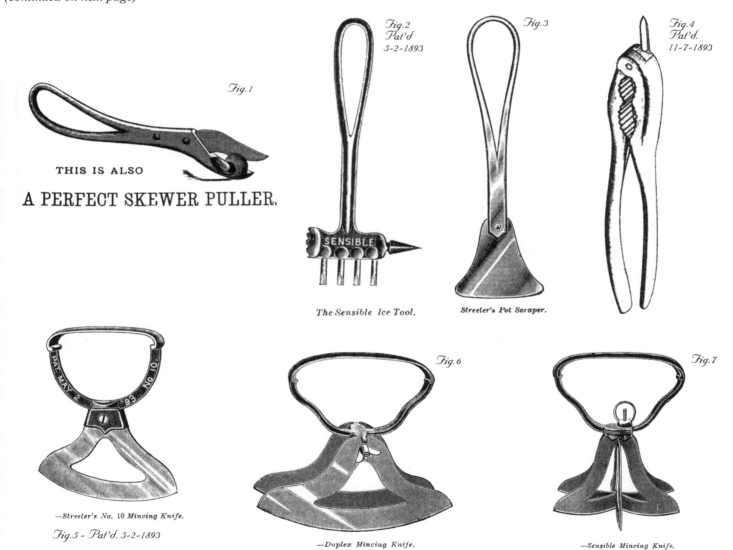

Fig.1

THIS IS ALSO
A PERFECT SKEWER PULLER.

Fig.2 Pat'd 5-2-1893

The Sensible Ice Tool.

Fig.3

Streeter's Pot Scraper.

Fig.4 Pat'd 11-7-1893

—*Streeter's No. 10 Mincing Knife.*
Fig.5 - Pat'd 5-2-1893

Fig.6
—*Duplex Mincing Knife.*

Fig.7
—*Sensible Mincing Knife.*

A line of improved *SENSIBLE* mincing knives (Figs.8-10) was introduced in 1894. The *SENSIBLE* bread toaster (Fig.11) was introduced in 1897; the *STERLING* slicer (Fig.12) in 1900; and a larger model *STERLING* slicer (Fig.13) in 1903.

Fig.8

--Sensible Mincing Knife No. 10.

Fig.9

—Sensible Mincing Knife No. 40.

Fig.10

-Sensible Mincing Knife No. 60.

Fig.11

—Toaster with Jaws Extended.

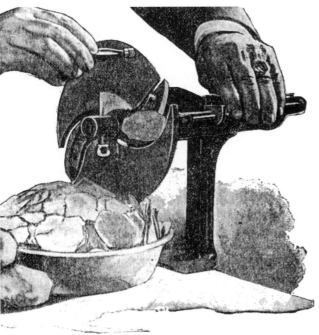

The Sterling Slicer.

Fig.12

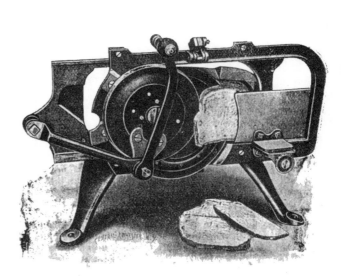

Fig.13

The Sterling Slicer No. 50.

STURGES & BURN MFG. CO., Chicago, IL

Operated by Frank Sturges (1842-1917). Maker of the *STURGES* steel churn, introduced in 1901 in 9 and 15 gallon sizes (Fig.1). The *JACK FROST* ice cream freezer (Fig.2), was introduced in 1907.

Fig.1

Fig.2

—*The Sturges Steel Churn*

STUART & PETERSON CO., Philadelphia, PA

Maker, in 1891, of a line of cast iron cookware. The *GOLDEN CROWN* line, with a folding prop for reducing heat, was introduced in 1893.

Oblong Boiler.

—*Golden Crown Ware.*

-*Colden Crown Ware in Use.*

SUMNER MFG. CO., Boston, MA

Maker of the *ECLIPSE* bread mixer and kneader, introduced in 1905. Later in 1905 production was taken over by Manning, Bowman & Co. *(Illustration at right)*

*Pat'd.
1-14-1902 &
9-27-1904*

The Eclipse Bread Mixer and Kneader.

SUN MFG. CO., Columbus, OH

Maker, in 1905, of a poultry beheader. *(Illustration at right)*

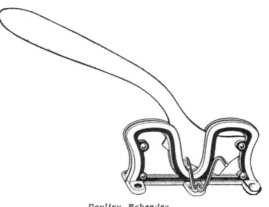

Poultry Beheader.

SUN MFG. CO., Greenfield, OH

Maker of coffee mills, including the 1893 *RECEPTACLE* mill with a built in canister which held a pound of unground beans (Fig.1) and the *OHIO* wall mount mill (Fig.2) introduced in 1902. 1903 offerings included two styles of box mills (Figs.3-4) and three styles of wall mount mills (Figs.5-7).

Fig.1

NO. 1080.

Fig.2

The Ohio Coffee Mill.

Fig.3

NO. 1070.

Fig.4

NO. 1088.

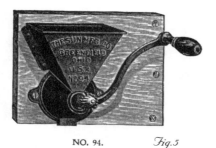

NO. 94. *Fig.5*

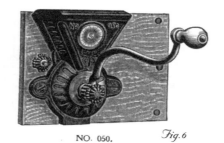

NO. 050. *Fig.6*

NO. 090. *Fig.7*

SUN STAMPING CO., Kalamazoo, MI

Maker, in 1891, of the *MORGAN* odorless broiler "made for broiling or toasting over a gas, oil, gasoline, wood or coal fire." By 1895, the same broiler was a product of the Morgan Mfg. Co. *(Illustration at right)*

SWEENEY MFG. CO., W.H., Brooklyn, NY

Maker of *ROYAL* nickel plated copper ware, including an engraved line, c1896-1905.

—*Royal Nickeled Copper Coffee Pot.*

—*Engraved Tea Pot.*

—*Engraved Coffee Pot.*

SYRACUSE MACHINE CO., Syracuse, NY

Maker of the *ECONOMY* food chopper, introduced in 1902. *(Illustration at right)*

Economy Meat and Food Chopper.

TAPLIN MFG. CO., New Britain, CT

Formed about 1892 by Clarence A. Taplin and Fred Goodrich (1844-1906). Maker, in 1902, of improved tumbler size DOVER (Fig.1) and MAMMOTH improved DOVER (Fig.2) eggbeaters. The center gear DOUBLE DASHER eggbeater (Fig.3) was introduced in 1908. The CLIPPER pot and kettle scraper (Fig.4) was introduced in 1903; VICTOR combination bottle opener and stopper (Fig.5) in 1904; and VICTOR lemon squeezer in 1908 (Fig.6). The CHAMPION egg opener, previously made by CHAMPION EGG OPENER CO., was offered in 1905.

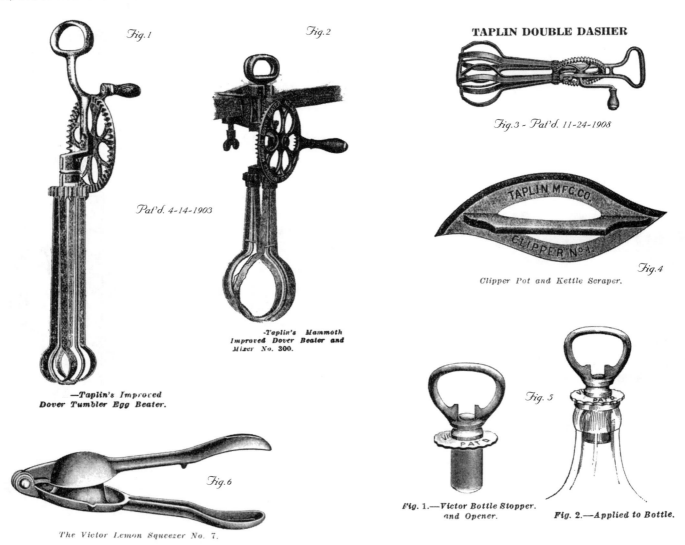

TAPLIN DOUBLE DASHER

Fig.3 - Pat'd. 11-24-1908

Clipper Pot and Kettle Scraper. *Fig.4*

Pat'd. 4-14-1903

—Taplin's Improved Dover Tumbler Egg Beater.

Taplin's Mammoth Improved Dover Beater and Mixer No. 300.

Fig.6

The Victor Lemon Squeezer No. 7.

Fig. 5

Fig. 1.—Victor Bottle Stopper and Opener.

Fig. 2.—Applied to Bottle.

TARBOX & BORGART MFG. CO., Cleveland, OH

Maker of the *T & B* fruit jar wrench (Fig.1), introduced in 1901. A fruit jar holder (Fig.2) was introduced in 1902. *(Illustrations on next page)*

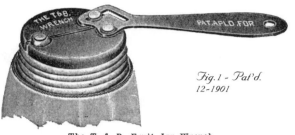

Fig.1 - Pat'd.
12-1901

Fig.2

—The T. & B. Fruit Jar Holder.

The T. & B. Fruit Jar Wrench.

TATUM CO., S.C., Cincinnati, OH

Founded by Samuel C. Tatum about 1877. Main products were hand tools and hardware items. In 1894, the firm introduced the Gooch's patent, *OHIO* ice cream freezer (Fig.1), made in 13 sizes from two to 25 quarts. The *QUEEN* (Fig.2), made in 11 sizes from one to 25 quarts and the *PEARL* (Fig.3), made in 12 sizes, from two to 10 quarts, were introduced in 1899.

Fig.1

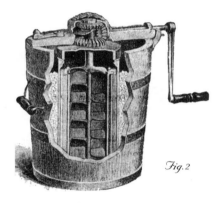

Fig.2

—Sectional View of Queen Freezer, with Crank.

Fig.3

— Pearl Freezer, with Crank.

The Ohio Freezer.

TAYLOR MFG. CO., Hartford, CT

Maker of the *YANKEE* can and bottle opener (Fig.1) introduced in 1906; and the *LITTLE GEM* can and bottle opener (Fig.2), introduced in 1907.

-The Yankee Can and Bottle Opener.

Fig.1 - Pat'd. 1-28-1902 & 12-26-1906

PATENTED

Little Gem Can and Bottle Opener.

Fig.2

TAYLOR MFG. CO., New Britain, CT

Maker of a potato parer, patented June 18, 1878. The parer is marked SARATOGA CHIPS, 75 CENTS, and SOLD THROUGH AGENTS.

The Taylor Fruit Press.

TAYLOR NOVELTY CO., Muscatine, IA

Maker of a fruit press introduced in 1891. The press could also be used as a sausage stuffer or for stuffing poultry. *(Illustration at right)*

Locke's Automatic Pie Turner and Lifter.

THOMAS & CO., W.E., Boston, MA

Maker of *LOCKE'S* pie turner and lifter, introduced in 1890. *(Illustration at left)*

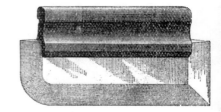

The Boosinger Scraper.

THOMAS, HARRIS E., Lansing, MI

Maker of the *BOOSINGER* scraper, introduced in 1894. *(Illustration at right)*

THOMSEN & CO., AUGUST, Brooklyn, NY

Maker, in 1924, of the ATECO cake and pastry decorator. *(Illustration at left)*

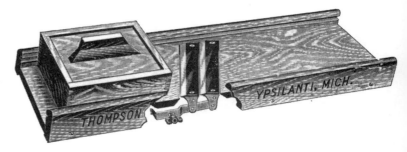

THOMSON & SONS, O.E., Ypsilanti, MI

Maker, beginning about 1905, of *YPSILANTI* slaw and kraut cutters with adjustable cutting knives. *(Illustration at right)*

TREADWELL, JOHN G., Albany, NY

Inventor and maker of a gridiron. Designed for use on coal or wood stoves, it was made with wire gauze under the grate. This was claimed to "cut off the flame arrising from the fire and thus prevent it from burning the meat." The tin cover had two small, mica, windows.

Pat'd. 12-20-1859

TREMAN, KING & CO., Ithaca, NY

Maker of an automatic (non-rotary) ice cream freezer, offered in four sizes, 3 to 8 pints, and introduced in 1891. *(Illustration at right)*

TREMONT MFG. CO., Tremont, NY

Maker of *DELMONICO* cake pans in 1896.

TRIPP BROS. & CO., Sodus, NY

Operated by Henry A. & Walter Tripp. Maker of the *OSCILLATOR* apple parer and corer (Fig.1); the *OSCILLATOR NO. 2* which pared two apples at a time (Fig.2) introduced in 1892; and the *CHALLENGE* hand or power operated parer and corer, introduced in 1895 (Fig.3). *(Illustrations continued on next page)*

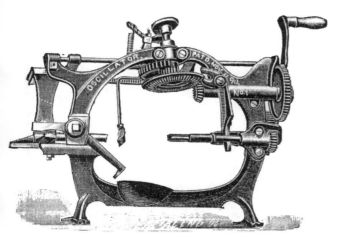
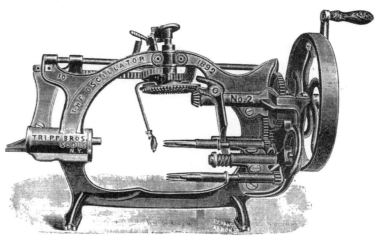

Apple Paring and Coring Machine.

Fig.1 - Pat'd. 6-13-1882 & 11-11-1890

Fig.2   *The Oscillator No. 2.*

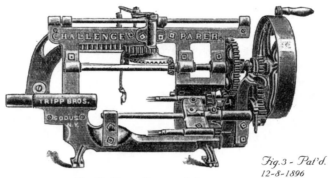

Fig.3 - Pat'd.
12-8-1896

The Challenge Parer and Corer.

TROY NICKEL WORKS, Albany, NY

Maker, in 1898, of the *ALASKA* stove lifter and, in 1902, *HALL'S PEERLESS* mincer.

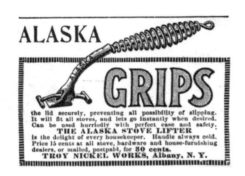

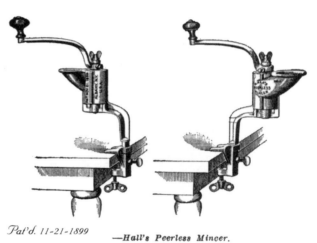

Pat'd. 11-21-1899

—*Hall's Peerless Mincer.*

TUCKER & DORSEY MFG. CO., Indianapolis, IN

Operated by Robert L. Dorsey. Maker of a variety of wooden kitchen and household items beginning about 1880.

Products offered in 1886 included kraut and slaw cutters (Fig.1). New models with corrugated blades (Fig.2) were introduced in 1894 and the *INDIANAPOLIS* model with a lid for the sliding box (Fig.3). *(continued on next two pages)*

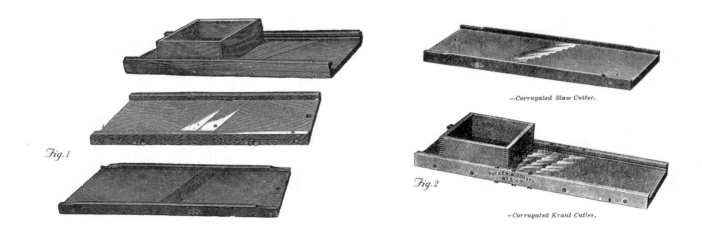

Fig.1

—*Corrugated Slaw Cutter.*

Fig.2

—*Corrugated Kraut Cutter.*

SANITARY models, with metal covered beds, were offered by 1920 (Figs.4 -6). Other offerings in 1911 included lemon squeezers, patented (Fig.7); vegetable cutters (Fig.8); and ST. REGIS fruit and vegetable slicers (Fig.9). T & D bread and meat slicers (Fig.10) were introduced in 1895 with an improved model available by 1920 (Fig.11). The BOSS bread and meat slicer (Fig.12) was introduced in 1904. Product additions in the mid-1920's included the ASTOR (Fig.13) and SWISS (Fig.14) fruit and vegetable slicers. (Illustrations continued on next page)

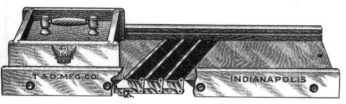

Indianapolis Kraut Cutter. Fig.3 - Pat'd. 7-11-1905

Fig.4 **T. & D. SPECIAL SANITARY**

With Plain Sliding Box
Triple Coated Pure Block Tin Plate Bed, Maple Frame, Well Sharpened Adjustable Steel Knives, 24 Degree Shear.

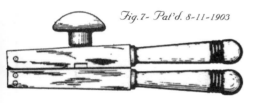

INDIANAPOLIS SANITARY
Fig.5

With Automatic Safety Sliding Box
Triple Coated Pure Block Tin Plate Bed, Maple Frame, Keenly Sharpened and Highly Polished Adjustable Steel Knives, 45 Degree Shear.

SLAW CUTTERS
Fig.6

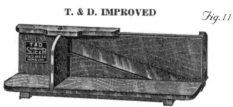

No. 631.

No. 632.

With Sanitary Metal Bed
Triple Coated Pure Block Tin Plate Bed, White Hard Maple Frame, Adjustable Stiff Polished Steel Knives, Forged Wing Nuts.

T. & D. IMPROVED Fig.11

Fig.7- Pat'd. 8-11-1903

Fig.8

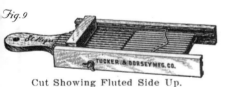

Fig.9

Cut Showing Fluted Side Up.

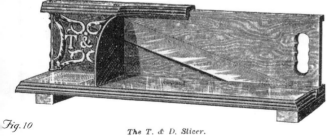

Fig.10 The T. & D. Slicer.

Fig.12 - Pat'd. 6-23-1903

235

Fig. 13

Fig. 14

TURNER & SEYMOUR MFG. CO., Torrington, CT

Founded by Elisha Turner in 1848. After several name changes, the firm became Turner & Seymour Mfg. Co. in 1874 and offered a variety of hardware items, including egg beaters and can openers, beginning in 1889. Later products included the *BLUE WHIRL* eggbeater (Fig.1); *MERRY WHIRL* eggbeater, patented November 28, 1916; *BLUE STREAK* can openers (Fig.2); and a grapefruit corer, patented May 28, 1923, and August 18, 1925.

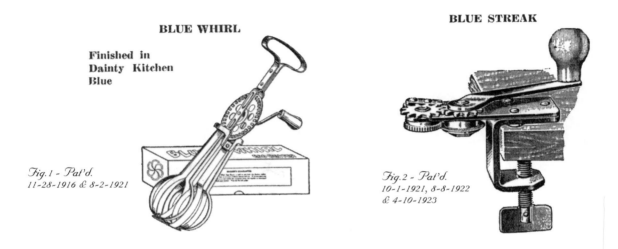

BLUE WHIRL

Finished in
Dainty Kitchen
Blue

Fig.1 - Pat'd.
11-28-1916 & 8-2-1921

BLUE STREAK

Fig.2 - Pat'd.
10-1-1921, 8-8-1922
& 4-10-1923

TUTHILL & AVERY, New York, NY

Maker, in 1868, of a patent reversible griddle. In use the circular spaces were filled with batter and, when done, that half of the griddle was turned over to dump the cakes into the other half for cooking the other side. The next batch could then be started in the first half.

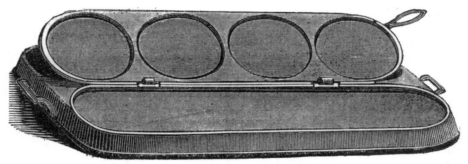

AN IMPROVED PATENT REVERSIBLE GRIDDLE.

TWISS, BENJAMIN, Meriden CT

Twiss began making clocks in 1825 and shortly after added coffee pots to his line. He may also have been the maker of coffee mills, patented June 19, 1837, by H. Twiss.

UNION LOCK & HARDWARE CO., Lancaster, PA

Maker, in 1897, of the pepper grinding box shown at right.

Pepper Grinding Box.

UNION LUNCH BOX CO., New York, NY

Maker of the *BON-VEE-VON* lunch box, introduced in 1903. Aimed at "fastidious people," the imitation leather covered box was furnished with a plate "for engraved name or initials." The box was 8" wide, 7" high and 5" deep and supplied with an alcohol lamp for use as a stove.

Fig. 1.—Bon-Vee-Von Lunch Box, Closed.

Fig. 2.—Interior Metal Box, Front Dropped.

UNION MFG. CO., Buffalo, NY

Maker of the *PERFECTION* raisin seeder, introduced in 1899.
(Illustration at right)

Perfection Raisin Seeder.

UNION MFG. & PLATING CO., Freeport, IL

Formed about 1893 with J.J. Comstock, president and C.B. Barrett, secretary and treasurer. The firm was no longer listed in the Freeport City Directory after 1898. Maker of a timble iron (Fig.l) introduced in 1893 and the *ARCADE* cork extractor (Fig.2), introduced in 1894. Both products were later made by the Arcade Mfg. Co.

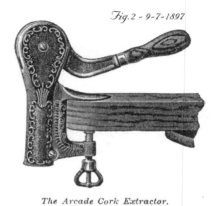

Fig.2 - 9-7-1897

Timbale Iron.   *Fig.1*

The Arcade Cork Extractor.

UNIQUE MFG. CO., New York, NY

Maker of a pickle grabber introduced in 1893.

UNITED ROYALTIES CORP., New York, NY

Maker of *LADD* eggbeaters. *(Illustration at right)*

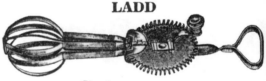

LADD

Pat'd. 7-7-1908 & 2-2-1915

U.S. MFG. CO., Fond du Lac, WI

Maker of the *INDESTRUCTIBLE* fire kindler, introduced in 1897. The device used asbestos pads which were soaked in kerosene. *(Illustration at left)*

U. S. Indestructible Fire Kindler and Oil Can.

U.S. STAMPING CO., Portland, CT

Maker of a variety of stamped tin ware and wire goods. Products in 1883 included *ERNSHAW'S* flour scoop and sifter (Fig.1); the *NATIONAL* flour sifter (Fig.2); *MAGIC* flour sifter (Fig.3); asparagus boilers (Fig.4); and fish boilers (Fig.5). *(Illustrations continued on next page)*

Fig.1 - Pat'd. 7-25-1865

Fig.2

Fig.3

Fig.4

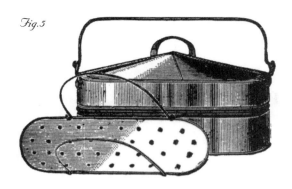

Fig.5

UNIVERSAL HARDWARE WORKS, Mount Joy, PA

Formed in 1909 as a reorganization of the Rollman Mfg. Co., the new company continued most of the *ROLLMAN* products, such as cherry stoners, ice cream freezers, etc., and introduced the *NEW STANDARD* food chopper *(at left)* in 1910.

The firm was reorganized as the New Standard Hardware Works about 1915.

UPSON & HART, Unionville, CT

A partnership of Andrew S. Upson and Herbert C. Hart, formed about 1890 and merged into the Upson Nut Co. in 1898. Products included cutlery and nut crackers. *(Illustration at right)*

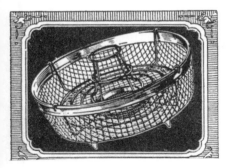

UTILITY MFG. CO., Baltimore, MD

Maker, in 1924, of a line of kitchen wire goods, including the dish drainer shown at left.

VAN ETTEN, F.M., Chicago, IL

Maker, in 1881, of *SCHOFIELD'S* patent cake griddle. Made of cast iron and weighing four pounds, it sold for $1.25. *(Illustration at right)*

239

VAUGHAN NOVELTY MFG. CO., Chicago, IL

Maker of apple corers, pie trimmers, and sealers, patented May 10, 1921.

VERMONT FARM MACHINE CO., Bellows Falls, VT

Maker, from 1880 to after the turn of the century, of the *DAVIS* swing churn. It was made in nine sizes, from three to 50 gallons.

DAVIS' SWING CHURN.

Pat'd. 5-1-1877 & 9-6-1879

This cut illustrates the action of the cream in the Davis Swing Churn when in operation.

VOGEL, WILLIAM W., Chicago, IL

Inventor and maker of a fruit jar cap wrench.
(Illustration at right)

Pat'd. 12-3-1907

VOLLRATH MFG. CO., Sheboygan, WI

Founded in 1874 by Jacob J. Vollrath to make a line of enameled ware, including the first grey enameled products. The firm incorporated in 1884 and continued to made enameled ware in great variety, some of which are shown below. By 1910 the firm was noted for its white enameled ware, with blue accents, and its *TULIP* enameled ware in colbalt blue. *(Illustrations continued on next page)*

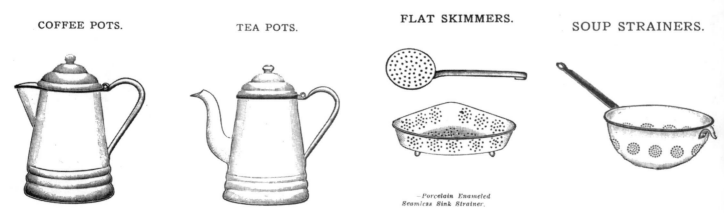

COFFEE POTS.   TEA POTS.   FLAT SKIMMERS.   SOUP STRAINERS.

—Porcelain Enameled Seamless Sink Strainer.

BASTING SPOONS.

Fig. 2.—*The Vollrath Double Roaster.*

Fig. 1.—*Vrooman Sink Strainer.*

Fig. 2.—*Wire Stand for Sink Strainer.*

VROOMAN, F.H. & E.B., Chicago, IL

Maker of a sink strainer introduced in 1905. By 1907, the same strainer was a product of Andrews Wire & Iron Co. *(Illustration at left)*

WADDEL MFG. CO., JOHN M., Greenfield, OH

Maker of a variety of coffee mills, including *WADDEL'S* improved coffee mill, with or without a handle for holding and carrying, introduced in 1889 (Fig.1)and the No. 44 coffee mill, introduced in 1890 (Fig.2). The *IDEAL* coffee mill was introduced in 1893 (Fig.3) and the *LONE STAR* wall mounted, folding coffee mill was also introduced in 1890 (Fig.4).

Fig.1-Pat'd.
5-15-1888

—*Waddel's Improved Coffee-Mill.*

—*Waddel's Improved Coffee-Mill with Handle.*

241

Fig.2

No. 44 Coffee Mill.

Ideal Coffee Mill.
Fig.3 - Pat'd. 1-21-1890

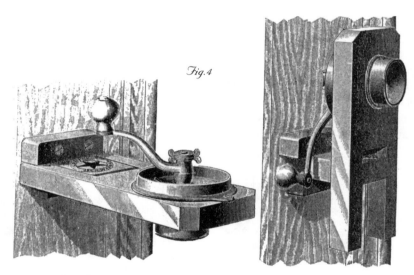

Fig.4

—Lone Star Side Mill.

—The Lone Star Folded Up.

WAGNER BROTHERS, Sidney, OH, <u>later</u>
WAGNER MFG. CO., Sidney, OH

 Founded in 1891 as a partnership of Milton M. Wagner and his brother Bernard P. Wagner to make cast iron cook ware. A third brother, W.H. Wagner, joined the firm in 1893, shortly before it was incorporated as the Wagner Mfg. Co.

 Nickel plated cast iron ware was introduced in 1894 and cast aluminum ware about 1901. By 1920, product offerings had expanded to include sausage and lard presses and a variety of builder's hardware. *(continued on next three pages)*

Cast iron products included waffle irons (Figs.1-3) in several types; tea kettles, including a swing lid type (Fig.4), introduced in 1892; the *WAGNER* improved broiler (Fig.5), introduced in 1901; and a great variety of hollow ware (Figs.6-13). By 1910, the firm offered a line of polished hollow ware "free from sand holes and gate marks" (Figs.14-18).

Cast aluminum ware was introduced in 1901 and included a self-opening tea kettle (Fig.19) and waffle irons (Figs.20-21). By 1910, the line was extensive and included Card (Fig.22) and Patty moulds (Fig.23), and a variety of hollow ware and griddles (Figs.24-38). The aluminum *KRUSTY KORN KOB* pan (Fig.39) was introduced about 1920.

Fig.1

Fig.2

Fig.3

REGULAR POTS.

Fig.4

Fig.5

Fig.6

Wagner Improved Broiler.

LOW BULGED POTS.

Fig.7

REGULAR KETTLES.

Fig.8

FLAT BOTTOM KETTLES.

Fig.9

LOW KETTLES.

Fig.10

SCOTCH BOWLS.

Fig.11

DUTCH OVENS.

Fig.12

OVAL ROASTERS.

Fig.13

LONG GRIDDLES.
Fig. 14

BAILED GRIDDLES.
Fig. 15

HANDLED GRIDDLES.
Fig. 16

Fig. 17   SKILLETS.

ROUND SAD IRON HEATERS.
Fig. 18

TEA KETTLES.
Fig. 19

Fig. 20
AMERICAN PATTERN, ALUMINUM PANS, IRON RINGS, SATIN FINISH.

Fig. 21
HIGH FRAME, SQUARE, FOR VAPOR AND GAS STOVE.

Fig. 22   CRISP CARD MOULDS

Fig. 23   CRISP PATTY MOULDS

TEA POTS.
Fig. 24
CAST IN ONE PIECE, RUBBEROID HANDLE.

COFFEE POTS.
Fig. 25
CAST IN ONE PIECE, RUBBEROID HANDLE.

RICE BOILERS.
Fig. 26

LIPPED KETTLES.
Fig. 27
CAST IN ONE PIECE.

BERLIN KETTLES.
Fig. 28
WITH CAST ALUMINUM COVER.

ROASTERS.
Fig. 29
CAST ALUMINUM.

DUTCH OVENS.
Fig. 30
CAST ALUMINUM.

BAILED GRIDDLES.

Fig. 31

HANDLED GRIDDLES.

Fig. 32

LONG GRIDDLES.

Fig. 33

NURSERY SAUCE PANS.

Fig. 34

RUBBEROID HANDLE.

DEEP SAUCE PANS.

Fig. 35

OBLONG BREAD OR CAKE PANS.

Fig. 36

POLISHED OUTSIDE.

CORN OR CUP CAKE. *Fig. 37*

FRENCH ROLL. *Fig. 38*

CAST KRUSTY KORN KOB MOULDS

Fig. 39

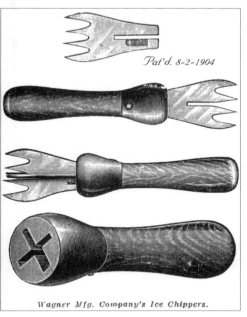

Pat'd. 8-2-1904

Wagner Mfg. Company's Ice Chippers.

WAGNER MFG. CO., Cedar Falls, IA

Maker of ice chippers, patented by Adam Wagner. *(Illustration at left)*

WALKER CO., C.L., Erie, PA

Formed in 1918 by C.L. Walker as a reorganization of the Erie Specialty Co. The new firm continued to make the *QUICK & EASY* ice dippers previously by the Erie Specialty Co.

WARE-STANDARD MFG. CO., New York, NY

Maker, in 1905, of food holders designed for under shelf or wall mounting. *(Illustration at right)*

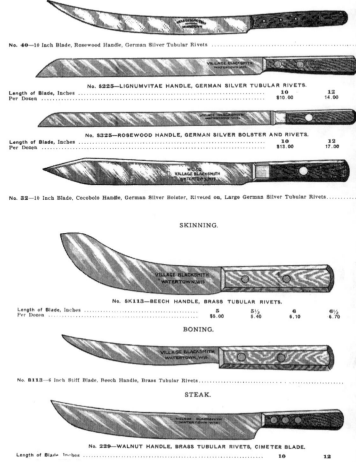

Fig. 2.—Holders Attached to Wall.

WARNER MFG. CO., Freeport, IL

Maker of a combination corn popper and coffee roaster, patented April 7, 1868 and July 19, 1870. Later products included coffee mills, patented October 22, 1889 and October 7, 1890.

WASHBURN CO., Worcester, MA

A holding company formed in 1922 to operate the Wire Goods Co., Andrews Wire & Iron Co., and Cassady-Fairbank Co.

WATERTOWN CUTLERY CO., Watertown, WI

Maker, in 1910, of a line of *VILLAGE BLACKSMITH* kitchen cutlery, some of which are shown below. Other products included butcher cutlery, scrapers, etc.

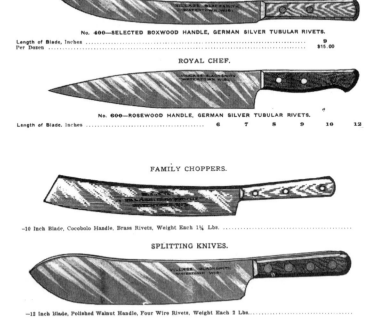

COOK.

No. 400—SELECTED BOXWOOD HANDLE, GERMAN SILVER TUBULAR RIVETS.

| Length of Blade, Inches | 9 |
| Per Dozen | $15.00 |

ROYAL CHEF.

No. 600—ROSEWOOD HANDLE, GERMAN SILVER TUBULAR RIVETS.

| Length of Blade. Inches | 6 | 7 | 8 | 9 | 10 | 12 |

FAMILY CHOPPERS.

–10 Inch Blade, Cocobolo Handle, Brass Rivets, Weight Each 1¼ Lbs. ....

SPLITTING KNIVES.

–12 Inch Blade, Polished Walnut Handle, Four Wire Rivets, Weight Each 2 Lbs...

SLICERS.

No. 40—10 Inch Blade, Rosewood Handle, German Silver Tubular Rivets ....

No. S225—LIGNUMVITAE HANDLE, GERMAN SILVER TUBULAR RIVETS.

| Length of Blade, Inches | 10 | 12 |
| Per Dozen | $10.00 | 14.00 |

No. S325—ROSEWOOD HANDLE, GERMAN SILVER BOLSTER AND RIVETS.

| Length of Blade, Inches | 10 | 12 |
| Per Dozen | $13.00 | 17.00 |

No. 32—10 Inch Blade, Cocobolo Handle, German Silver Bolster, Riveted on, Large German Silver Tubular Rivets..........

SKINNING.

No. SK113—BEECH HANDLE, BRASS TUBULAR RIVETS.

| Length of Blade, Inches | 5 | 5½ | 6 | 6½ |
| Per Dozen | $5.00 | 5.40 | 6.10 | 6.70 |

BONING.

No. B113—6 Inch Stiff Blade, Beech Handle, Brass Tubular Rivets.........................

STEAK.

No. 229—WALNUT HANDLE, BRASS TUBULAR RIVETS, CIMETER BLADE.

| Length of Blade. Inches | 10 | 12 |

BREAD.

~8 Inch Blade, Rosewood Handle, German Silver Bolster, Riveted On, Large German Silver Tubular Rivets........

8 Inch Blade, Rosewood Handle, German Silver Tubular Rivets ....

~9½ Inch Extra Wide Blade, Ground Thin, Rosewood Handle, German Silver Tubular Rivets....................

~8 Inch Blade, Lignumvitae Handle, German Silver, Tubular Rivets ....

WATROUS, E.L., Des Moines, IA

Maker of a hot pan lifter, introduced in 1904. *(Illustration at right)*

Fig. 1.—Hot Pan Lifter.

The Weaver Match Safe.

WEAVER NOVELTY CO., Detroit, MI

Maker of the *FEEDS ONE MATCH* match safe, introduced in 1901. *(Illustration at left)*

WEISKETTEL & SON, A., Baltimore, MD

Maker of a gas flame chicken singer, introduced in 1897. *(Illustration at right)*

Chicken Singer.

WELLINGTON SASH LOCK CO.,
Worcester, MA

Maker of the *IDEAL* can opener, introduced in 1897.
(Illustration at right)

Ideal Can Opener.

WHEELER, E.A., Omaha, NE, <u>later</u>
WHEELER CAN OPENER CO., St. Louis, MO

Maker, in 1888, of a can opener (Fig.1). By 1890, the Wheeler Can Opener Co. had been formed and was offering the can opener in a slightly modified form (Fig.2).

The Wheeler Can Opener.

Fig.1 - Pat'd. 8-17-1886

Fig.2

The Wheeler Can Opener.

WHEELING CORRUGATING CO., Wheeling, WV

Maker, in 1916, of a variety of stamped household ware, including the *OVAL OAK* seamless roaster (Fig.1) and the *CRESCENT* roaster and baker (Fig.2). In 1921 the firm introduced a coffee percolator (Fig.3).

"OVAL OAK" SEAMLESS ROASTER

Fig.1

"CRESCENT" ROASTERS AND BAKERS.

Fig.2

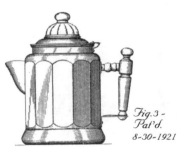

Fig.3 - Pat'd. 8-30-1921

WHITAKER MFG. CO., Chicago, IL

Maker of the *AGRIPPA* fruit jar wrench, introduced in 1904.
(Illustration at right)

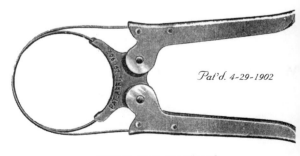

Pat'd. 4-29-1902

Agrippa Fruit Jar Wrench.

Fig. 1.—*Sure Cut Can Opener and Bottle Cap Lifter, No. 501.*

WHITE & SON CO., IRA F., Newark, NJ

Maker of the *SURE CUT* can opener, introduced in 1909. It was made with and without a corkscrew. *(Illustration at right)*

Fig. 2.—*Sure Cut Can and Bottle Opener, No. 95.*

Pat'd.
7-19-1904

WHITE MOUNTAIN FREEZER CO., Nashua, NH

Founded by Thomas Sands (1833-1900) at Laconia, NH. The factory burned in 1881 and was rebuilt in Nashua. Sands retired in 1890 but was granted patents for ice cream freezers as late as June 13, 1899.

Its most common product was the Sand's patent *WHITE MOUNTAIN* triple motion ice cream freezer (Fig.1). It was made in 10 sizes, from 2 to 50 quarts, and under subsequent patents dated April 5, 1881, April 10, 1883, and as late as June 12, 1923.

Other products included Sands' *FAMILY* ice crusher (Fig.2); *ARCTIC* ice cream freezers, made in seven sizes from one to ten quarts (Fig.3); and *JUNIOR* single motion freezers made only in one pint size (Fig.4). The *GRANITE STATE* double action freezer, in five sizes from 2 to 8 quarts, (Fig.5) was introduced in 1890. *(Illustrations continued on next page)*

White Mountain Freezer Co.,

MANUFACTURERS OF

SANDS' PATENT TRIPLE MOTION

White Mountain Ice-Cream Freezer.

The only Freezer in the world having three distinct motions inside the can, thereby, of course, **producing Finer, Smoother Cream** than any other Freezer on the market. Machinery easily adjusted and operated. Tubs waterproof. **Over 300,000 in use.** Send for catalogue and price-list of this celebrated Freezer.

WHITE MOUNTAIN FREEZER CO.,
NASHUA, N. H.

Fig.1 - Pat'd. 2-27-1872 & 3-31-1874

SANDS' FAMILY ICE CRUSHER.

Fig.2

Fig.3 - Pat'd. 12-3-1889

Fig.4

Fig.5

White Mountain factory in 1886

COWLES' PATENT CHURN.

WHITING, W.& W., Baldwinsville, MA

Maker, in 1857, of *COWLES'* churn. The churn had two interlocking dashers which, through gearing, rotated in opposite directions.

Pat'd. 3-3-1857

WHITNEY & VAN VALKENBERG, Effingham, IL

Maker of *WHITNEY'S* coffee roaster. A small, circular, glass window allow the beans to be checked without opening the roaster. *(Illustration at right)*

Pat'd. 2-5-1867

WHITNEY'S COFFEE ROASTER.

WHITTEMORE BROTHERS, Worcester, MA, <u>later</u>
WHITTEMORE, D.H., Worcester, MA

Formed in 1857 to make apple parers (Fig.1). Later apple parer patents were issued to D.H. Whittemore on November 20, 1866, and August 10, 1869; and to E.L. Pratt on October 6, 1863, and January 12, 1864. Nutcrackers (Fig.2) were introduced in 1868.

The name was changed to D.H. Whittemore by 1871 and the firm's last listing in the Worcester City Directory was in 1879. Products offered in 1871 included peach stoners and halvers; peach parers, patented August 23, 1864; apple parers, corers and slicers; and the *UNION* apple parer.

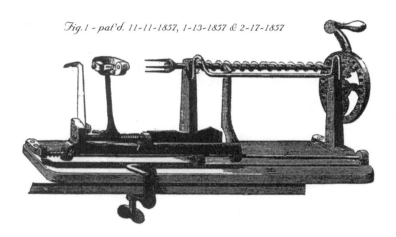

Fig.1 - pat'd. 11-11-1857, 1-13-1857 & 2-17-1857

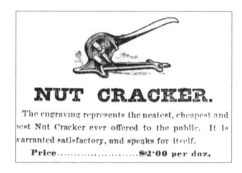

NUT CRACKER.

The engraving represents the neatest, cheapest and best Nut Cracker ever offered to the public. It is warranted satisfactory, and speaks for itself.

Price......................$2·00 per doz.

Fig.2 - Pat'd. 3-31-1868

WILCOX, JAMES, Philadelphia, PA

Maker, in 1857, of a rotary knife cleaner. The trough beneath the lower roller was filled with a polishing powder; cranking caused the powder to fill woolen disks on both rollers which polished the knife as it was passed through. *(Illustration at right)*

Pat'd. 12-4-1855

WILCOX JAR CO., New Haven, CT

Maker, in 1868, of a fruit jar, patented by B.B. Wilcox. The patent covered the yoke and ring which held the lid in place and the use of the yoke as a bail in carrying the jar. *(Illustration at left)*

Pat'd. 3-26-1857

WILDER, J.L., Augusta, ME

Inventor and maker of *WILDER'S* meat and fruit press, patented December 4, 1906.

WILL & WEBER, Toledo, OH

Maker of the *RESSLER* roaster and baker, introduced in 1894. *(Illustration at right)*

The Ressler Roaster and Baker.

Pat'd. 6-4-1867

WILLETT, JOHN B., West Meriden, CT

Inventor and maker of a plate lifter. The three wires retracted to grab the plate when the lever was depressed and extended when it was released.
(Illustration at left)

WILLIAMS CO., A.C., Ravenna, OH

Operated by Alan C. Williams. Maker of a variety of cast iron kitchen tools including the *COLUMBIA* pan and stove lid lifter, introduced in 1894 (Fig.1); BOSS raisin seeder, introduced in 1896 (Fig.2); and *MODEL* lemon squeezers made ca.1905-1915 (Fig.3).

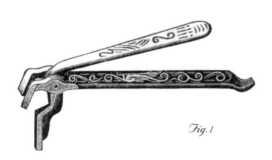

Fig.1

—*The Columbia Lifter.*

MODEL.

The Boss Raisin Seeder.
Fig.2 - Pat'd. 8-4-1896

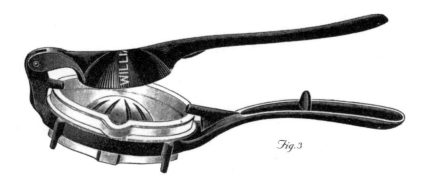

Fig.3

WILLIAMSON CO., C.T., Newark, NJ, <u>later</u>
WILLIAMSON WIRE NOVELTY CO., C.T., Newark, NJ

Formed in 1885 by Cornelius Williamson, when the partnership of Clough & Williamson separated into the Rockwell Clough Co. and the C.T. Williamson Co. Maker of a large variety of corkscrews, including several previously made by Clough & Williamson. New products included folding corkscrews, patented June 18, 1889; *WILLIAMSON'S* hand power corkscrew for cork, crowns and Baltimore seals (Fig.1); and bottle shaped pocket corkscrews (Fig.2).

By 1901, the firm name had changed to Williamson Wire Novelty Co. which offered a champagne tap (Fig.3) in 1901 and the New Era cork puller (Fig.4) in 1902. Offerings in 1910 included a folding pocket model (Fig.5); the *NEWARK* wooden case pocket model, (Fig.6); and two types of hand corkscrews (Fig.7-8).

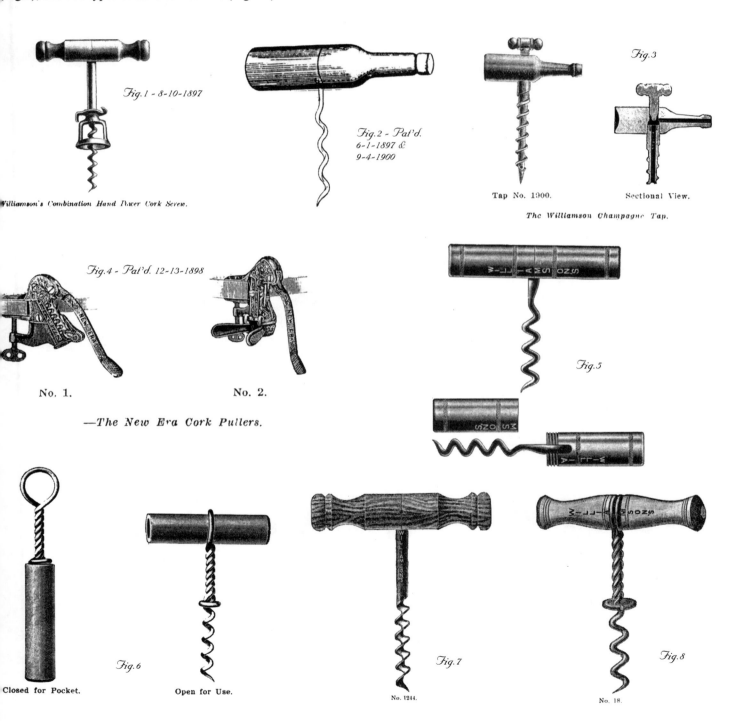

Fig.1 - 8-10-1897

Williamson's Combination Hand Power Cork Screw.

Fig.2 - Pat'd. 6-1-1897 & 9-4-1900

Tap No. 1900.

Fig.3

Sectional View.

The Williamson Champagne Tap.

Fig.4 - Pat'd. 12-13-1898

No. 1.   No. 2.

—The New Era Cork Pullers.

Fig.5

Fig.6

Closed for Pocket.   Open for Use.

Fig.7

No. 1244.

Fig.8

No. 18.

Pat'd. 12-4-1888

WILSON & CO., F.C., Chicago, IL
Maker of the *MUHAMMAD* coffee biggin, introduced in 1889. *(Illustration at right)*

—*The Muhammad Coffee Biggin.*

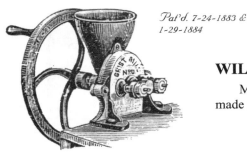

*Pat'd. 7-24-1883 &
1-29-1884*

WILSON, FRANK, Easton, PA
Maker of line of hand driven mills, primarily for farm use. The *FAMILY* grist mill was made for kitchen use "for grinding graham flour or corn meal." *(Illustration at left)*

No. o.   Family grist mill.

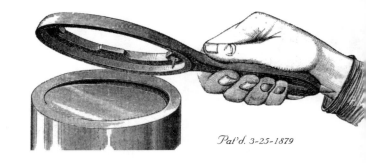

WILSON, T.F., Washington, DC
Inventor and maker of a can opener. *(Illustration at right)*

Pat'd. 3-25-1879

WOOD BACK, COFFEE MILLS.

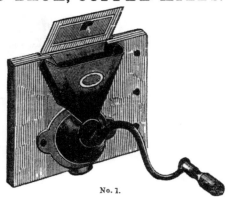

WILSON, INCREASE, New London CT
Inventor and maker of coffee mills. Wilson incorporated his firm in 1855 and continued operation until his death in 1861.
(Illustration at left)

No. 1.

WILSON TOASTER & SPECIALTY MFG. CO., Minneapolis, MN

Maker of the *WILSON* bread toaster, introduced in 1904. A perforated top shelf could be used for "making coffee or poaching eggs while toasting bread, thus economizing fuel."
(Illustration at right)

Wilson Bread Toaster.

WINCHELL MFG. CO., GEORGE D., Cincinnati, OH

Maker of a porcelain cup milk or rice boiler, introduced in 1892. *(Illustration at left)*

WHIPWELL

WINSTED HARDWARE MFG. CO., Winsted, CT

Maker of the *WHIPWELL* egg beater. *(Illustration at right)*

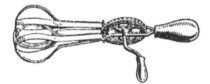

Pat'd. 3-23-1920 & 5-2-1921

WIRE GOODS CO., Worcester, MA

Founded in 1880 by Charles G. Washburn and incorporated in 1882 with a capital of $20,000. Maker of a wide variety of formed wire kitchen utensils. The firm acquired Andrews Wire & Iron Works in 1917 and Cassady-Fairbank Mfg. Co. in 1914. The three companies merged in 1922 to form the Washburn Co. *(continued on next page)*

Products included a plate lifter (Fig.1); the *YR* sink brush and dishwasher (Fig.2), introduced in 1900; *CROSS CUT* (Fig.3), *FLEXIBLE* (Fig.4), *SURPRISE* (Fig.5), and *ELECTRIC* (Fig.6) egg whips, introduced in 1908. The *SPIRAL* egg beater (Fig7), *SENSIBLE* pot chain and scraper (Fig.8), and wire pot chains in 1/2" ring (Fig.9) and 3/4" ring (Fig.10) models were offered by 1910. The *VICTOR* flour sifter (Fig.11); *SHERWOOD* corn popper (Fig.12); *BOSTON* toaster (Fig.13); and several styles of *DOVER* egg beaters (Fig.14) were offered by 1920. *(Illustrations continued on next page)*

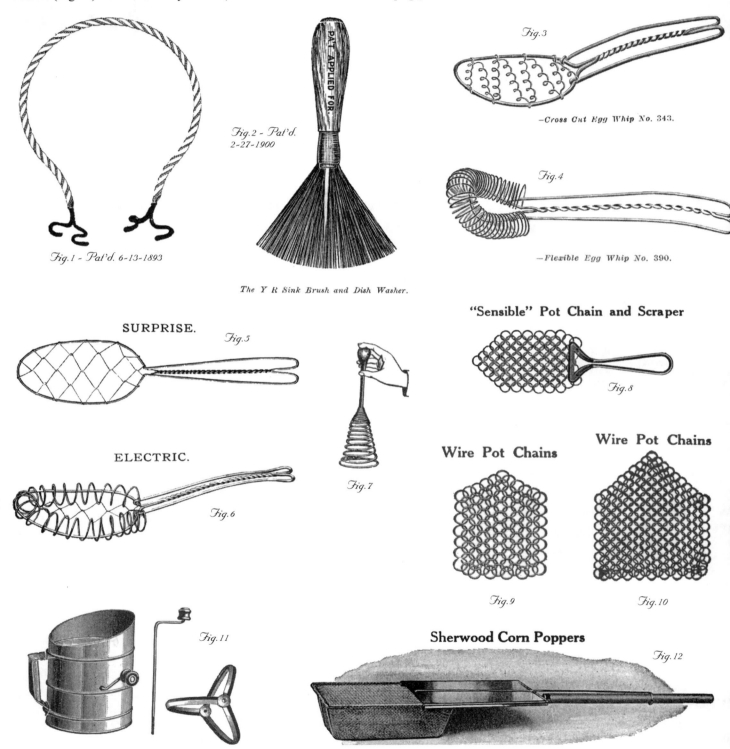

Fig.3

—Cross Cut Egg Whip No. 343.

Fig.2 - Pat'd.
2-27-1900

Fig.4

—Flexible Egg Whip No. 390.

Fig.1 - Pat'd. 6-13-1893

The Y R Sink Brush and Dish Washer.

SURPRISE.
Fig.5

"Sensible" Pot Chain and Scraper
Fig.8

ELECTRIC.
Fig.6

Fig.7

Wire Pot Chains

Wire Pot Chains

Fig.9

Fig.10

Fig.11

Sherwood Corn Poppers
Fig.12

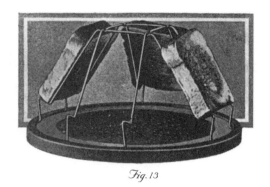

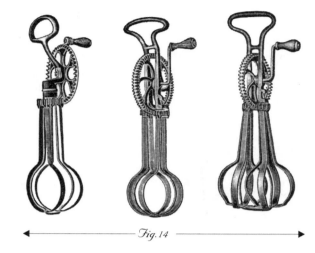

Fig. 13

Fig. 14

WISE & SON, JOHN, Butler, OH

Maker of a combined baker and roaster, introduced in 1890. *(Illustration at left)*

Combined Roaster and Baker.—

WITHERS & WOLFE, Atlanta, GA

Maker, in 1880, of a cast iron tea kettle, patented by W.S. Withers. A linkage from the handle to the kettle top caused the top to be locked in place when the bail was upright and self opening when the bail was horizontal. They also noted that the handle, kept upright when the kettle was on the stove, "cannot become heated."
(Illustration at right)

WOLFF APPLIANCE CORP., Long Island City, NY

Maker of the *WOLFF* visible toaster, patented September 21, 1920.

WOLVERINE SUPPLY CO., Pittsburgh, PA

Maker of the *WOLVERINE* fruit jar holder and opener, introduced in 1905.
(Illustration at left)

Holder.   Opener.

Pat'd. 5-27-1902

The Wolverine Fruit Jar Holder and Opener.

WOODRUFF & EDWARDS CO., Elgin, IL

Maker, beginning in 1907, of a line of *ELGIN NATIONAL* coffee mills, used primarily in stores. Offerings included iron hopper models with six ounce capacity (Fig.1), one pound capacity (Fig.2), one and a quarter pound capacity (Fig.3), and five larger sizes from 1 1/2 to 4 1/2 pounds. Nickel hopper models were made in two pound (Fig.4), and six other sizes from 2 1/4 to 9 pounds (Fig.5).

Floor models were made in iron hopper style (Fig.6) with 4 1/2 and 6 3/4 pound capacities; and nickel hopper style (Fig.7) with a capacity of seven pounds. *(The illustrations are arranged in vertical columns.)*

IRON HOPPER, STEEL GRINDERS.

NICKEL HOPPER, STEEL GRINDERS.

IRON HOPPER, STEEL GRINDERS.

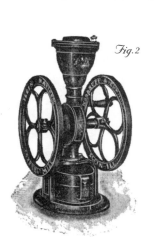

IRON HOPPER, STEEL GRINDERS.

IRON HOPPER, STEEL GRINDERS.

NICKEL HOPPER, STEEL GRINDERS.

NICKEL HOPPER, STEEL GRINDERS.

WOODRUFF, OLIVER D., Pottstown, PA

Maker of the *NEW CONNECTICUT* meat chopper, introduced in 1900. By 1906, the meat chopper was a product of Colebrookdale Iron Co.

—The New Connecticut Meat Chopper.

Pat'd. 4-10-1894, & 10-8-1895
Improvements pat'd. 1-6-1903

No. 1.

No. 2.

No. 3.

Rotors of the New Connecticut Meat Chopper.

WOODS, BACON & CO., New York, NY

Maker of the *WOODS* can opener, introduced in 1900. The opener was made well into the 1920's.

Pat'd. 3-5-1901
& 10-8-1901

Woods' Adjustable Can Opener.

WOODS, SHERWOOD & CO., Lowell, MA, <u>later</u>
WOODS-SHERWOOD CO., Lowell, MA

A partnership of E.P. Woods and Daniel Sherwood, formed about 1860. Maker of kitchen items formed from wire, including coffee strainers, patented July 9, 1861; wire gauze strainers, patented November 18, 1862; dish stands, patented December 31, 1867 and April 27, 1869; toast racks, patented July 13, 1869 and February 8, 1870. Wooden fruit jar holders (Fig.1) were offered in 1880. *(continued on next page)*

Fig.1 - Pat'd. 3-25-1879
& 8-26-1879

TRIUMPH PLATE
LIFTERS.

Fig.2

SHERWOOD'S

SPIRAL.

Fig.3

SHERWOOD'S

Later products included *TRIUMPH* plate lifters (Fig.2) and *SPIRAL* egg beaters (Fig.3) offered in 1886; and a folding dish drainer and plate warmer, introduced in 1888 (Fig.4). In 1909 the firm introduced the *LOCK LIP* strainer (Fig.5); *WHIPIT* egg beater, vegetable skimmer and egg separator (Fig.6); and a screw rim tea or coffee ball (Fig.7). The company was absorbed by the Wire Goods Co. about 1915.

Folding Dish Drainer and Plate Warmer.

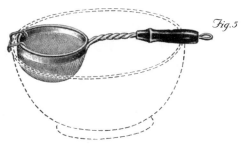

Lock Lip Strainer. Which Locks Itself on a Bowl or Other Receptacle.

—Whipit Egg Beater, Vegetable Skimmer, Egg Separator, &c.

Screw Rim Tea or Coffee Ball, Obviating the Use of Strainer.

The Anchor Potato Parer.

WOODWELL, W.E. & J., Pittsburgh, PA

Maker of the *ANCHOR* potato peeler, introduced in 1890. *(Illustration at left)*

WORTHINGTON MFG. CO., Elyria, OH

Maker, in 1908, of the *ELYRIA* knife sharpener. Equipped with the usual hardened steel rollers, it differed from many other sharpeners only in the hand grips formed on both ends.
(Illustration at right)

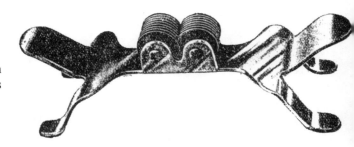

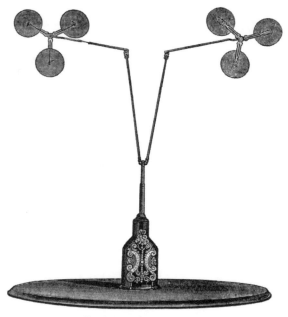

Revolving Disc Fly Fan.

WREN, WHITEHURST & CO., Norfolk, VA

Maker of a very elaborate fly fan, introduced in 1891. It was claimed to run for two hours on a single winding. *(Illustration at right)*

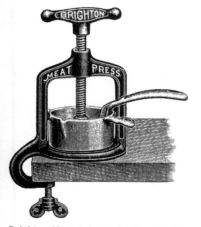

WRIGHTSVILLE HARDWARE CO., Wrightsville, PA

Maker of the *BRIGHTON* meat juice extractor, introduced in 1909. *(Illustration at left)*

Brighton Meat Juice Extractor, No. 12.

YAWMAN & KNAPP MFG. CO., Rochester, NY

Maker of a pineapple eyer, introduced in 1906.

Yawman Pineapple Eyer.

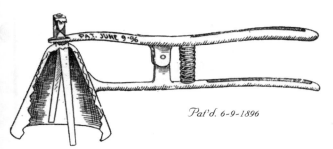

Pat'd. 6-9-1896

Automatic Ice Cream Disher.

YOUNGSTOWN SPECIALTY MFG. CO., Youngstown, OH

Maker, in 1898, of an ice cream disher.

APPENDIX A

TRADE NAMES WITH MAKERS

Many kitchen collectibles are marked with trade names or abbreviations rather than the actual maker's name. Reference to the list below will identify the maker(s) using that mark.

Note that the same trade name was often used by more than one maker. A short description of the collectible, shown after a trade name used by more than one maker, will help find the proper maker. In those cases where the trade name was used by multiple firms for an identical item (usually as a result of a company taking over the products of another company) the trade name is not repeated for each company.

TRADE NAME	MAKER
ACW	A.C. Williams Co.
A & W	Adams & Westlake Co.
ACME (lemon squeezer)	F.F. Adams Co.
ACME (cold handle)	Brittan, Graham & Mathes Co.
ACME (can opener)	Goodell Co.
ACME (flour sifter)	National Enameling & Stamping Co.
ACME (freezer)	Polar Star Co.
	Acme Freezer Co.
ACME (fry pan)	New York Stamping Co.
ACME (freezer)	Palmer Hardware Co.
ACME (corn popper)	Quincy Hardware Mfg. Co.
ACME (bean cutter)	L. Salomon
AGATE	Lalance & Grosjean Mfg. Co.
AGRIPPA	Whitaker Mfg. Co.
ALADDIN	Cleveland Metal Products Co.
ALASKA (freezer)	Alaska Freezer Co.
ALASKA (stove lifter)	Troy Nickel Works
ALBUM	Beaumont & Callahan
	Album Mfg. Co.
ALL STEEL	New Standard Hardware Works
ALPHA	Elizabeth Mfg. Co.
ALWAYS READY	Meadville Vise Co.
AMERICAN (cheese cutter)	American Cheese Cutter Co.
AMERICAN (bread knife)	American Cutlery Co.
AMERICAN (ice chisel)	American Machine Co. (freezer)
AMERICAN (tobacco cutter)	American Machine Co.
	North Brothers Mfg. Co.
AMERICAN (waffle iron)	Griswold Mfg. Co.
AMERICAN (lemon squeezer)	Logan & Strobridge Iron Co.
AMERICAN (knife sharpener)	Mossberg Mfg. Co.
AMERICAN QUEEN	Logan & Strobridge Iron Co.
AMERICAN TWIN	North Brothers Mfg. Co.
AMERICAN WONDER	George Borgfeldt & Co.
AMES	Edmumd Brown
ANCHOR	W.E. & J. Woodwell

TRADE NAME	MAKER
ANDROCK	Andrews Wire & Iron Works
ANGER	Sargent & Co.
ARCADE (various)	Arcade Mfg. Co.
ARCADE (cork puller)	Union Mfg. & Plating Co.
ARCTIC (jar wrench)	Fanner Mfg. Co.
ARCTIC (freezer)	White Mountain Freezer Co.
ARMITAGE	Republic Supply Co.
AROMA	Bronson-Walton Co.
ASTOR	Tucker & Dorsey Mfg. Co.
ATECO	August Thomsen & Co.
ATLAS	Household Necessities Mfg. Co.
AUNT DINAH'S	Andrews Wire & Iron Works
AUTOSPIN	Fred J. Burr
BADGER	Badger Wire & Iron Works
BALDWIN'S	Chicago Nickel Works
BALL'S	Aluminum Novelty Co.
BARDEN'S	Granville Mfg. Co.
BARLER	Sidney Shepard & Co.
BAY STATE (can opener)	Boston Mfg. Assoc.
BAY STATE (apple parer)	Goodell Co.
BELL	Arcade Mfg. Co.
BELLE	J. McDermaid
BEST	William G. Browne Mfg. Co.
BEST OF ALL	Charles Lehmann
BEST YET (can opener)	Hasbrouck Alliger
BEST YET (knife sharpener)	F.H. Smith Mfg. Co.
BLIZZARD	North Brothers Mfg. Co.
BLOOD'S	Dover Stamping Co.
BLUE STREAK	Turner & Seymour Mfg. Co.
BLUE WHIRL	Turner & Seymour Mfg. Co.
BLUST	Constance Co.
BONANZA	Goodell Co.
BON-VEE-VON	Union Lunch Box Co.
BOOSINGER	Harris E. Thomas
BOSS (fire kindler)	Clark Mfg. Co.
BOSS (freezer)	Gooch Freezer Co.
BOSS (jar holder and wrench)	Kline & Co.
BOSS (lemon squeezer)	John Somer's Son
BOSS (bread slicer)	Tucker & Dorsey Mfg. Co.
BOSS (raisin seeder)	A.C. Williams Co.
BOSTON (roaster)	Hill & Whitney Mfg. Co.
BOSTON (can opener)	Maltby, Henly & Co.
BOSTON (toaster)	Wire Goods Co.
BOVINIZER	W.G. Henis' Sons Co.
BRIGHTON (various)	Logan & Strobridge Iron Co.
BRIGHTON (meat press)	Wrightsville Hardware Co.
BRIGHTON SPECIAL	Logan & Strobridge Iron Co.
BRIGHTON STAR	Logan & Strobridge Iron Co.
BROOKLYN (fry pan)	New York Stamping Co.

TRADE NAME	MAKER
BROOKLYN (various)	Silver & Co.
BROWN BEAUTY	Bronson-Walton Co.
BRYANT'S	Paine, Diehl & Co.
BUFFALO	Sidney Shepard & Co.
BUFFER	Blanchard, Parker & Co.
BULLDOG	Cassady-Fairbank Mfg. Co.
BUTTERFLY	E.M. La Roche & Co.
C-B-CO	Comstock-Bolton Co.
CMP	Cleveland Metal Products Co.
C.P. CO.	Charles Parker Co.
CSC	Cincinnati Stamping Co.
CALIFORNIA	Goodell Co.
CAPEE	Manning, Bowman & Co.
CENTAUR	Centaur Mfg. Co.
CENTENNIAL	Clipper Mfg. Co.
CHALLENGE (coffee mill)	Sun Mfg. Co.
CHALLENGE (apple parer)	Tripp Bros. & Co.
CHAMPION (ice chisel)	American Axe & Tool Co.
CHAMPION (beef shaver)	Enterprise Mfg. Co.
CHAMPION (lemon squeezer)	Arcade Mfg. Co.
CHAMPION (cork puller)	Beaumont & Callahan
CHAMPION (egg opener)	Taplin Mfg. Co.
CHAMPION (tobacco cutter) (coffee mill)	Enterprise Mfg. Co.
CHAMPION (roaster)	Leach Roaster & Baker Co.
CHAMPION (egg beater) (freezer)	Reid-Edelmuth Mfg. Co.
CHAMPION (grater)	Specialty Novelty Co.
CHICAGO	Illinois Stamping Co.
CLASSIC	Griswold Mfg. Co.
CLEAN CUT	A.F. Beese
CLEVELAND RAPID	Harris Mfg. Co.
CLEWELL	Valentine Clad
CLIMAX (apple corer)	Goodell Co.
CLIMAX (grater)	Hamilton Metal Products Co.
CLIPPER (cork puller)	Arcade Mfg. Co.
CLIPPER (ice cream scoop)	Giles & Nielsen Nickel Works
CLIPPER (tobacco cutter)	Sargent & Co.
CLIPPER (pot scraper)	Taplin Mfg. Co.
CLOUGH'S	Rockwell-Clough Co.
COLONIAL	Logan & Strobridge Iron Co.
COLUMBIA (fly fan)	Matthai, Ingram & Co.
COLUMBIA (can opener)	A.F. Meisselbach & Bro.
COLUMBIA (spoon)	M.L. Schroch
COLUMBIA (pan lifter)	A.C. Williams Co.
COLUMBIAN (enamel ware)	Bellaire Stamping Co.
COLUMBIAN (roaster)	Sidney Shepard & Co.
COMET (knife)	Christy Knife Co.
COMET (can opener)	Charles Messenger

TRADE NAME	MAKER
COMMON SENSE (can opener)	Alford & Berkele
	New England Specialty Co.
COMMON SENSE (toaster)	Frank B. Schuyler
COMMON SENSE (kettle)	Sidney Shepard & Co.
CONE CUP	Bradley, Blinn & Lyon
CONNECTICUT	Colbrookdale Iron Co.
	O.D. Woodruff
CONVENIENT	John Stortz & Son
CORKEE	Freeport Novelty Co.
	Manning, Bowman & Co.
CORONA	Enterprise Enamel Co.
COTNER	Home Novelty Co.
COWLES	W.& W. Whiting
CRACKER JACK	Beaumont & Callahan
CREAM CITY	Geuder, Paeschke & Frey Co.
CREASEY'S	Novelty Machine Works
CRESCENT	Wheeling Corrugating Co.
CRISPY	Clark Hardware Co.
CROSSCUT	Wire Goods Co.
CROWN (ice chipper)	American Machine Co.
(freezer)	North Brothers Mfg. Co.
CROWN (roaster)	Enterprise Enamel Co.
CROWN (griddle)	Hall & Carpenter
CROWN (coffee mill)	Landers, Frary & Clark
CRUSTY	Niles Mfg. Co.
CRYSTAL (coffee mill)	Arcade Mfg. Co.
CRYSTAL (freezer)	J.B. Foote Foundry Co.
CRYSTAL (lemon squeezer)	J.P. Manny
CRYSTAL (food holder)	Ware-Standard Mfg. Co.
CYCLONE (churn)	Anthony Wayne Mfg. Co.
CYCLONE (can opener)	Bridgeport Mfg. Co.
CYCLONE (egg beater)	William G. Browne Mfg. Co.
CYCLONE (can opener)	Chieftain Co.
CYCLONE (kraut cutter)	J.H. Day & Co.
CYCLONE (dish washer)	Z.S.& C.L. Randleman
D.S. CO.	Dover Stamping Co.
DAISY (cork puller)	Arcade Mfg. Co.
DAISY (lemon squeezer)	James D. Frary
DAISY (mincing knife)	A.S. Henn & Co.
DAISY (apple parer)	Hudson Parer Co.
DAISY (shaker)	Stevens, Woodman & Co.
DANDY (can opener)	
(apple parer)	Goodell Co.
DANDY (mincing knife)	A.S. Henn & Co.
DANDY (cherry stoner)	New Standard Hardware Works
DAVIS (corkscrew)	Detroit Corkscrew Co.
DAVIS (churn)	Vermont Farm Machine Co.
DELMONICO (ice cream disher)	
(lemon squeezer)	Nicol & Co.

TRADE NAME	MAKER
DELMONICO (meat tenderer)	Pullman Sash Balance Co.
DELMONICO (can opener)	Albert B. Schofield
DELMONICO (cake pan)	Tremont Mfg. Co.
DERBY	Plumb Novelty Co.
DEWEY'S SLUGS	Albert Pick & Co.
DIAMOND (cleaver)	Wm. Beatty & Son
DIAMOND (ice pick)	Bradley Mfg. Co.
DIAMOND (knife)	Maltby, Henly & Co.
DIAMOND (grater)	Scott Mfg. Co.
DIAMOND (ice shave)	Charles B. Stevens
DIAMOND POINT	Easley Mfg. Co.
DIEHL	Paine, Diehl & Co.
DIXIE	Standard Stamping Co.
DOUBLE ACTION	Albert B. Schofield
DOUBLE DASHER	Taplin Mfg. Co.
DOUBLE DELIGHT	H.D. Smith & Co.
DRAW CUT	Murray Iron Works
DRESDEN	George Havell
DRUM	Manning, Bowman & Co.
DUCHESS	Vollrath Co.
DUPLEX (serving fork)	Cassady-Fairbank Mfg. Co.
	Duplex Fork Co.
DUPLEX (knife sharpener)	John Chatillon & Sons
DUPLEX (broiler)	Dundee Mfg. Co.
DUPLEX (churn)	Duplex Mfg. Co.
DUPLEX (can opener)	Lawrence Hardware Works
DUPLEX (mincing knife)	N.R. Streeter & Co.
E-Z MIXER	National Mfg. & Supply Co.
EAGLE	Charles Parker & Co.
EARLE'S	Dover Stamping Co.
EARNSHAW'S	U.S. Stamping Co.
EASY (dough mixer)	R.W. Jamieson Co.
EASY (can opener)	R.W. Loll Mfg. Co.
EASY (freezer)	Wm. A. Sexton Co.
ECLISPE (can opener)	Brooklyn Novelty Co.
ECLISPE (bread maker)	Manning, Bowman & Co.
	Sumner Mfg. Co.
ECONOMY (fruit press)	Northwestern Kitchenware Mfg. Co.
ECONOMY (food chopper)	Syracuse Machine Co.
EDIE	Smith & Egge Mfg. Co.
EDLUND, JR.	Edlund Co.
ELECTRIC (can opener)	Alford & Berkele
ELECTRIC (veg. parer)	Augusta Machine Works
ELECTRIC (cider press)	O.E. Davidson & Co.
ELECTRIC (egg whip)	Wire Goods Co.
ELGIN NATIONAL	Woodruff & Edwards Co.
ELYRIA	Worthington Mfg. Co.
EMPIRE	New York Stamping Co.
EMPRESS WARE	New York Stamping Co.

TRADE NAME	MAKER
ENTERPRISE	Enterprise Mfg. Co.
ERIE	Griswold Mfg. Co.
ESTATE	Estate Stove Co.
EUREKA (churn)	Wm. L. Bradley
EUREKA (fruit pitter)	Farnsworth & Co.
EUREKA (apple parer)	Goodell Co.
EUREKA (toaster)	Kilbourne Mfg. Co.
EVAPORATOR	Goodell Co.
EVER-READY (coffee mill)	Bronson-Walton Co.
EVER-READY (grater)	Geuder, Paeschke & Frey Co.
EXCELSIOR	M.F. Koenig & Co.
EXPERT	Penn Hardware Co.
EZY	American Specialty Co.
FAMILY (apple parer)	Goodell Co.
FAMILY (beef press)	Silver & Co.
FAMILY (grater)	Specialty Novelty Co.
FAMILY (ice crusher)	White Mountain Freezer Co.
FAMOUS	Charles F. Spery
FAULTLESS	Quaker Novelty Co.
FAVORITE	Arcade Mfg. Co.
FAYWAY	Blanton & McKay Co.
FEEDS ONE MATCH	Weaver Novelty Co.
FELTHAUSEN'S	Scott Mfg. Co.
FIFTH AVENUE	James D. Frary
FLANDERS	Hamblin & Russell Mfg. Co.
FLEXIBLE	Wire Goods Co.
4-IN-1	J.C. Forster & Son
FOUR POUR	Cassady-Fairbank Mfg. Co.
FOWLER	Matthai, Ingram & Co.
FRANCO-AMERICAN	Logan & Strobridge Iron Co.
FREZO	Dana Co.
FROST KING	Richmond Cedar Works
G.P.& F.	Geuder, Paeschke & Frey Co.
GARNET	Geuder, Paeschke & Frey Co.
GEM (ice pick)	American Enamel Co.
GEM (freezer)	American Machine Co.
	North Brothers Mfg. Co.
GEM (batter mixer)	American Machine Co.
	North Brothers Mfg. Co.
GEM (nutmeg grater)	Caldwell Mfg. Co.
GEM (veg. masher)	Chieftain Mfg. Co.
GEM (toaster)	Clark Hardware Co.
GEM (slicer)	Horton & Link Mfg. Co.
GEM (cooker)	Illinois Pure Aluminum Co.
GEM (cake pan)	North Brothers Mfg. Co.
GEM (food chopper)	Sargent & Co.
GIANT	James D. Frary
GIANT LIGHTNING	Shepard Hardware Co.
GOLD MEDAL	Monroe Brothers

TRADE NAME	MAKER
GOLDEN CROWN	Stuart & Peterson Co.
GRANITE STATE	White Mountain Freezer Co.
GRANT'S	Gaynor & Mitchell Mfg. Co.
GREAT AMERICAN	W.J. Lloyd Mfg. Co.
GREENFIELD	Jon. M. Waddel Mfg. Co.
HALE	Russell & Erwin Mfg. Co.
HALL'S PEERLESS	Troy Nickel Works
HANDY (ice shave)	A.E. Faber
HANDY (can opener)	Handy Things Mfg. Co.
HANDY (corkscrew)	Little Giant Letterpress Co.
HANDY (strainer)	Sidney Shepard & Co.
HANDY (grater)	F.E. Snyder
HAWTHORNE (julep strainer)	Manning, Bowman & Co.
HELPING HAND	Hamblin & Russell Mfg. Co.
HENIS	Royal Mfg. Co.
HERCULES	Moses L. Hawks
HERO	Clement & Dunbar
HERO in diamond	Hero Stamping Works
HERSEY	Dover Stamping Co.
HOLD-FAST	Hamblin & Russell Mfg. Co.
HOME (coffee mill)	Arcade Mfg. Co.
HOME (nut cracker)	
(cherry stoner)	Schroeter Bros. Hdw. Co.
HOUSEHOLD JEWEL	Gravity Twine Box Co.
HOUSEWIFES' DELIGHT	F.E. Kohler & Co.
HOXIE'S	John Freimuth
HUDSON'S	Northwestern Consolidated Iron & Steel Mfg. Co.
HUNTER'S	Fred J. Meyers Mfg. Co.
HURLEY'S	F.F. Adams Co.
IXL	Arcade Mfg. Co.
I.X.L.	W.G. Browne Mfg. Co.
ICE KING	Dover Stamping Co.
ICELAND	Peerless Freezer Co.
IDEAL (coffee pot)	Aluminum Cooking Utensil Co.
IDEAL (freezer)	John A.E. Anderson
IDEAL (nutcracker)	Frank B. Cook Co.
IDEAL (bread pan)	Matthai, Ingram & Co.
IDEAL (coffee pot) (freezer)	New England Enameling Co.
IDEAL (meat chopper)	Peck, Stow & Wilcox Co.
IDEAL (various)	Stover Mfg. & Engine Co.
IDEAL (coffee mill)	Waddel Mfg. Co.
IDEAL (can opener)	Wellington Sash Lock Co.
IMPERIAL (coffee mill)	Arcade Mfg. Co.
IMPERIAL (coffee mill)	Lalance & Grosjean Mfg. Co.
IMPROVED BAY STATE	Goodell Co.
IMPROVED NEVER SLIP	Browne & Dowd Mfg. Co.
INDESTRUCTIBLE	U.S. Mfg. Co.

TRADE NAME	MAKER
INDIANAPOLIS	Tucker & Dorsey Mfg. Co.
INFANTA	Meriden Malleable Iron Co.
INVINCIBLE	Hugo Reisinger
JACK FROST (freezer)	American Automatic Vending Machine Co.
	Jack Frost Freezer Co.
JACK FROST (freezer)	Sturges & Burn Mfg. Co.
JENNIE MAY	Hamblin & Russell Mfg. Co.
JEWEL (coffe mill)	
(cake turner)	Arcade Mfg. Co.
JEWEL (toaster)	Detroit Stove Works
JEWEL (can opener)	Jewel Tool Co.
JIM'S	Harkin & Willis
JUICY FRUIT	O.P Schriver & Co.
JUMBO	Caldwell Mfg. Co
JUNIOR	White Mountain Freezer Co.
K W	Keiner-Williams Stamping Co.
KANTBREAK	Pike Mfg. Co.
KEEN KUTTER	Simmons Hardware Co.
KEENO	Keeno Corp.
KEYSTONE (can holder)	F.F. Adams Co.
KEYSTONE (food chopper)	Colbrookdale Iron Co.
KEYSTONE (beater)	Keystone Beater Co.
	North Brothers Mfg. Co.
KEYSTONE (beater)	
(freezer)	Paine, Diehl & Co.
KLEAN-EM	L.C. Pond Co.
KLONDIKE	Hall Mfg. Co.
KNEAD-FULL	Gem Mfg. Co.
KING (can opener)	Browne & Dowd Mfg. Co.
KING (lemon squeezer)	
(egg beater)	Alfred Rex & Co.
KIN-HEE	James Heekin & Co.
KITCHEN FRIEND	American Cutlery Co.
KITCHEN JEWEL	Harkins Foundry Co.
KITCHEN KUMFORT	Lasher Mfg. Co.
	Andrews Wire & Iron Works
KITCHEN PAL	Scientific Specialty Co.
KLONDIKE	Duplex Mfg. Co.
KRAUT KUTTER	Tucker & Dorsey Mfg. Co.
KRISPY	Andrews Wire & Iron Works
KRUSTY KORN KOB	Wagner Mfg. Co.
KWICKSHARP	Spengler-Loomis Mfg. Co.
L.F.& C.	Landers, Frary & Clark
LADD	United Royalties Corp.
LEADER	Leader Specialty Co.
LEBANON	Seltzer Specialty Co.
LIGHTNING (can opener)	R.M. Ball
LIGHTNING (churn)	Porter Blanchard's Sons
LIGHTINNG (can opener)	Chieftain Co.

TRADE NAME	MAKER
LIGHTNING (bread knife)	Clark & Parsons
LIGHTNING (cork puller)	Gilchrist Mfg. Co.
LIGHTNING (mixing spoon)	J. Allen Glover
LIGHTNING (peach parer)	Goodell Co.
LIGHTNING (bread cutter)	
(potato slicer)	Hoxie & Clark
LIGHTNING (egg beater)	Lightning Dasher Egg Beater Co.
LIGHTNING (kettle cleaner)	Lightning Dish & Kettle Cleaner Co.
LIGHTNING (mincing knife)	Logan & Strobridge Iron Co.
LIGHTNING (cream whip)	Matthai, Ingram & Co.
LIGHTNING (beater)	National Co.
LIGHTNING (ice shave)	North Brothers Mfg. Co.
LIGHTNING (freezer)	Shepard Hardware Co.
	North Brothers Mfg. Co.
LINK	H.M. Quackenbush
LITTLE GEM	Taylor Mfg. Co.
LITTLE GIANT	Peck, Stow & Wilcox Co.
LITTLE HUSTLER	Silver & Co.
LITTLE STAR	Hudson Parer Co.
LOCK LIP	Woods, Sherwood & Co.
LOCKE'S	W.E. Thomas & Co.
LONE STAR	Waddel Mfg. Co.
LOWNDES	John Chatillon & Sons
LUSK	Dayton Co.
M.B. MEANS BEST	Manning, Bowman & Co.
MACKLETT STAR	Farwell, Ozmun, Kirk & Co.
MAGIC (churn)	American Woodenware Co.
MAGIC (corkscrew)	Charles L. Griswold
MAGIC (veg. parer)	New York Glass Enameling Co.
MAGIC (toothpick holder)	Sidney Shepard & Co.
MAGIC (flour sifter)	U.S. Stamping Co.
MAGUIRE	Comstock-Bolton Co.
MAHOGANY	Bronson-Walton Co.
MAMMOTH	Taplin Mfg. Co.
MARION HARLAND	Silver & Co.
MARVEL	Kalischer Mfg. Co.
MARYLAND	Matthai, Ingram & Co.
MASSER'S	E. Ketchum & Co.
MASTER BAKE POT	Cadmus Products Co.
MATADOR	Gwinner Mfg. Co.
MATCHLESS	Hill & Whitney Mfg. Co.
MEAKER	Ireland & Matthews Mfg. Co.
MEDALLION	Scott Mfg. Co.
MERIDEN	Manning, Bowman & Co.
MERRY WHIRL	Turner & Seymour Mfg. Co.
METEOR	Manning, Bowman & Co.
MIKADO	Manning, Bowman & Co.
MILLER	Hamblin & Russell Mfg. Co.
MIRRO	Aluminum Goods Mfg. Co.

TRADE NAME	MAKER
MODEL	A.C. Williams Co.
MODERN	Gilchrist Mfg. Co.
MONARCH (can opener)	Electric Letter Box Co.
MONARCH (broiler)	Maltby, Henly & Co.
MONARCH (apple parer)	L.A. Sayre
MONITOR (coffee pot)	E. Blunt
MONITOR (coffee mill)	Bronson-Walton Co.
MONROE'S	Dover Stamping Co.
MORGAN	Morgan Mfg. Co.
	Sun Stamping Co.
MRS. VROOMAN'S	Andrews Wire & Iron Works
MUDGE	John L. Gaumer Co.
MUHAMMAD	F.C. Wilson & Co.
N. & CO.	Nicol & Co.
N.R.S. & CO.	N.R. Streeter & Co.
N.Y.S. CO.	New York Stamping Co.
NATIONAL (fly fan)	Bridgeport Brass Co.
NATIONAL (various)	National Specialty Mfg. Co.
NATIONAL (coffee mill)	Charles Parker & Co.
NATIONAL (lemon squeezer)	Matt Redlinger
NATIONAL (flour sifter)	U.S. Stamping Co.
NESCO	National Enameling & Stamping Co.
NEVER BREAK	Bronson-Walton Co.
NEVER BURN	Bronson-Walton Co.
NEVER SLIP (can opener)	Browne & Dowd Mfg. Co.
NEVER SLIP (jar wrench)	Paxton Hardware Mfg. Co.
NEW BOSS	John Somer's Son
NEW BRIGHTON	Logan & Strobridge Iron Co.
NEW CENTURY (apple parer)	Goodell Co.
NEW CENTURY (nutcracker)	Matt Redlinger
NEW CONNECTICUT	O.D. Woodruff
NEW ENGLAND	Smith & Hemenway Co.
NEW ERA	Williamson Co.
NEW IDEA (hot cake iron)	Franklin Specialty Co.
NEW IDEA (can opener)	Scott Mfg. Co.
NEW MODEL	New Union Mfg. Co.
NEW PATTERN	H.M. Quackenbush
NEW TRIUMPH	Peck, Stow & Wilcox Co.
NEWARK	Williamson Co.
NEWSAM	William Newsam
NEWIRE	Rockwell-Clough Co.
99	Rockwell-Clough Co.
NIP-IT	Windsor Stephens & Co.
NONE-SUCH (coffee mill)	Bronson-Walton Co.
NONE-SUCH (can opener)	W.G. Browne Mfg. Co.
NORTH POLE	Alaska Freezer Co.
NORTH'S	American Vapor Stove Co.
O.K.	John S. Carter
OCEAN	Illinois Cutlery Co.

TRADE NAME	MAKER
OHIO (coffee mill)	Sun Mfg. Co.
OHIO (freezer)	S.C. Tatum & Co.
OLD STYLE	Cincinnati Stamping Co.
ONE-MINUTE (egg beater)	F.W. Loll Mfg. Co.
ONE-MINUTE (churn)	Standard Churn Co.
ONYX	Columbian Enameling & Stamping Co.
OPENRIGHT	M.& L. Ehrlich
OPLEX	Bronson-Walton Co.
ORIGINAL	Enterprise Mfg. Co.
ORIOLE	Scott Mfg. Co.
OSCILLATOR	Tripp Bros. & Co.
OSSCO	Ohio State Stove Co.
OVAL OAK	Wheeling Corrugating Co.
OXFORD	George Havell
P.S.& W.	Peck, Stow & Wilcox
PALACE	Chicago Nickel Works
PARISIAN	Lalance & Grosjean Mfg. Co.
PEARL	S.C. Tatum & Co.
PEERLESS (enamel ware)	Enterprise Enamel Co.
PEERLESS (freezer)	Gooch Freezer Co.
PEERLESS (knife sharpener)	Goodell Co.
PEERLESS (bread cutter)	Green & Noble Brothers
PEERLESS (eyer)	John D. Houck
PEERLESS (meat tenderer)	Lavigne & Scott Mfg. Co.
PEERLESS (cork screw)	Francis H. Loss
PEERLESS (cork screw)	Maltby, Henly & Co.
	Smith & Hemenway Co.
PEERLESS (coffee pot)	Peerless Cooker Co.
PEERLESS (can opener)	Albert B. Schofield
PEERLESS ICELAND	Dana & Co.
PERCO-POT	Perco-Ware Co.
PERCY	Hamblin & Russell Mfg. Co.
PERFECT (cork puller)	Alford & Berkele
PERFECT (lemon squeezer)	Arcade Mfg. Co.
PERFECT (can opener)	Luther S. Hull
PERFECT (bread mixer)	R.W. Jamieson Co.
PERFECTION (meat cutter)	American Machine Co.
	North Brothers Mfg. Co.
PERFECTION (veg. peeler)	American Specialty Co.
PERFECTION (coal tongs)	Cincinnati Tool Co.
PERFECTION (jar wrench)	
(jar holder)	Drake & Mills
PERFECTION (corn holder)	Imperial Metal Mfg. Co.
PERFECTION (egg beater)	Nelson Lyon
PERFECTION (tea strainer)	Manning, Bowman & Co.
PERFECTION (roaster)	National Enameling & Stamping Co.
PERFECTION (cherry stoner)	Edwin D. Parker
PERFECTION (corn forks)	F.P. Pfleghar & Co.

TRADE NAME	MAKER
PERFECTION (cake tin)	Richardson Mfg. Co.
	Sidney Shepard & Co.
PERFECTION (flour bin)	Sherman, Tangenberg & Co.
PERFECTION (raisin seeder)	Union Mfg. Co.
PERK'S	Schroeter Bros. Hdw. Co.
PERRY'S	Peck, Stow & Wilcox Co.
PET	Gooch Freezer Co.
PHENIX	Sargent & Co.
PHILADELPHIA	John Stortz & Son
PHOENIX	Arcade Mfg. Co.
PICNIC	Ohio Tin & Copper Co.
PIX	Arcade Mfg. Co.
POLAR	Estes & Co.
POLAR STAR	Polar Star Co.
	Smith & Hemenway Co.
PREMIER (lemon squeezer)	Logan & Strobridge Iron Co.
PREMIER (knife sharpener)	Premier Mfg. Co.
PRIDE	Cassady-Fairbank Mfg. Co.
PRISCO	Pritchard-Strong Co.
PROSPECT	Bronson-Walton Co.
PUDDLEFOOT	Detroit Corkscrew Co.
PULLMEE	Freeport Novelty Co.
	Manning, Bowman & Co.
PURITAN	Bronson-Walton Co.
PURITAN (cooker)	
(egg poacher)	Eustis Mfg. Co.
QUEEN (slaw cutter)	E.C. Atkins & Co.
QUEEN (percolator)	Bellaire Stamping Co.
QUEEN (can opener)	Browne & Dowd Mfg. Co.
QUEEN (flour sifter)	Geuder, Paeschke & Frey Co.
QUEEN (freezer)	S.C. Tatum & Co.
QUEEN CITY	Sidney Shepard & Co.
QUICK AS A WINK	Converse, M.D.
QUICK CUT	Gibbs Mfg. Co.
QUICK & EASY	Erie Specialty Co.
QUICKSAFE, JR.	Quicksafe Mfg. Co.
QUINCY	Quincy Hardware Mfg. Co.
RADIANT	Andrews Wire & Iron Works
RAPID (veg. cutter)	Bluffton Slaw Cutter Co.
RAPID (cork puller)	Meriden Malleable Iron Co.
REDTOP	Redtop Electric Co.
REGAL	Landers, Frary & Clark
RELIABLE (corkscrew)	Francis H. Loss
RELIABLE (corkscrew)	Maltby, Henly & Co.
	Smith & Hemenway Mfg. Co.
RESSLER	Will & Weber
REVERSIBLE (toaster)	Andrews Wire & Iron Works
REVERSIBLE (electric toaster)	Manning, Bowman & Co.
REX	Abbott & Boutell

TRADE NAME	MAKER
REYNOLD'S	Cassady-Fairbank Mfg. Co.
RIGHT HAND	Goodell Co.
RIVAL (apple parer)	Kelsea & Boutell
RIVAL (egg beater)	Standard Co.
ROSELAND	Rockford Can Co.
ROYAL (ice pick)	American Enamel Co.
ROYAL (coffee mill)	Arcade Mfg. Co.
ROYAL (veg. masher)	William G. Browne Mfg. Co.
ROYAL (cherry stoner)	Royal Mfg. Co.
ROYAL (roaster)	Silver & Co.
ROYAL (coffee pot)	M. Stransky & Co.
ROYAL (nickel plated ware)	W.H. Sweeney Mfg. Co.
RUSSWIN	Russell & Erwin Mfg. Co.
S.H.CO.	Simmons Hardware Co.
SAFETY (can opener)	Cassady-Fairbank Mfg. Co.
SAFETY (can opener)	David H. Coles
SAFETY (match safe)	E.P. Hasbrouck
SAFETY FILL	Griswold Mfg. Co.
SAFETY GRIP	George W. Hobbs
ST. REGIS	Tucker & Dorsey Mfg. Co.
SALAMANDER	Iron-Clad Mfg. Co.
SAND'S	White Mountain Freezer Co.
SANITARY (sink basket)	Silver & Co.
SANITARY (slaw cutter)	Tucker & Dorsey Mfg. Co.
SANITROX	Columbian Enameling & Stamping Co.
SARATOGA	Goodell Co.
SAVORY	Republic Metal Ware Co.
SCHOFIELD'S	F.M. Van Etten
SCOOPS ALL	Geuder, Paeschke & Frey Co.
SCIENTIFIC	Onodaga Mfg. & Promoting Co.
SEASIDE	James D. Frary
SELFSEAL	Selfseal Pressure Cooker Co.
SENSIBLE (various)	N.R. Streeter & Co.
SENSIBLE (pot scrubber)	Wire Goods Co.
78	Reading Hardware Co.
SHAKER	Sidney Shepard & Co.
SHARPIT	Dazey Churn & Mfg. Co.
SHARP'S	Fred J. Meyers Mfg. Co.
SHEAR CUT CLIPPER	William G. Browne Mfg. Co.
SHERWOOD	Wire Goods Co.
SHOMEE	Freeport Novelty Co.
	Manning, Bowman & Co.
SHOOT-A-LITE	Cassady-Fairbank Mfg. Co.
SILVER LAKE	Bronson-Walton Co.
SIMPLEX	Manning, Bowman & Co.
SKIMIT	Skimit Mfg. Co.
SLICK-OPE	Irwin Mfg. Co.
SLY-SIR	Jennings-Hall-Sperry Co.
SMITH'S PAT.	Centaur Mfg. Co.

TRADE NAME	MAKER
SNOW BALL	Richmond Cedar Works
SOLITAIRE	Charles F. Henis Co.
SPIRAL	Wire Goods Co.
	Woods, Sherwood & Co.
SPRAGUE	Sargent & Co.
SPRING	H.M. Quackenbush
STAR (freezer)	American Machine Co.
STAR (food cutter)	Charles D. Brown
STAR (rasin seeder)	F.H. Chase & Co.
STAR (knife)	Goodell Co.
STAR (chopping knife)	C.T. Ludwig
STAR (meat pounder)	Nicol & Co.
STAR (meat tenderer)	Parker Wire Goods Co.
STAR (jar holder)	L.H. Schmidt
STAR (coffee pot)	Silver & Co.
STAR-RITE	Fitzgerald Mfg. Co.
STEEL FRAME	Richmond Cedar Works
STERLING (lemon squeezer)	Logan & Strobridge Iron Co.
STERLING (bread slicer)	N.R. Streeter & Co.
STODDARD	Moseley & Stoddard Mfg. Co.
STORK	Stork Mfg. Co.
STOW'S	Russell & Erwin Mfg. Co.
STRAIGHT FLUSH	Edward S. Hotchkiss
SUCCESS (orange parer)	Goodell Co.
SUCCESS (can opener)	Peck, Stow & Wilcox Co.
SULLIVAN	James D. Frary
SUN (dinner pail)	W.B. Bertels, Son & Co.
SUN (apple slicer)	C.M. Heffron
SUPREME	Cassady-Fairbank Mfg. Co.
SURPRISE	Wire Goods Co.
SURE CUT	Ira F. White & Son Co.
SURE GRIP	A.S. Henn & Co.
SURE-SHARP	Edlund Co.
SURPRISE	Peck, Stow & Wilcox Co.
SWIFT	Lane Bros.
SWISS	Tucker & Dorsey Mfg. Co.
T.A.C.U.	The Aluminum Cooking Utensil Co.
T.& D.	Tucker & Dorsey Mfg. Co.
TELEPHONE	Arcade Mfg. Co.
TELLER	Andrews Wire & Iron Works
TENNESSEE	A.H. Patch
THERMAX	Landers, Frary & Clark
THERMOMETER	R.M. Ball
TIGER	Bronson-Walton Co.
TOLEDO	Maher & Grosh
TOP-OFF	Edlund Co.
TRIUMPH (jar wrench)	Forbes Chocolate Co.
TRIUMPH (broiler)	Maltby, Henly & Co.
TRIUMPH (hollow ware)	Patton Mfg. Co.

TRADE NAME	MAKER
TRIUMPH (meat chopper)	Peck, Stow & Wilcox Co.
TRIUMPH (churn)	J. Phynott
TRIUMPH (plate lifter)	Woods, Sherwood & Co.
TULIP	Geuder, Paeschke & Frey Co.
	Vollrath Mfg. Co.
TURBINE	Cassady-Fairbank Mfg. Co.
TURN TABLE 98	Goodell Co.
20TH CENTURY (lemon squeezer)	Album Mfg. Co.
20TH CENTURY (sharpener)	Pike Mfg. Co.
20TH CENTURY (churn)	Rippley Hardware Co.
TWENTIETH CENTURY (can opener)	Premo-Hall Mfg. Co.
TWIN REVERSIBLE	Perfection Electric Products Co.
TWO KNIFE	Reading Hardware Co.
UNION (coffee mill)	Charles Parker & Co.
UNION (apple parer)	D.H. Whittemore
UNIQUE (skewer puller)	F.W. Hall
UNIQUE (ice cream dipper)	Mosteller Mfg. Co.
UNIQUE (nutmeg grater)	Steel Edge Stamping & Retinning Co.
UNIVERSAL (various)	Landers, Frary & Clark
UNIVERSAL (corkscrew)	Snow & Petrelli Mfg. Co.
VAN DEUSEN	C.A. Chapman
VANTAGE	Rockford Metal Specialty Co.
VENICE	George Havell
VICTOR (mincing knife)	Corbin & Kenyon
	Clauss Shear Co.
VICTOR (veg. parer)	Goodell Co.
VICTOR (flour sifter)	Milwaukee Wire Works
VICTOR (flour sifter)	National Mfg. Co.
VICTOR (coffee mill)	Charles Parker & Co.
VICTOR (apple parer)	Scott Mfg. Co.
VICTOR (lemon squeezer) (bottle stopper)	Taplin Mfg. Co.
VICTOR (flour sifter)	Wire Goods Co.
VICTORIA	Scott Mfg. Co.
VIKO	Aluminum Goods Mfg. Co.
VILLAGE BLACKSMITH	Watertown Cutlery Co.
VIOLET	Geuder, Paeschke & Frey Co.
VROOMAN	F.H.& E.B. Vrooman
	Andrews Wire & Iron Works
VULCAN	William M. Crane Co.
W.C.CO.	Watertown Cutlery Co.
WAGNER (sausage stuffer)	Salem Tool Co.
WALDORF-ASTORIA	Smith & Hemenway Co.
WALKER'S (variety)	Erie Specialty Co.
WALKER'S (pineapple slicer)	Scott Mfg. Co.
WEAR EVER	Aluminum Cooking Utensil Co.
WEBB	Bradley Mfg. Co.
WEST'S	T.G. Ellsworth
WHHIPIT	Woods, Sherwood & Co.

TRADE NAME	MAKER
WHIPWELL	Winsted Hardware Mfg. Co.
WHITE MOUNTAIN (apple parer)	Goodell Co.
WHITE MOUNTAIN (ice pick)	Nashua Iron & Brass Foundry Co.
WHITE MOUNTAIN (freezer)	White Mountain Freezer Co.
WHITE'S	C.S. Osborne & Co.
WILDER'S	J.L. Wilder
WILSON	Wilson Toaster & Specialty Mfg. Co.
WOLVERINE	Wolverine Supply Co.
WONDER	Household Novelty Works
WORLD	C.M. Heffron
WORLD'S BEST	William W. Lyman
X-RAY (coffe mill)	Arcade Mfg. Co.
X-RAY (raisin seeder)	East Mfg. Co.
X-RAY (lemon squeezer)	Freeport Novelty Co.
	Manning, Bowman & Co.
YALE	Johnson Foundry & Machine Works
YANKEE (cork puller)	
(lemon squeezer)	Gilchrist Co.
YANKEE (nutmeg grater)	Grand Rapids Grater Co.
YANKEE (strawberry huller)	Hamblin & Russell Mfg. Co.
YANKEE (can opener)	Taylor Mfg. Co.
YPSILANTI	O.E. Thompson & Sons
YR	Wire Goods Co.
ZERO	Gooch Freezer Co.
ZIP	Phillips Laffitte Co.

PATENT DATES WITH MAKERS

Many kitchen collectibles are marked with a patent date only. Reference to the following list will identify the maker which made products under patents issued on a given date.

Note that the same patent date will often be found on the products of more than one maker. Where the same patent date has been used by multiple makers, these makers will be listed after that date without a repeat of the date. In those cases where different patents of the same date are listed, a short definition of the item will be included after the date to help identify the proper maker.

PATENT DATE	MAKER
1818/3/6	Increase Wilson
1832/6/22	Charles Parker & Co.
1848/12/15	E. Ketcham & Co.
1855/12/4	James Wilcox
1856/11/11	Whittemore Brothers
1857/1/13	Whittemore Brothers
1857/3/3	W.& W. Whiting
1857/10/13	Edmund Brown
1858/1/19	E. Ketcham & Co.
1858/7/6	Russell & Erwin Mfg. Co.
1858/9/14	M. Newman
1859/3/15	Russell & Erwin Mfg. Co.
1859/4/5	Russell & Erwin Mfg. Co.
1859/4/19	Dover Stamping Co.
1859/5/17	Dover Stamping Co.
1859/5/17	R. Frisbie
1859/6/7	DeWitt Stevens
1859/12/20	John G. Treadwell
1860/1/10	Peck, Stow & Wilcox
1860/2/7	Charles Parker & Co.
1860/5/1	K.E. Ashley
1860/5/15	S.J. Smith
1860/5/22	Charles W. Packer
1860/9/25	William T. Nicholson
1860/11/6	Beaumont & Guernsey
1861/4/23	E. Ketchum & Co.
1861/6/18	Dover Stamping Co.
1861/7/23	William T. Nicholson
1861/9/17 (sifter)	Dover Stamping Co.
1861/9/17 (strainer)	Edmund Brown
1861/10/29	Charles Parker & Co.
1862/12/2	Hudson Parer Co.
1863/7/7	Dover Stamping Co.
1863/10/6	Goodell Co.
	Whittemore Brothers

PATENT DATE	MAKER
1864/1/12	Whittemore Brothers
1864/4/19	George H. Snow
1864/8/23	Goodell Co.
	Whittemore Brothers
1864/8/30	Dover Stamping Co.
1864/11/1	J.R. Champlin & Co.
1864/12/27	G.W. Putnam
1865/5/23	Athol Machine Co.
1865/7/4	Peck, Stow & Wilcox
1865/7/25	U.S. Stamping Co.
1865/10/31	John A. McNeil
1865/11/14	J.J. Doyle
1865/12/12	Russ & Eddy
1866/1/9	Dover Stamping Co.
1866/1/30	Wm. L. Bradley
1866/2/20	William C. McGill
1866/4/3	William C. McGill
1866/4/10	William C. McGill
1866/4/24	Dover Stamping Co.
1866/5/8	William C. McGill
1866/6/26 (eggbeater)	K.E. Ashley
1866/6/26 (freezer)	J.R. Champlin & Co.
1866/7/24	Russ & Eddy
1866/8/21	Monroe Brothers
1866/10/2	E.R. Stilwell
1866/10/23	Longshore & Bro.
1866/10/9	Champion Grater Co.
1866/10/16	Lane Bros.
1866/11/20	Whittemore Brothers
1867/1/8	L.V. Badger
1867/2/5	Whitney & Van Valkenberg
1867/3/26	Wilcox Jar Co.
1867/4/2	Champion Grater Co.
1867/4/9	Geer & Hutchinson
1867/6/4	John B. Willett
1867/6/11	Charles Gooch
1867/6/18	Goodell Co.
1867/7/23	Charles W. Packer
1867/10/22	Charles Messinger
1867/12/10	John Chatillon & Sons
1868/1/14 (coffee mill)	Lane Bros.
1868/1/14 (cork puller)	James Morton
1868/1/21	Charles Gooch
1868/3/31	Whittemore Brothers
1868/4/7	T.C. Smith
1868/5/5 (apple parer)	Reading Hardware Co.
1868/5/5 (coffee mill)	Charles Parker & Co.
1868/6/30	Meriden Britannia Co.
1868/7/21	American Broiler Mfg. Co.

PATENT DATE	MAKER
1868/10/20	Meriden Britannia Co.
1868/11/3	E. Blunt
1869/2/16	Goodell Co.
1869/3/9	Peck, Stow & Wilcox
1869/3/16	J.R. Champlin & Co.
1869/8/10	Goodell Co.
	Whittemore Brothers
1869/8/17	Goodell Co.
1869/10/5	Philadelphia Patent & Novelty Co.
1869/10/19 (broiler)	American Broiler Mfg. Co.
1869/10/19 (can opener)	W.M. Bleakley
1870/5/10	Goodell Co.
1870/5/31	Dover Stamping Co.
1870/6/21	Enterprise Mfg. Co.
1870/7/12	W.W. Lyman
1870/7/19 (can opener)	W.W. Lyman
1870/7/19 (coffee pot)	Manning, Bowman & Co.
1870/8/30	A.R. Silver
1870/11/15	N. Linden
1870/11/22	Goodell Co.
1871/7/4	Charles Gooch
1871/7/11	A.R. Silver
1871/8/15	M.L. Edwards
1872/2/27	White Mountain Freezer Co.
1872/3/5	Hudson Parer Co.
1872/3/26	Reading Hardware Co.
1872/4/30	Houchin Mfg. Co.
1872/9/10	Charles Lehmann
1872/11/26	Silver & Deming Mfg. Co.
1872/12/10	Goodell Co.
1873/4/15	Athol Machine Co.
1873/5/6	Dover Stamping Co.
1873/6/3	M.L. Edwards
1873/6/10	Landers, Frary & Clark
1873/7/22	Reading Hardware Co.
1873/8/12	A.R. Silver
1873/10/28	Heinz & Munschauer
1873/12/16	Lane Brothers
1874/1/27	Charles Gooch
1874/2/10	Charles Lehmann
1874/3/31	White Mountain Freezer Co.
1874/6/20	Lane Brothers
1874/7/21	Sargent & Co.
1874/8/4	Goodell Co.
1874/11/24	M.L. Edwards
1875/2/9	Lane Brothers
1875/4/13	Enterprise Mfg. Co.
1875/5/2	Reading Hardware Co.
1875/8/17 (comb. tool)	American Mfg. Co.

PATENT DATE	MAKER
1875/8/17 (flour sifter)	Milwaukee Wire Works
1875/9/14	Matthai, Ingram & Co.
1875/10/5	Enterprise Mfg. Co.
1875/10/19	Reading Hardware Co.
1875/11/14	Reading Hardware Co.
1875/12/28	Robert Crane
1876/1/4	John Chatillon & Sons
1876/1/25	Samuel Poole
1876/2/1	Clough & Williamson
	Rockwell Clough Co.
1876/5/23	Willis H. Sherwood
1876/5/30	St. Louis Stamping Co.
1876/6/27	Joshua Barnes
1876/6/27 (corkscrew)	Joshua Barnes
1876/6/27 (potato slicer)	A. Herring
1876/6/27 (coffee pot)	Willis H. Sherwood
1876/11/14	New York Stamping Co.
1876/12/12	Chicago Nickel Works
1877/5/1	Vermont Farm Machine Co.
1877/5/22	Reading Hardware Co.
1877/7/3	St. Louis Stamping Co.
1877/7/10	Willis H. Sherwood
1877/12/25 (grater)	Standard Co.
1877/12/25 (nut cracker)	Samuel Poole
1878/4/30 (coffee mill)	Peck, Stow & Wilcox
1878/5/28	A.W. Sperry
1878/6/11	Landers, Frary & Clark
1878/6/18	Taylor Mfg. Co.
1878/10/29	Novelty Machine Works
1878/11/12	Valentine Clad
1878/11/19	Enterprise Mfg. Co.
1879/3/25 (can opener)	T.F. Wilson
1879/3/25 (jar holder)	Woods, Sherwood & Co.
1879/8/5	J.M. Hunter
	Fred J. Meyers Mfg. Co.
1879/8/26	Woods, Sherwood & Co.
1879/9/16	Vermont Farm Machine Co.
1879/9/30	Enterprise Mfg. Co.
1880/1/20	Charles W. Packer
1880/3/9	Peck, Stow & Wilcox
1880/6/29	Standard Co.
1880/9/21	Standard Co.
1880/10/5	Peck, Stow & Wilcox
1880/11/16	N.S. Chandler
1880/12/14	J. McDermaid
1881/3/6	Standard Co.
1881/4/5	White Mountain Freezer Co.
1881/5/3 (churn)	Moseley & Stoddard Mfg. Co.
1881/5/3 (apple parer)	Reading Hardware Co.

PATENT DATE	MAKER
1881/6/7	Clough & Williamson
1881/6/21	R.M. Ball
1881/7/12	Enterprise Mfg. Co.
1881/11/1	Charles F. Hennis Co.
1881/11/15	Joseph E. Hoff
1881/12/13	Landers, Frary & Clark
1882/1/24	C.E. Hudson
1882/2/7 (lemon squeezer)	William B. Dean
1882/2/7 (can opener)	Fred J. Meyer Mfg. Co.
1882/2/7 (coffee mill)	Charles Parker & Co.
1882/2/28	Landers, Frary & Clark
1882/3/7	A.W. Lyman
1882/4/4	Penn Hardware Co.
1882/4/11 (apple parer)	Penn Hardware Co.
1882/4/11 (lemon squeezer)	Alfred C. Rex & Co.
1882/6/13	Tripp Bros. & Co.
1882/7/11	C.E. Hudson
1882/9/12	Enterprise Mfg. Co.
1882/12/19	New England Specialty Co.
1883/1/30	Enterprise Mfg. Co.
1883/2/6	Selden & Griswold Mfg. Co.
1883/2/20 (ice cream freezer)	Charles W. Packer
1883/2/20 (coffee mill)	Charles Parker & Co.
1883/3/27	Clough & Williamson
1883/4/10 (lard press)	Enterprise Mfg. Co.
1883/4/10 (ice cream freezer)	White Mountain Freezer Co.
1883/4/24	Enterprise Mfg. Co.
1883/5/15	Ellrich Hardware Mfg. Co.
1883/6/12	Charles Parker Co.
1883/7/17	Alfred C. Rex & Co.
1883/7/24	Frank Wilson
1883/8/14	Manning, Bowman & Co.
1883/9/4	Logan & Strobridge Iron Co.
1883/9/11	L.A. Sayre & Co.
1883/10/9	Kelsea & Boutell
1884/1/8	Valentine Clad
1884/1/29 (can opener)	Fred J. Meyer Mfg. Co.
1884/1/29 (grist mill)	Frank Wilson
1884/3/18 (ice crusher)	Bradley Co.
1884/3/18	Goodell Co.
1884/3/22 (wrong date, but so marked)	Dame, Stoddard & Kendall
1884/4/8	American Machine Co.
	North Brothers Mfg. Co.
1884/4/22	Thomas Curley
1884/5/13	Alfred C. Rex & Co.
1884/7/22 (corkscrew)	Clough & Williamson
1884/7/22 (corkscrew)	Charles L. Griswold
1884/8/12	James D. Frary
1884/9/16	Kelsea & Boutell

PATENT DATE	MAKER
1884/11/4	Charles F. Hennis Co.
1885/1/6	Goodell Co.
1885/1/13	Adams & Westlake Co.
1885/1/20	Enterprise Mfg. Co.
1885/2/17	Lalance & Grosjean Mfg. Co.
1885/3/10	Charles W. Packer
1885/3/31	American Axe & Tool Co.
1885/4/28	Paine, Diehl & Co.
1885/5/26	J.L. Newcomer
1885/6/2	Paine, Diehl & Co.
1885/6/9	C.E. Hudson
1885/8/25	J.P. Manny
1885/7/14	Sidney Shepard & Co.
1885/10/27	New Union Mfg. Co.
1885/11/5	Silver & Co.
1885/11/24	Albert Friedmann
1885/12/1	Paine, Diehl & Co.
1885/12/15	North Brothers Mfg. Co.
1885/12/29	New Union Mfg. Co.
1886/4/13	Enterprise Mfg. Co.
1886/4/27 (apple parer)	Goodell Co.
	L.A. Sayre & Co.
1886/4/27 (press)	Shephard Hardware Co.
1886/5/11	Silver & Co.
1886/7/27	John L. Gaumer Co.
1886/8/17	Wheeler Can Opener Co.
1886/8/24	Fred J. Meyers Mfg. Co.
1886/9/14	Peck, Stow & Wilcox
1886/9/28	Paine, Diehl & Co.
1886/10/19	Chicago Coffee Mill Co.
1886/11/9	Silver & Co.
1886/11/16	Goodell Co.
1887/1/4	Champion Egg Opener Co.
1887/4/5	C.E. Hudson
1887/4/12	Clark Novelty Co.
1887/5/17	Tripp Brothers & Co.
1887/5/24	O.W. Bullock
1887/6/28	Paine, Diehl & Co.
1887/7/19	American Vapor Stove Co.
1887/7/26	Brewington, Bainbridge & Co.
1887/8/9	American Machine Co.
1887/10/18	Silver & Co.
1887/12/6	American Machine Co.
1887/12/20	F.F. Adams Co.
1887/12/27	Sidney Shepard & Co.
1888/1/31	C.E. Hudson
1888/2/14	Erie Specialty Co.
1888/3/6	B.J. Greely
1888/3/13	Goodell Co.

PATENT DATE	MAKER
1888/4/3	Dover Stamping Co.
1888/5/8	Goodell Co.
1888/5/15	John M. Waddel Mfg. Co.
1888/6/5	Enterprise Mfg. Co.
1888/6/19	Gilchrist Mfg. Co.
1888/6/26	Shephard Hardware Co.
1888/7/10	Easley Mfg. Co.
1888/9/4	L.M. Devore & Co.
1888/9/25 (cork puller)	L.M. Devore & Co.
1888/9/25 (coffee mill)	Arcade Mfg. Co.
1888/9/25 (freezer)	Shephard Hardware Co.
1888/10/9	John McDermaid
1888/10/30	Gilchrist Mfg. Co.
1888/11/28	Adams & Westlake Co.
1888/12/4	F.C. Wilson & Co.
1888/12/18	Chicago Nickel Works
1889/1/29	H.M. Quackenbush
1889/2/12	Koenig & Co.
1889/3/19 (coffee mill)	Arcade Mfg. Co.
1889/3/19 (churn)	John McDermaid
1889/3/39 (meat chopper)	Peck, Stow & Wilcox
1889/3/19 (grater)	Steel Edge Stamping & Retinning Co.
1889/4/16	Empire Knife Co.
1889/5/7 (meat cutter)	American Machine Co.
1889/5/7 (can opener)	Lehman, Bolen & Co.
1889/5/14	Brewington, Bainbridge & Co.
1889/5/21	Manning, Bowman & Co.
1889/6/18	Wiliamson Co.
1889/6/25	Kelsea & Boutell
1889/9/10	Shepard Hardware Co.
1889/10/22	Warner Mfg. Co.
1889/11/12	Christy Knife Co.
1889/12/3	White Mountain Freezer Co.
1890/1/14	Ellrich Hardware Mfg. Co.
1890/1/21	Waddel Mfg. Co.
1890/2/4	Smith & Egge Mfg. Co.
1890/2/11	Albert B. Schofield
1890/3/4	Peck, Stow & Wilcox
1890/3/11	Brewington, Bainbridge & Co.
1890/3/25	Means Mfg. Co.
1890/4/1	Enterprise Mfg. Co.
1890/6/10	C.M. Heffron
1890/7/1	W.J. Lloyd Mfg. Co.
1890/7/29 (can opener)	Hasbrouck Alliger
1890/7/29 (cake pan)	North Brothers Mfg. Co.
1890/10/7	Warner Mfg. Co.
1890/11/11	Tripp Bros. & Co.
1890/12/2	J.P. Manny
1890/12/30	C.T. Ludwig

PATENT DATE	MAKER
1891/1/13	Arcade Mfg. Co.
1891/2/24	Little Giant Letterpress Co.
1891/3/17 (ice cream freezer)	Shepard Hardware Co.
1891/3/17 (lid lifter)	L.M. Devore & Co.
1891/3/24 (grater)	Burton H. Cook
1891/3/24 (coffee mill)	Logan & Strobridge Iron Co.
1891/4/14	Eustis Mfg. Co.
1891/4/21	Meriden Malleable Iron Co.
1891/5/19	Erie Specialty Co.
1891/6/9	L.A. Sayre & Co.
1891/7/7	Detroit Corkscrew Co.
1891/7/14	Detroit Corkscrew Co.
1891/8/4	Bradley, Blinn & Lyon
1891/8/18	Edgar Mfg. Co.
1891/9/8	John McDermaid
1891/10/6	Christy Knife Co.
1891/10/27	John Chatillon & Sons
1891/10/20	Arcade Mfg. Co.
1891/11/24	Dover Stamping Co.
1891/12/15	Thomas Curley
1892/1/5	Gaynor & Mitchell Mfg. Co.
1892/2/2	John Freimuth
1892/2/9	Hudson Parer Co.
1892/2/23 (grater)	Burton H. Cook
1892/2/23 (freezer)	Shepard Hardware Co.
1892/3/8 (lunch pail)	W.B. Bertels, Sons & Co.
1892/3/8 (food chopper)	Sargent & Co.
1892/4/19 (lemon squeezer)	Meriden Malleable Iron Co.
1892/4/19 (food chopper)	Peck, Stow & Wilcox Co.
1892/4/26	Geuder, Paeschke & Co.
1892/5/3	Rockwell Clough Co.
1892/5/10 (food chopper)	Ellrich Hardware Mfg. Co.
1892/5/10 (knife)	Maltby, Henley & Co.
1892/5/17 (can opener)	Browne & Dowd Mfg. Co.
1892/5/17 (food chopper)	Ellrich Hardware Mfg. Co.
1892/5/24	Quincy Hardware Mfg. Co.
1892/5/31	Parker Ice Tool Co.
1892/6/7	Arcade Mfg. Co.
1892/8/2	Enterprise Mfg. Co.
1892/8/30	Enterprise Mfg. Co.
1892/9/6	Enterprise Mfg. Co.
1892/9/27	Acme Shear Co.
1892/10/11	Manning, Bowman & Co.
1892/11/1	Clauss Shear Co.
1892/11/8	Enterprise Mfg. Co.
1892/12/6	Silver & Co.
1892/12/20	Albert B. Schofield
1893/2/14	Shepard Hardware Co.
1893/3/2	New York Stamping Co.

PATENT DATE	MAKER
1893/4/11 (coffee mill)	Arcade Mfg. Co.
1893/4/11 (can opener)	Peck, Stow & Wilcox
1893/5/2	N.R. Streeter & Co.
1893/6/13 (can opener)	F.E. Kohler & Co.
1893/6/13 (plate lifter)	WIre Goods Co.
1893/6/20	Gravity Twine Box Co.
1893/7/4	Enterprise Mfg. Co.
1893/7/11 (can opener)	Browne & Dowd Mfg. Co.
1893/7/11 (corkscrew)	Detroit Corkscrew Co.
1893/7/25	Erie Specialty Co.
1893/8/15	Illinois Cutlery Co.
1893/9/23	A.F. Meisselbach & Bro.
1893/10/10	Everett Specialty Co.
1893/11/7	N.R. Streeter & Co.
1893/11/21	Lavigne & Scott Mfg. Co.
1893/11/28	Enterprise Mfg. Co.
1894/1/2	Everett Specialty Co.
1894/2/6	M.L. Schoch
1894/2/27	Erie Specialty Co.
1894/3/13	C.A. Chapman
1894/3/20	Bradley Mfg. Co.
1894/4/10	Colbrookdale Iron Co.
	Oliver D. Woodruff
1894/6/5 (freezer)	Butler, Pattenhorn & Ellsworth
1894/6/5 (cherry stoner)	Enterprise Mfg. Co.
1894/6/19	Peck, Stow & Wilcox
1894/8/28	O.E. Davidson & Co.
1894/9/4	Gooch Freezer Co.
1894/11/27	A.B.C. Can Opener Co.
1895/1/1 (cork puller)	Meriden Malleable Iron Co.
1895/1/15	Arcade Mfg. Co.
1895/1/29	George Borgfeldt & Co.
1895/2/2	William F. Easley Mfg. Co.
1895/3/19	John Chatillon & Sons
1895/4/2	F.H. Chase & Co.
	Enterprise Mfg. Co.
1895/4/9	Darling Filter Co.
1895/5/21	American Specialty Co.
1895/6/11 (can opener)	Browne & Dowd Mfg. Co.
1895/6/11 (bread knife)	Christy Knife Co.
1895/6/11 (can opener)	Handy Things Mfg. Co.
1895/7/16	Gibbs Mfg. Co.
1895/7/23	Erie Specialty Co.
1895/8/20	Enterprise Mfg. Co.
1895/9/3	Peck, Stow & Wilcox Co.
1895/9/17 (food chopper)	Enterprise Mfg. Co.
1895/9/17 (coffee maker)	New York Stamping Co.
1895/10/8 (cheese cutter)	Enterprise Mfg. Co.
1895/10/8 (food chopper)	Oliver D. Woodruff

PATENT DATE	MAKER
1895/10/15	North Brothers Mfg. Co.
1895/11/12	Arcade Mfg. Co.
1895/12/24	East Mfg. Co.
1896/3/24	Landers, Frary & Clark
1896/4/7	Erie Specialty Co.
1896/4/28	Hall & Carpenter
1896/5/5	Michael H. Sexton
1896/5/12	Parker Wire Goods Co.
1896/6/2	Landers, Frary & Clark
1896/6/9 (cork puller)	Arcade Mfg. Co.
1896/6/9 (ice cream disher)	Youngstown Specialty Mfg. Co.
1896/6/23	Meriden Malleable Iron Co.
1896/7/21	Brittan, Graham & Mathes Co.
1896/8/4 (grater)	Specialty Novelty Co.
1896/8/4 (rasin seeder)	A.C. Williams & Co.
1896/10/20	Thomas Curley
1896/11/10	Edgar Mfg. Co.
1896/12/8	Tripp Bros. & Co.
1897/2/2	Albert B. Schofield
1897/2/9	Erie Specialty Co.
1897/3/9	Charles Parker Co.
1897/3/23 (cork puller)	Erie Specialty Co.
1897/3/23 (waffle iron)	Griswold Mfg. Co.
1897/4/20	Silver & Co.
1897/6/1	Williamson Co.
1897/6/15	Fanner Mfg. Co.
1897/7/27	A.E. Faber
1897/8/3	Matthai, Ingram & Co.
1897/8/17	Specialty Novelty Co.
1897/8/10	Williamson Co.
1897/8/31	Hero Stamping Works
1897/9/7 (cork puller)	Union Mfg. & Plating Co.
	Arcade Mfg. Co.
1897/9/7 (egg beater)	Nelson Lyon
1897/10/12	Landers, Frary & Clark
1897/11/9	Beaumont & Callahan
	Album Mfg. Co.
1897/11/30	Sidney Shepard & Co.
1897/12/21	Logan & Strobridge Mfg. Co.
1898/2/1	Luther S. Hull
1898/2/22	Nelson Lyon
1898/5/24	Goodell Co.
1898/7/19	Eustis Mfg. Co.
1898/8/16	William G. Browne Mfg. Co.
1898/9/20	Erie Specialty Co.
1898/10/4	Matthai, Ingram & Co.
1898/11/15	W.F. Easly Mfg. Co.
1898/12/13 (coffee mill)	Griswold Mfg. Co.
1898/12/13 (corkscrew)	Williamson Co.

PATENT DATE	MAKER
1898/12/27 (flour bin)	Glascock Bros. Mfg. Co.
1898/12/27 (coffee mill)	Griswold Mfg. Co.
1899/1/31	Landers, Frary & Clark
1899/2/14	Meriden Malleable Iron Co.
1899/2/21	Rockwell-Clough Co.
1899/3/14	Arcade Mfg. Co.
	Beaumont & Callahan
1899/3/28 (nutpick holder)	Freeport Novelty Co.
1899/4/11	Peck, Stow & Wilcox
1899/4/18	Landers, Frary & Clark
1899/5/6	M.D. Converse
1899/5/30	Arcade Mfg. Co.
1899/6/13	White Mountain Freezer Co.
1899/7/4	Manning, Bowman & Co.
1899/8/8	Arcade Mfg. Co.
1899/8/22	Holt-Lyon Co.
1899/8/29	Arcade Mfg. Co.
1899/10/10	Freeport Novelty Co.
1899/11/14	Fred J. Burr
	New England Enameling Co.
1899/11/21	Troy Nickel Works
1899/12/5	Freeport Novelty Co.
1899/12/12	John A.E. Anderson
1900/2/27	Wire Goods Co.
1900/3/6	W.F. Easly Mfg. Co.
1900/4/3	Holt-Lyon Co.
1900/4/17	Erie Specialty Co.
1900/5/15	Erie Specialty Co.
1900/5/22	James Heekin & Co.
1900/5/29	Christy Knife Co.
1900/6/12 (crumb crusher)	Ogden Bolton
1900/6/12 (lemon squeezer)	Freeport Novelty Co.
1900/6/12 (churn)	Smith & Egge Mfg. Co.
1900/6/26 (coffee mill)	Arcade Mfg. Co.
1900/6/26 (can opener)	William G. Browne Mfg. Co.
1900/7/17	William G. Browne Mfg. Co.
1900/7/31	Freeport Novelty Co.
1900/8/28	Charles D. Brown
1900/9/4	Williamson Co.
1900/10/30	Cassady-Fairbank Mfg. Co.
1900/11/13	Landers, Frary & Clark
1901/1/15	Freeport Novelty Co.
1901/1/22	Enterprise Mfg. Co.
1901/2/19	Freeport Novelty Co.
	Manning, Bowman & Co.
1901/3/5	Woods, Bacon & Co.
1901/3/12	Leader Specialty Co.
1901/4/9	Anneta Mfg. Co.
1901/5/14 (fork)	Goodell Co.

PATENT DATE	MAKER
1901/5/14 (waffle iron)	Griswold Mfg. Co.
1901/5/28	Freeport Novelty Co.
	Manning, Bowman & Co.
1901/6/11 (grater)	Elwin S. Anderson
1901/6/11 (cork puller)	Erie Specialty Co.
1901/6/18	W.H. Plumb Novelty Co.
1901/6/25	William G. Browne Mfg. Co.
1901/7/9	Bronson-Walton Co.
1901/7/16	William G. Browne Mfg. Co.
1901/7/23	Freeport Novelty Co.
1901/8/6	Enterprise Mfg. Co.
1901/9/10	H.F. Osborne Co.
1901/9/17	Arcade Mfg. Co.
1901/9/24	Standard Churn Co.
1901/10/1	Landers, Frary & Clark
1901/10/8 (ice breaker)	C.A. Hiles & Co.
1901/10/8 (can opener)	Woods, Bacon & Co.
1901/11/19	Arcade Mfg. Co.
1901/12/31 (cork puller)	Arcade Mfg. Co.
1901/12/31 (cork puller)	Freeport Novelty Co.
1902/1/14	Manning, Bowman & Co.
	Sumner Mfg. Co.
1902/1/28	Taylor Mfg. Co.
1902/2/4	Eustis Mfg. Co.
1902/2/11	Erie Specialty Co.
1902/2/18	Abbott & Boutell
1902/3/25	Silver & Co.
1902/4/1	Freeport Novelty Co.
1902/4/29 (nut cracker)	H.M. Quackenbush
1902/4/29 (jar wrench)	Whitaker Mfg. Co.
1902/5/27	Wolverine Supply Co.
1902/7/1	Freeport Novelty Co.
1902/8/5	Goodell Co.
1902/8/12	Moses L. Hawks
1902/9/30	Goodell Co.
1902/10/21	Bronson-Walton Co.
1902/10/28	Silver & Co.
1902/11/4	National Enameling & Stamping Co.
1902/11/11	Erie Specialty Co.
1903/1/6	Oliver D. Woodruff
1903/1/20	Goodell Co.
1903/1/27	Edwin D. Parker
1903/2/10	4-S Food Press Co.
1903/3/17	Matt Redlinger
1903/3/24	Kalischer Mfg. Co.
1903/3/31	Enterprise Mfg. Co.
1903/4/7	Goodell Co.
1903/4/14	Taplin Mfg. Co.
1903/5/5 (food chopper)	Griswold Mfg. Co.

PATENT DATE	MAKER
1903/5/5 (food chopper)	Rollman Mfg. Co.
1903/5/19	Arcade Mfg. Co.
1903/6/2	Landers, Frary & Clark
1903/6/23 (food press)	Fanner Mfg. Co.
	Silver & Co.
1903/6/23 (slicer)	Tucker & Dorsey Mfg. Co.
1903/6/30	National Mfg. & Supply Co.
1903/7/7	Premo-Hall Mfg. Co.
1903/8/11	Tucker & Dorsey Mfg. Co.
1903/11/3 (jar wrench)	Forbes Chocolate Co.
1903/11/10	Bronson-Walton Co.
1903/11/17	Schroeter Brothers Hdw. Co.
1903/11/24 (can opener)	Moses L. Hawks
1903/11/24 (can opener)	Lawrence Hardware Works
1903/12/8	Stork Mfg. Co.
1903/12/22	Champion Egg Opener Co.
1904/1/26	Bronson-Walton Co.
1904/4/19 (champagne tap)	Erie Specialty Co.
1904/4/19 (eye clip)	Patterson & Co.
1904/6/14	F.E. Snyder
1904/6/28	R.J. Berthoud
1904/7/19	Ira F. White & Son Co.
1904/8/2	Wagner Mfg. Co.
1904/9/6 (knife)	Goodell Co.
1904/9/6 (bread mixer)	Landers, Frary & Clark
1904/9/27	Manning, Bowman & Co.
	Sumner Mfg. Co.
1904/11/29	Landers, Frary & Clark
1905/2/7	Giles & Nielsen Nickel Works
	Geer Mfg. Co.
1905/2/14	Landers, Frary & Clark
1905/2/21	Landers, Frary & Clark
1905/2/28	Logan & Strobridge Iron Co.
1905/3/28 (lemon squeezer)	Gilchrist Co.
1905/3/28 (coffee mill)	Logan & Strobridge Iron Co.
1905/4/4	Home Supply Mfg. Co.
1905/4/18 (ice chipper)	C.W. Halsey
1905/4/18 (cake mixer)	Landers, Frary & Clark
1905/4/25	Gilchrist Co.
1905/5/16 (veg. masher)	Erie Specialty Co.
1905/5/16 (filter)	Silver & Co.
1905/6/27 (sausage stuffer)	Enterprise Mfg. Co.
1905/6/27 (washer)	Z.S. & C.L. Randleman
1905/7/11 (baking pan)	Silver & Co.
1905/7/11 (slaw cutter)	Tucker & Dorsey Mfg. Co.
1905/7/18	Landers, Frary & Clark
1905/8/1	Irona Mfg. Co.
1905/11/7 (ice cream disher)	Keiner-Williams Stamping Co.
1905/11/7 (cake mixer)	Landers, Frary & Clark

PATENT DATE	MAKER
1906/1/2	Mosteller Mfg. Co.
1906/3/6	Hugo Reisinger
1906/4/24	Bronson-Walton Co.
1906/5/15	J.S. Dunlap
1906/5/22	Landers, Frary & Clark
1906/5/29	Landers, Frary & Clark
1906/6/19	Gilchrist Co.
1906/6/26	Andrews Wire & Iron Works
1906/7/3	Mosteller Mfg. Co.
1906/7/17 (saussage stuffer)	Enterprise Mfg. Co.
1906/7/17 (coffee pot)	Landers, Frary & Clark
1906/10/9	F.W. Loll Mfg. Co.
1906/10/23	Bronson-Walton Co.
1906/10/30	Rollman Mfg. Co.
	Universal Hardware Works
1906/12/4	J.L. Wilder
1906/12/18	Windsor Stephens & Co.
1906/12/25 (coffee pot)	Landers, Frary & Clark
1906/12/25 (can opener)	Taylor Mfg. Co.
1907/2/26 (cork puller)	Arcade Mfg. Co.
1907/2/26 (egg beater)	J.S. Dunlap
1907/3/5	J.L. De Steiger
1907/3/26	Arcade Mfg. Co.
1907/4/30	National Specialty Mfg. Co.
1907/5/28	National Specialty Mfg. Co.
1907/6/25 (cork puller)	Gilchrist Co.
1907/6/25 (apple parer)	Goodell Co.
1907/7/16	Landers, Frary & Clark
1907/7/30	J.S. Dunlap
1907/8/20	W.G. Henis' Sons & Co.
1907/8/27	Mosteller Mfg. Co.
1907/10/15	A.& J. Mfg. Co.
1907/11/19	J.S. Dunlap
1907/12/3	William W. Vogel
1907/12/17	J.L. Sommer Mfg. Co.
1908/4/21	Mosteller Mfg. Co.
1908/6/23	National Specialty Mfg. Co.
1908/7/7 (apple parer)	Boutell Mfg. Co.
1908/7/7 (ice cream disher)	Erie Specialty Co.
1908/7/7 (fruit pitter)	Mosteller Mfg. Co.
1908/7/7 (eggbeater)	United Royalties Corp.
1908/8/11	H.M. Quackenbush
1908/8/18	Browne & Dowd Mfg. Co.
1908/8/25	Mosteller Mfg. Co.
1908/9/1	Andrews Wire & Iron Works
1908/9/29	Gilchrist Co.
1908/11/3	Browne & Dowd Mfg. Co.
1908/11/24 (mill)	Landers, Frary & Clark
1908/11/24 (eggbeater)	Taplin Mfg. Co.

PATENT DATE	MAKER
1909/1/5	Autospin Co.
	New England Enameling Co.
1909/1/26	John D. Houck
1909/2/9	Imperial Metal Mfg. Co.
1909/4/27	John D. Houck
1909/5/11	Bronson-Walton Co.
1909/6/1	Goodell Co.
1909/7/20 (strainer)	Andrews Wire & Iron Works
1909/7/20 (tea-ball)	Simmons, Bro. & Co.
1909/8/10	H.M. Quackenbush
1909/8/31	Landers, Frary & Clark
1909/9/28	Gilchrist Co.
1909/11/9 (pot)	Hamblin & Russell Mfg. Co.
1909/11/9 (lemon squeezer)	Mosteller Mfg. Co.
1909/11/16	Landers, Frary & Clark
1909/12/28 (cherry pitter)	John Houck
1909/12/28 (toaster)	Frank B. Schuyler
1910/2/15	Polar Star Co.
	Acme Freezer Co.
1910/3/8	Mosteller Mfg. Co.
1910/3/22	Gilchrist Co.
1910/3/29	Landers, Frary & Clark
1910/5/24	Goodell Co.
1910/6/28	Erie Specialty Co.
1910/7/19	Erie Specialty Co.
1910/9/13	J.C. Foster & Son
1910/10/4	Andrews Wire & Iron Works
1910/11/1 (apple parer)	Boutell Mfg. Co.
1910/11/1 (can opener)	Irwin Mfg. Co.
1911/1/3 (lemon squeezer)	Gilchrist Co.
1911/1/3 (percolater)	Landers, Frary & Clark
1911/1/24	Arcade Mfg. Co.
1911/2/21	Landers, Frary & Clark
1911/5/30	Mak-Mor Sales Co.
1911/6/27	Estate Stove Co.
1911/8/1	Charles Parker Co.
1911/8/15	Griswold Mfg. Co.
1911/7/11	Sommer Mfg. Co.
1911/11/14	Goodell Co.
1911/11/28	Dazey Churn & Mfg. Co.
1911/12/26 (bottle opener)	Crown Throat & Opener Co.
1911/12/26 (ice cream disher)	Erie Specialty Co.
1912/1/2	Auto Vacuum Freezer Co.
1912/3/12	Sommer Mfg. Co.
1912/3/26	Frank Mossberg Co.
1912/4/30	Crown Throat & Opener Co.
1912/6/18 (dish drainer)	Andrews Wire & Iron Works
1912/6/18 (knife)	Federal Tool Co.
1912/7/16	Arcade Mfg. Co.

PATENT DATE	MAKER
1912/7/23	Acme Freezer Co.
1912/9/10 (can opener)	Boye Needle Co.
1912/9/10 (toaster)	Pelouze Scale & Mfg. Co.
1912/10/29	John D. Houch
1912/11/26	Sommer Mfg. Co.
1913/2/11	Landers, Frary & Clark
1913/3/18	Andrews Wire & Iron Works
1913/3/25	Erie Specialty Co.
1913/4/8 (cork puller)	Gilchrist Co.
1913/4/8 (lunch box)	Landers, Frary & Clark
1913/4/29	Landers, Frary & Clark
1913/5/13	Landers, Frary & Clark
1913/6/17	Crown Throat & Opener Co.
1913/8/12	Boye Needle Co.
1913/8/19	Boye Needle Co.
1913/9/9 (tea kettle)	Griswold Mfg. Co.
1913/9/9 (bread slicer)	Hamblin & Russell Mfg. Co.
1913/11/25	Crown Throat & Opener Co.
1913/12/9	Landers, Frary & Clark
1914/3/3	Manning, Bowman & Co.
1914/4/6	Harper Supply Co.
1914/4/28 (bottle opener)	Sommer Mfg. Co.
1914/4/28 (tea kettle)	Sterling Machine & Stamping Co.
1914/5/12	David H. Coles
1914/7/21	Erie Specialty Co.
1914/7/14	Landers, Frary & Clark
1914/7/28	Landers, Frary & Clark
1914/8/18	Sommer Mfg. Co.
1914/8/25	Sommer Mfg. Co.
1914/9/1	Gilchrist Co.
1914/9/29	Boye Needle Co.
1914/10/13	Silex Co.
1914/10/20	Landers, Frary & Clark
1914/11/3	Erie Specialty Co.
1914/11/24	Sommer Mfg. Co.
1914/12/8	Crown Throat & Opener Co.
1915/1/5	Landers, Frary & Clark
1915/2/2 (toaster)	Manning, Bowman & Co.
1915/2/2 (eggbeater)	United Royalties Corp.
1915/2/16	Landers, Frary & Clark
1915/2/23	Sommer Mfg. Co.
1915/3/23	Gilchrist Co.
1915/4/27	Landers, Frary & Clark
1915/5/11	Erie Specialty Co.
1915/6/1	Landers, Frary & Clark
1915/7/6	Crystal Percolator Co.
1915/8/17	Erie Specialty Co.
1915/8/24 (cork puller)	Arcade Mfg. Co.
1915/8/24 (nut cracker)	Schroeter Brothers Hdw. Co.

PATENT DATE	MAKER
1915/9/14	Byron S. Rosenblatt
1915/10/5 (lemon squeezer)	Arcade Mfg. Co.
1915/10/5 (toaster)	
(ice shave)	Landers, Frary & Clark
1915/11/30	Erie Specialty Co.
1915/12/7	Erie Specialty Co.
1916/2/8 (dish stand)	Eustis Mfg. Co.
1916/4/4	Landers, Frary & Clark
1916/4/18	Landers, Frary & Clark
1916/8/15	Erie Specialty Co.
1916/11/28 (jar wrench)	Boye Needle Co.
1916/11/28 (egg beater)	Turner & Seymour Mfg. Co.
1916/12/26	J.C. Forster & Son
1917/5/8	Best S. Co.
1917/5/22	Boye Needle Co.
1917/7/3	Landers, Frary & Clark
1917/8/17	Schroeter Brothers Hdw. Co.
1917/8/30	Cassady-Fairbank Mfg. Co.
1917/12/18	Dazey Churn & Mfg. Co.
1918/3/12	Landers, Frary & Clark
1918/6/4	Hamblin & Russell Mfg. Co.
1918/6/18	Landers, Frary & Clark
1918/8/6	Frank B. Cook Co.
	Cook Electric Co.
1918/10/15	Hamblin & Russell Mfg. Co.
1918/10/22	Cassady-Fairbank Mfg. Co.
1918/12/3	Hamblin & Russell Mfg. Co.
1919/3/4	Sommer Mfg. Co.
1919/12/23	New England Enameling Co.
1920/2/10	Rockford Metal Specialty Co.
1920/3/23	Winsted Hardware Mfg. Co.
1920/4/6	Boye Needle Co.
1920/5/18	Griswold Mfg. Co.
1920/6/15	Boye Needle Co.
1920/8/10	Kit-Chin-Kit Corp.
1920/9/14	Loeb-Strongson Corp.
1920/9/21	Wolff Appliance Corp.
1920/11/9	Kit-Chin-Kit Corp.
1920/11/16 (toaster)	Landers, Frary & Clark
1920/11/16 (toaster)	Perfection Electric Products Co.
1920/12/28	Manning, Bowman & Co.
1921/5/3	Winsted Hardware Mfg. Co.
1921/5/10	Kit-Chin-Kit Corp.
1921/8/2	Turner & Seymour Mfg. Co.
1921/8/30	Wheeling Corrugating Co.
1921/10/18	United Royalties Corp.
1921/10/25	Landers, Frary & Clark
1921/12/20 (cap lifter)	Sommer Mfg. Co.
1921/12/20 (churn)	Dazey Churn & Mfg. Co.

PATENT DATE	MAKER
1922/1/31	Landers, Frary & Clark
1922/2/14	Dazey Churn & Mfg. Co.
1922/2/21	M.& L. Ehrlich
1922/3/14	Landers, Frary & Clark
1922/5/23	Perfection Electric Products Co.
1922/7/11	Griswold Mfg. Co.
1922/8/8	Turner & Seymour Mfg. Co.
1922/12/26	Landers, Frary & Clark
1923/4/10	Turner & Seymour Mfg. Co.
1923/5/28	Turner & Seymour Mfg. Co.
1923/6/12	White Mountain Freezer Co.
1923/10/9	A.& J. Mfg. Co.
1923/12/4	Manning, Bowman & Co.
1924/1/8	Landers, Frary & Clark
1924/1/22	Landers, Frary & Clark
1924/7/1	Landers, Frary & Clark
1924/11/18	Landers, Frary & Clark
1924/12/9	Taplin Mfg. Co.
1925/3/17	Landers, Frary & Clark
1925/3/31	Landers, Frary & Clark
1925/4/21	Edlund Co.
1925/5/12	Edlund Co.
1925/6/27	Estate Stove Co.
1925/8/18	Turner & Seymour Mfg. Co.

APPENDIX C

MARKS ON FOREIGN-MADE KITCHEN COLLECTIBLES

Foreign made kitchen collectibles are often marked with terms and abbreviations unfamiliar to American collectors. Reference to the following list will give the meaning of these marks and, in most cases, identify the country where the items were made.

Beginning in 1891, American law required that all merchandise imported into the U.S. through normal trade channels be marked with the country of origin. Lack of this mark, however, does not necessarily mean that the item was made prior to 1891. Post 1891 items brought into the U.S. by immigrants, returning American tourists, and American servicemen will usually not be marked.

MARK	COUNTRY	MEANING
A.G.	Germany	Aktiergesellschaft (joint stock company)
BAYR	Germany	Bayrisch (Bavarian)
BREV.	Italy	Brevetto (patent)
BRTE or BRVT or BRVTE	French speaking	Brevete (patent)
B.S.G.D.G. or Bte. S.G.D.G.	France	Brevete Sans Garantie Du Gouvernement (patent without government guarantee)
Bte or Bvt.	French speaking	Brevete (patent)
Cia.	Spanish speaking	Compania (company)
Cie.	French speaking	Compagnie (company)
Cie.	German speaking	Companie (company)
D.R.G.M.	Germany	Deutsches Reich Gebrauchsmuster (German government registered design)
D.R.P. or D.R.Pa.	Germany	Deutsches Reichpatent (German government patent)
D.R.P.u.A.P. or D.R.P.u.AUS PAT	Germany	Deutsches Reichpatent und Ausland Patenten (German and foreign patents)
ET. or ETR.	France	Etrangere (foreign, usually referring to patents)
FABB.	Italy	Fabbrica (factory)
FABCA. or Fca.	Spanish speaking	Fabrica (factory)

296

MARK	COUNTRY	MEANING
Frs.	French speaking	Freres (brothers)
Geb. or Gebr.	Germany	Gebruder (brothers)
Ges.	Germany	Gesellschaft (company)
GmbH	Germany	Gesellschaft Mit Beschlanter Haftung (limited liability company)
G S	German speaking	Guss Stahl (cast steel)
Her. or HERMs or Hrs	Spanish speaking	Hermanos (brothers)
Ine. or Inv. or Invr.	French speaking	Inventeur (inventor)
Ma'Fa	France	Manufacture (factory)
PAT. I.A.	Germany	Patent in Alle Kultrustatten (patented in all civilized countries)
SA or S.A.	Belgium	Societe Anonyme (stock company)
S.A.	Spanish speaking	Sociedad Anonima (stock company)
S.G.D.G.	France	Sans Guarentie de Gouvernment (without government guarantee)
SPOL	Czechoslovakia	Spolecnost (company)

INDEX